David H. Blake

NORTHEASTERN UNIVERSITY

Robert S. Walters

UNIVERSITY OF PITTSBURGH

THE POLITICS OF GLOBAL ECONOMIC RELATIONS

Second Edition

PRENTICE-HALL, INC., Englewood Cliffs, New Jersey 07632

Library of Congress Cataloging in Publication Data

BLAKE, DAVID H.
    The politics of global economic relations.

    Includes index.
    1. International economic relations.   I. Walters,
Robert S., [date.]   II. Title.
HF1411.B6 1983   337   82-5369
ISBN 0-13-684449-9   AACR2

Editorial production/supervision: *Edith Riker*
Cover design: *Wanda Lubelska Design*
Manufacturing buyer: *Edmund W. Leone*

To
DAVID, JENNIFER, KIMBERLY, SCOTT, and CLAIRE

ISBN 0-13-684449-9

Prentice-Hall International, Inc., *London*
Prentice-Hall of Australia Pty. Limited, *Sydney*
Prentice-Hall Canada Inc., *Toronto*
Prentice-Hall of India Private Limited, *New Delhi*
Prentice-Hall of Japan, Inc., *Tokyo*
Prentice-Hall of Southeast Asia Pte. Ltd., *Singapore*
Whitehall Books Limited, *Wellington, New Zealand*

CONTENTS

CHAPTER SEVEN
OPEC AND OTHER STRATEGIES FOR STATES IN THE PERIPHERY OF THE GLOBAL POLITICAL ECONOMY   *167*

CHAPTER EIGHT
FOREIGN ECONOMIC POLICYMAKING IN THE UNITED STATES   *204*

CHAPTER NINE
INTERNATIONAL POLITICAL ECONOMY: CURRENT PROBLEMS AND FUTURE NEEDS   *230*

LIST OF ILLUSTRATIONS

FIGURES

PREFACE

The second edition of *The Politics of Global Economic Relations* represents considerably more than an updating of events since the early and mid-1970s. At least a third of the volume has been rewritten completely. The chapters on monetary relations and technology transfers have been recast completely to bring these important dimensions of political-economic relations into sharper focus. Important segments have been added or recast in our treatment of trade relations, multinational corporations, economic assistance, OPEC, the new international economic order, and the foreign economic policymaking in the United States. Of course, throughout the volume we have attempted to incorporate timely examples and more recent data in developing those ideas that seem to remain as appropriate today as they did with the appearance of the first edition.

While much of the second edition is rewritten, the substantive issues covered and the interplay of radical and liberal concepts in analyzing the issues have been retained. We would not argue that these two analytical orientations alone are adequate to explain the dynamics of the contemporary global political economy. On the other hand, we chose to retain the "dialogue" between these world views as an extraordinarily useful tool in introducing students to the complexities of a broad range of international economic relationships. We are gratified by the positive reaction that this approach has evoked among our students and colleagues over the years.

The assumption of administrative duties by both of us and David Blake's move to Northeastern University made this edition harder to produce than the first. Despite the obstacles, we were delighted that the challenge of drafting a second edition enabled us to renew a truly special professional collaboration focused around this volume.

We wish to thank Mary Hamler, Mary Ann Salapa, Melanie Katilius, Kendall Stanley, and Evelyn Keefe for providing their excellent secretarial skills in the face of trying demands we sometimes placed upon them. Robert Stephens provided valuable research assistance in connection with these revisions. Stan Wakefield's understanding and continued support in producing a second edition after more than one failure on our part to meet self-imposed deadlines is greatly appreciated. Above all, we want to acknowledge our substantial debt to the students and colleagues who have in a variety of contexts reacted to the various strengths and weaknesses they found in our work. Without their encouragement this new edition would not have emerged.

D.H.B. and R.S.W.

CHAPTER ONE
INTRODUCTION
*Economic Transactions
and
World Politics*

We are currently in the midst of a key transition in American foreign policy that in some respects is even more profound than the dramatic foreign policy moves made by the United States immediately following World War II. The Bretton Woods system, membership in the United Nations, the Truman Doctrine, Marshall aid, NATO, and the construction of a complex of alliance systems ringing the Communist world are commonly viewed as evidence of that turning point in United States history when we abandoned our tradition of isolationism (however different its face in different parts of the globe). Through these instruments the United States was seen as having moved into a series of multilateral commitments that saddled it with tremendous responsibilities abroad and circumscribed American freedom of action in ways that the United States had found unacceptable in the past. But the United States during the 1970s and 1980s has confronted a series of foreign economic challenges that are likely to result in even more constraints on its freedom of action than did the agreements in the 1940s.

As an isolationist, the United States could maximize freedom of action in its international relations (economic and political) by avoiding formal commitments; this was a basic theme, for example, in opposition to American membership in the League of Nations. Following World War II, when the United States did bind itself by numerous multilateral commitments in the economic and political spheres, it did so from a clearly preeminent po-

1

sition and, thus, was able in substantial measure to shape the various agreements to conform to American interests. The postwar multilateral agreements were typically of a sort that committed all member states to abide by specified global norms of behavior, which, while ensuring benefits for these countries, would also facilitate the perpetuation of American preeminence. These commitments had the net effect of ensuring America's freedom of action in the globe rather than circumscribing it.

Now, however, the United States is in the process of having to reformulate its foreign economic and political relations to take into account new global realities. America has moved from virtual self-sufficiency in energy to extensive reliance on oil imports from the Middle East. Europe, through the creation of the Common Market, has transformed itself from a junior partner of America to a giant economic rival/partner. Japan's economic miracle and vigorous promotion of exports now threaten the vitality of key industries (such as automobiles, steel, and semiconductors) and hundreds of thousands of jobs in the United States. The world's confidence in the dollar as the top international currency has been shaken repeatedly since 1971. These and other developments have combined to necessitate the construction of a new global economic and political order within which the United States will occupy a significantly less preeminent status. In short, it has been in the 1970s and 1980s, not in the 1940s, that the United States is of necessity engaging itself with the rest of the world, as opposed to maintaining its freedom of action by either avoiding formal multilateral commitments or shaping them unilaterally.

The political significance of global economic relations goes well beyond this contemporary transition in the international position of the United States. The increased sensitivity in economic interdependence among virtually all states compels us to assess the political implications of international economic transactions everywhere. Even if economic transactions between states have grown at a slower rate than have economic transactions within them,[1] the volume and speed with which economic resources can now be transferred between states places tremendous economic and political strains upon them. For example, modern communications and the management capabilities of giant international banks and corporations, which command assets greater than the gross national products of most states, allow massive capital transfers in response to even small disparities in the market conditions and the political milieus of various states.[2] Long-term investments by

---

[1]See K. Deutsch and A. Eckstein, "National Industrialization and the Declining Share of the International Economic Sector, 1890–1959," *World Politics*, 13, no. 2 (January 1961), 267–99; and K. Waltz, "The Myth of National Interdependence," in *The International Corporation*, ed. C. Kindleberger (Cambridge, Mass.: M.I.T. Press, 1970), p. 208.

[2]For an elaboration of the sensitivity of international economic interdependence and its substantive implications, see Richard Cooper, "Economic Interdependence and Foreign Policy in the Seventies," *World Politics*, 24, no. 2 (January 1972), 159-81. See also Chapter 7 of this book.

these economic actors and the movement of their liquid assets in international monetary markets can undermine domestic economic and political programs and produce severe conflicts between states. Indeed, some observers of these banks and corporations feel that they may ultimately undermine the contemporary nation-state system itself.[3]

Although international economic relations among private and public actors necessitate profound alterations in contemporary American foreign policy and in political relations among states everywhere, American students of international politics have until recently paid little attention to interrelationships between economic transactions and international politics. This situation must be remedied if we are to understand contemporary global politics and the transition of America's role in the world. A major obstacle to our understanding of these problems, however, is the poverty of conceptual frameworks with which to address systematically the various interrelationships between international political behavior and international economic behavior. It is important to ask why this is the case and what can be done to increase our analytical capabilities for examining these problems.

Analysts of international politics develop conceptual frameworks in order that they may better address what they perceive to be substantive problems of overriding importance. Almost without exception, American specialists in international politics for two decades following World War II saw the Cold War and the defense of the non-Communist world as the substantive focus of U.S. foreign relations. As a consequence, they relied heavily upon paradigms in which security and power relations among states were postulated as constituting the quintessence of world politics. The dominant paradigm (political realism) led to a focus upon states as sole or primary actors in world politics,[4] and except insofar as economic instruments (such as aid and trade) were employed directly in power struggles between states, the distribution of benefits from domestic and international economic relations were seen as lying outside the boundaries of international politics.[5] Within this analytical tradition, international economic transactions such as trade and monetary affairs were typically looked upon as essentially nonpolitical relationships. They were seen as being managed, in the non-Communist world at least, according to politically neutral, technical criteria and administered by functionally specific ("nonpolitical") international organizations such as the General Agreement on Tariffs and Trade and the International Monetary Fund. The study of such affairs was left to international economists, international lawyers, and students of international organizations—most of whom neglected to analyze the significance

[3] See Frank Tannenbaum, "The Survival of the Fittest," *Columbia Journal of World Business,* 3, no. 2 (March–April, 1968), 13–20.

[4] See Hans Morgenthau, *Politics Among Nations,* 4th ed. (New York: Knopf, 1967).

[5] Ibid, pp. 25–26.

of such transactions (and of international economic organizations themselves) in world politics.

In short, until recently the conceptual frameworks used most frequently by American analysts tended to relegate economic relationships to the periphery of inquiry; the interrelationships between domestic and international politics were not examined systematically; and interests other than those of states (such as corporate, partisan, or class interests) received scant attention in studies of international politics. Marxist analyses dealing explicitly with interests and relationships that were of little concern to scholars representing the dominant analytical tradition of American scholarship on international politics were virtually ignored. These are some important reasons accounting for the poverty of conceptual frameworks useful in studying the politics of international economic relations.

However, some recent developments have brought the economic dimension of world politics back into prominence. New conceptual orientations are fostering sytematic analysis of the relationship between international economic and political behavior, in contrast to paradigms focusing exclusively on power and security aspects of world order. Economic security and stability have emerged alongside military security as top-priority foreign policy challenges for numerous states. Multinational corporate activities, instability of both the dollar and gold in international financial relations, supply interruptions and price escalations for critical resources such as oil and food, and import surges that displace local production and jobs as well as threaten to unleash trade wars are fueling domestic as well as international political disorders of profound importance. Indeed, in many respects these disorders affect the personal lives of individuals throughout the world more directly than do most forms of international diplomacy focused on maintaining military security. These problem areas, as well as increased interest in revisionist interpretations of the Cold War and the phenomenon of American imperialism, are exciting substantive and theoretical areas of inquiry that are now perceived widely as being of overriding importance in contemporary world politics and U.S. foreign policy. None of them can be handled well within the conceptual frameworks used most frequently in the past by American international politics specialists. In response to these facts, and as a result of a logical evolution of focus, considerable progress has been made during recent years in the field of international relations theory. Instead of theories that focus on states as sole or primary actors, we now have new conceptual schemes that admit to a much broader range of actors and processes integral to the study of international politics than was the case just a few years ago.[6] These new schemes constitute the

---

[6]See particularly Robert Keohane and Joseph Nye, eds. *Transnational Relations and World Politics* (Cambridge, Mass.: Harvard University Press, 1976); and *Power and Independence* (Boston: Little, Brown, 1977); and Edward Morse, *Modernization and the Tranformation of International Relations* (New York: Free Press, 1976).

precondition necessary for addressing systematically the relationships between international economic and political behavior.

As a consequence of this gradual evolution in substantive and conceptual focus, specialists in international politics have become much more cognizant of the economic dimensions of world politics. Nonetheless, no theory has emerged that specifies adequately the relationships existing among various actors and processes now viewed as integral to the study of world politics. No attempt will be made in this volume to provide such a general theory. Instead, our aim is to describe more richly and explain more adequately the political significance of various economic relationships by contrasting assumptional bases that underlie alternative views of political and economic behavior. The chapters that follow examine the major substantive areas of trade, monetary relations, foreign investment, aid, technology transfers, alternative economic strategies for poor states, and the formulation of foreign economic policy in the United States. Each of these areas, and the interdependencies among them, will be described in terms of how they affect political relations among rich states as well as how they affect relations between rich and poor states. In addition, we will examine how various conceptual frameworks lead to alternative conclusions about which policies are most appropriate for resolving conflicts of interest among states and other actors.

Without attempting to force all analyses of global economic relations into one or the other of the following schools of thought, the major clash in description, explanation, prediction, and policy prescription relating to these problems appears to be between those analysts and decision makers subscribing to the assumptions of classical liberal economic thought and those subscribing to the assumptions of what Americans refer to as radical thought. The classical liberal economic approach is evident in the works of numerous analysts[7] as well as in the basic contemporary foreign economic policy orientations of the United States and other governments of advanced industrial societies in the West. They are evident as well in the policy orientations of key international economic institutions such as the General Agreement on Tariffs and Trade, the International Monetary Fund, and the International Bank for Reconstruction and Development. Examples of radical thought can be found in the works of Cold War revisionists, analysts of contemporary American imperialism, neo-Marxian political economists,

[7]Harry Johnson, *Economic Policies Toward Less Developed Countries* (Washington, D.C.: The Brookings Institution, 1967); "The Link that Chains," *Foreign Policy,* No. 8 (Fall 1972), 113–19; and "The Multinational Corporations as an Agency of Economic Development: Some Explanatory Observations," in *The Widening Gap,* ed. Barbara Ward (New York: Columbia University Press, 1971), pp. 242–52. See also, Richard Cooper, *The Economics of Interdependence* (New York: McGraw-Hill, 1968); and Leland Yeager, with David Tuerck, *Foreign Trade and U.S. Policy* (New York: Praeger, 1976).

and *dependencia* theories of Latin American relations in a capitalist international system.[8]

Although there are many differences of opinion among the statesmen and scholars within each of these two general schools of thought, there are nevertheless certain basic assumptions that are shared widely by the adherents of each school; these assumptions distinguish clearly the two orientations. In particular, there are important differences between the two schools' basic assessments of the primary values underlying actions taken by decision makers on behalf of states, the distribution of benefits from international economic relations, the degree and patterns of conflict inherent in international economic relations, and the location of the major obstacles to the achievement of national economic aspirations. The central tenets of these two analytical traditions are summarized in Table 1-1.

Adherents of classical liberal economic thought tend to see the focus of states' economic policies as the maximization of economic growth and efficiency. The basic value determining policy choice in regard to economic issues before the state should be the optimal allocation of resources for national growth in the context of a global economy that operates in accordance with the norms of liberal economic principles. Success or failure is usually stated in terms of aggregate measures of economic performance such as the level and growth of GNP, trade, investment, per capita income, and so forth.

In this context, global as well as national economic growth and efficiency dictate that all states open themselves to foreign goods and capital and that they specialize in the production of those goods in which they possess a comparative advantage. Existing international economic relationships are viewed as mutually beneficial, even if the distribution of benefits among states is not completely symmetrical.

To the extent that existing international relationships do not enhance growth and the efficient allocation of resources, this view blames the unwillingness of decision makers within states to pursue rational liberal economic policies. In other words, to the extent that the global economy as a

---

[8]William Appleman Williams, *The Tragedy of American Diplomacy* (New York: Dell, 1959); David Horowitz, *The Free World Colossus* (New York: Hill and Wang, 1971); Gabriel Kolko, *The Limits of Power* (New York: Harper & Row, 1972); Harry Magdoff, *The Age of Imperialism* (New York: Monthly Review Press, 1969); Susanne Bodenheimer, "Dependency and Imperialism: The Root of Latin American Underdevelopment," in *Readings in U.S. Imperialism,* ed. K. T. Fann and D. C. Hodges (Boston: Porter Sargent, 1971), pp. 155–82; André Gunder-Frank, "Sociology of Development and Underdevelopment of Sociology," in *Dependence and Underdevelopment* eds. J. Cockcroft, A. G. Frank, and D. Johnson (Garden City, N.Y.: Doubleday, 1972), pp. 321–98; Johan Galtung, "A Structural Theory of Imperialism," *Journal of Peace Research,* 8, no. 2 (1971), 81–117; Fernando Cardoso, with Enzo Faletto, *Dependency and Development in Latin America* (Berkeley: University of California Press, 1979); Arghiri Emmanuel, *Unequal Exchange: A Study of the Imperialism of Trade* (New York: Monthly Review Press, 1972); Samir Amin, *Accumulation on a World Scale: A Critique of the Theory of Development,* 2 vols. (New York: Monthly Review Press, 1974); and Immanuel Wallerstein, *The Modern World System* (New York: Academic Press, 1976).

TABLE 1-1   Central Tenets of Liberal Economic and Radical Thought

Basic Premise	Liberal Economic Thought	Radical Thought
1. Primary value being pursued by states	Maximum aggregate economic growth in national and global economies	Maximum national economic growth consistent with capacity for national self-determination and with equitable distribution of income within and between states
2. Distribution of benefits from global economic relations conducted according to liberal principles	Mutual benefit if not symmetrical distribution	Clearly asymmetrical distribution in favor of rich states.
3. Degree of conflict *inherent* in global economic relations conducted according to liberal principles	Minimal	Very great
4. Persistent cleavages *inherent* in global economic relations conducted in accordance with liberal principles	None	Cleavages between rich states and poor states
5. Major obstacle to achievement of national economic aspirations	Irrational state policies	Rules of behavior governing international economic relations
6. Overall result of activities of international economic institutions	Provision of infrastructure advantageous to all states in conduct of international economic relations	Provision of infrastructure for perpetuating dominance by rich, Western states
7. Characterization of existing international system	Sovereign, autonomous states with considerable decisional latitude on economic policies	Hierarchically organized system of dominant and subordinate states; autonomy and meaningful decisional latitude on economic policy for dominant states only
8. Preferred means of resource allocation	Market mechanisms	State-administered terms of exchange

whole, and individual states' policies, conform to classical liberal economic principles, *all* states' growth and economic efficiency will be maximized. Of course, world production will be maximized also.

Inherent in this positive-sum view of international economic relationships is minimal conflict of interest between states. For the adherents of classical liberal economic thought, policy prescription is universalist: no basic differentiation is made among policy prescriptions appropriate for different types of national actors (large or small, rich or poor). The formal rules of behavior in international economic relations, and the policies of international economic institutions enforcing these rules, are seen as politically neutral among all states.

Liberal economic analysts are prone to see a world composed of sovereign, autonomous states enjoying equal economic opportunity (though not equality of economic condition) in an open international system. All states are understood to possess considerable autonomy and decisional latitude in critical choices about their domestic and foreign economic policies. Resource allocation in economic exchange within and between states should be determined principally by market mechanisms. To the extent that market mechanisms generate socially unacceptable inequalities, the state's function is to ameliorate them through redistribution programs. States should be very wary of intruding on market mechanisms, for they are the key to efficiency for all economic transactions, in the view of liberal analysts.

The assumptional bases of radical thought are vastly different from those underlying the liberals' world view. Although growth and economic efficiency are seen as priority goals of states, national self-determination and equitable income distribution are just as crucial. Indeed, these last two goals would be ranked above economic growth by most radicals if, in the short run, the choice had to be made. The radical analyst tends to see income equality and the capacity for economic and political self-determination among poor states, at least, as incompatible with integration into the existing global economy, which operates in accordance with the norms of classical liberal economic thought. A poor state's open acceptance of foreign goods and capital, along with its specialization in the production of those goods in which it enjoys a comparative advantage, is felt to generate a form of international economic relations in which unequal economic units are afforded equal access to, and compete for, markets and resources around the globe.

The benefits of such international economic relations between rich and poor states are distributed asymmetrically, in favor of the rich. This continued asymmetry in the distribution of benefits forms a basically exploitative relationship between dominant and dependent states that is seen by adherents of radical thought as the explanation for the existence and the widening of the gap between rich and poor countries. Hence, in a fundamental sense the major obstacle to the achievement of the national aspirations of poor states (most states in the world) is seen to be the nature of the international economic system itself, rather than the policies of individual poor states. Even if a poor state does formulate economic policy in accordance with classical liberal economic thought, the asymmetrical distribution of benefits in its international economic relations will condemn it to perpetual poverty, foreign penetration, and continued dependence upon rich states.

Clearly great conflicts of interest between states are inherent in this basically zero-sum view of international economic relations. Policy prescription is not universalist. Policies appropriate for rich states in the center of the global economy are not appropriate for poor states in the periphery. Classical liberal economic thought is viewed by radical thinkers as compatible with the interests of rich states but not with those of poor states. The existing international economic system is not politically neutral, as the classical liberal economists argue. The policies of all the key international economic institutions and the distribution of benefits from most public and private economic transactions inherently favor rich states, ensuring their dominance in global economic and political relations.

Radical economic analysts visualize a hierarchically organized world with dependent, subordinate states relegated to the periphery of the international economy dominated by the leading capitalist states. Only the latter possess autonomy in critical choices about their domestic and foreign economic policies. States in the periphery of the global economy must accept their place in an international division of labor imposed upon them by the leading capitalist states. Market mechanisms allocating resources in international and domestic economic exchange reinforce political, social, and economic inequalities that radical analysts find abhorrent. They seek an active role for the state in managing markets to introduce a greater measure of equity in domestic and foreign economic relations.

Quite obviously, the analysts and decision makers who employ these alternative sets of primary assumptions will differ greatly in their assessment of, say, multinational corporations and in their prescriptions for the treatment of multinationals by nations, acting individually and in concert. The profound cleavage in their basic premises leads adherents of the two schools of thought to talk past each other in analyzing specific economic issues, such as multinational corporations. To the classical liberal, for example, foreign investment appears mutually beneficial; to the radical, it is exploitative. Analysts from both schools seldom examine the appropriateness of the different assumptional bases from which their perceptions and policy prescriptions flow. In the absence of this examination, political conflict over economic issues is exacerbated. The typical analyst or decision maker within each school of thought simply sees no necessity to question seriously the assumptions underlying one's own stance on the issue and continues to propose policies that are seen as harmful in their incidence or intent by adherents of the other analytical tradition.

The clash between these two schools of thought not only has important substantive implications for international relations; it also affords an opportunity to analyze the political implications of various dimensions of global economic relations. In the following chapters, we will refer frequently to these alternative perspectives, and we will develop them more fully in specific contexts.

We will utilize other conceptual frameworks as the subject matter requires. For example, the theory of collective goods[9] tells us that severe conflicts of interest will emerge even among actors that maintain congruent assumptions about the nature of international economic relations and that see the desirability of achieving a common goal from which all actors will benefit. Thus, however useful the juxtaposition of liberal economic and radical thought may be as a means to examine political implications of global economic relations, it would be misleading to assert that this "dialogue" is itself sufficient to address all aspects of these complex problems.

Our essential objective in this volume is to clarify major political problems associated with international economic relations rather than to offer specific solutions to them; the latter can be done intelligently only after the problems themselves are understood better. There is really a great deal at stake in the success of this enterprise, toward which this volume is only a beginning. We are entering an era in international relations during which political conflicts are widely perceived to be centered in economic relations. Yet as political scientists we are presently ill equipped substantively and conceptually to analyze behavior in such an era. By the same token, if economists are to be in a position to prescribe policies appropriate in an era of highly politicized international economic relations, they must begin to examine systematically the political efficacy of their various economic "solutions."

[9]See Mancur Olson, Jr., *The Logic of Collective Action* (New York: Schocken Books, 1968).

CHAPTER TWO
WORLD TRADE DILEMMAS

There is no area of international economic activity that demonstrates more clearly than trade relations the general thrust of the remarks in Chapter 1. During the past decade, trade issues have figured prominently in political controversies between less developed countries and rich states, between East and West, and among the United States, Europe, and Japan. U.S. trade now amounts to over 25 percent of our GNP compared with about 10 percent in 1960. Yet, at a time when America's trade is becoming increasingly important to its overall economic well-being, its loss of economic preeminence relative to that during the immediate postwar period makes it increasingly more difficult for the United States to shape international trade in conformity with its particular economic and political interests. Before examining trade issues of contemporary political importance, we need to look at certain basic characteristics of the global trade order as it has evolved since World War II.

THE POSTWAR ECONOMIC ORDER

Following the war the Western states, under vigorous American leadership were most anxious to construct an international economic order within which trade would flourish. In particular, efforts were devoted to avoiding the explicitly competitive "beggar-thy-neighbor" foreign economic policies that characterized international commerce during the 1930s.

> Intensive economic nationalism marked the . . . decade. Exports were forced; imports were curtailed. All the weapons of commercial warfare were brought into play; currencies were depreciated, exports were subsidized, tariffs raised, exchanges controlled, quotas imposed, and discrimination practiced through preferential systems and barter deals. Each nation sought to sell much and buy little. A vicious spiral of restrictionism produced a further deterioration in world trade.[1]

These policies contributed not only to a deterioration of world trade, but also to global economic depression. Trade and monetary policies emerged as primary instruments used by major states to reinforce a division of the world into tightly knit political-economic regions, which in turn helped to contribute to the outbreak of World War II. In light of the consequences of the foreign economic policies characteristic of the 1930s, the need to encourage relatively free international movement of goods and capital was felt widely to be essential for world peace as well as for global prosperity.

It was toward the ends of peace and prosperity that the major Western states created the General Agreement on Tariffs and Trade (GATT) in 1947. GATT is a legally binding codification of rules for the conduct of trade among its member states. This tiny institution, located in Geneva, Switzerland, has also provided the international infrastructure and the locus for all the major multilateral tariff-reduction negotiations since World War II. Its general goal is to maximize growth in world trade and the global economy through a reduction in trade barriers pursued on a nondiscriminatory basis.

GATT seeks to promote trade in ways that avoid "beggar-thy-neighbor" policies or the creation of highly competitive regional economic blocks of the sort characterizing the 1930s. Protection of domestic industry is to be carried out exclusively through tariff duties (as opposed to other trade barriers such as quotas, controls on the use of foreign exchange, and so forth), and the general level of tariff protection is in turn to be reduced through successive multilateral negotiations. The progressive lowering of tariffs under these circumstances is expected to stimulate international trade and production. Tariff reductions are to be implemented in a nondiscriminatory fashion in accordance with the "most-favored-nation" (MFN) principle. Accordingly, any state in GATT is assured that its goods will enter the markets of all GATT members at rates of duty no less favorable than those applied to similar products of any other country. The MFN principle is designed to accelerate the pace of tariff reductions and trade growth throughout the world as well as to avoid the creation of new preferential trade blocs pro-

---

[1]Clair Wilcox, *A Charter for World Trade* (New York: Macmillan, 1949), pp. 8–9.

tected by discriminatory tariff barriers, except under conditions specified in the General Agreement.[2]

The last point reflects the most significant contribution of GATT to the promotion of international economic order. The General Agreement establishes international norms of responsible trade policy against which the national trade policies of its member states can be evaluated. In cases where a national policy is found to be inconsistent with GATT principles, there are established procedures to settle grievances in a manner designed to minimize further restrictions of international trade. During the 1930s the absence of a permanent international institution with these functions undoubtedly contributed to the escalation of discriminatory trade policies during that period and to the more general deterioration in economic and political relations among states. Thus, GATT's primary utility has been to introduce a form of permanent international oversight and accountability for commercial policies that, prior to its existence, were viewed as exclusively national prerogatives.

GATT was complemented by the creation in 1944 of the International Monetary Fund (IMF), which was designed to promote the stability and liberalization of international monetary transactions.[3] The goals of GATT would have been impossible to achieve without both an adequate global supply of foreign exchange and provisions for capital mobility to finance trade flows. Through the IMF, states became to some extent internationally accountable for their monetary policies. These two institutions, along with the International Bank for Reconstruction and Development (IBRD),[4] became the foundation for multilateral efforts to prevent the political and economic consequences of economic nationalism that preceded World War II.

The United States provided the driving force for the construction of this postwar international economic order. It did so not only for the reasons discussed in the preceding paragraphs, but also because the United States was in a peculiarly advantageous position to benefit from international economic transactions conducted in accordance with the norms established by GATT and the IMF. Immediately following the war, with the economies of most countries in a state of devastation and disarray, the United States was in a commanding position as a source of global credit and exports. An international economic order based on the principles of free movement of goods and capital served perfectly America's domestic and foreign economic interests and capabilities. Such an economic order was an effective means of allowing the United States to penetrate the trade preference systems, especially Britain's sterling area, from which it had been excluded

[2]See *The General Agreement on Tariffs and Trade*, Article XXIV.

[3]The IMF and the political implications of international monetary transactions will be examined in Chapter 3.

[4]The IBRD is the dominant multilateral aid agency. Multilateral aid is discussed in Chapter 5.

prior to the war.[5] The economic and political preeminence of the United States during the 1940s and 1950s assured the creation of an international economic order that was tailor-made to American interests, however sensible such an economic order might also be, from the perspective of liberal thought, for maximizing world trade flows, global prosperity, and peace.

The framers of GATT would look with considerable pride upon the evolution of world trade and production within the context of the economic order established following World War II. The original GATT membership of twenty-three states has climbed to eighty-four. Tariffs on dutiable manufactured and semimanufactured goods were reduced through the first six rounds of GATT negotiations to an average level in 1971 of 8.3 percent for the United States, 8.4 percent for the European Economic Community (EEC) of the Six, 10.2 percent for Britain, and 10.9 percent for Japan. In the case of the United States, this represented a substantial reduction of its level of tariff protection, which had averaged 60 percent in 1934 and 25 percent in 1945. In 1979 a seventh round of tariff negotiations (the Tokyo Round) was completed and will reduce tariff barriers to trade an additional 31 percent by the end of the 1980s. Partly as a consequence of these tariff reductions, world exports increased from $94 billion in 1955 to over $2 trillion in 1980. Since 1955 global GNP has grown from $1.1 trillion to $11.8 trillion. On the basis of these aggregate indicators, it appears that the lessons of the 1930s have been learned; international oversight of national foreign economic policies has been successful in promoting production and in curtailing the excesses of economic nationalism with its negative economic and political consequences.

As remarkable as these developments in world trade may be, they nevertheless present a false picture of the extent to which trade issues have been defused as a source of tension in international relations. International institutional arrangements in trade and monetary policy have facilitated rapid growth in world trade, but the benefits have not been distributed symmetrically across products and geographical regions. Trade problems are reemerging as questions of high politics among all variety of states. That is, trade issues are once again occupying the attention of presidents and prime ministers as priority problems of foreign and domestic politics. These issues contribute significantly to the overall tone of states' foreign relations and to the success of domestic economic policies. They are too important to be treated as essentially technical problems to be handled by nonpolitical experts. We will examine trade policy as foreign policy in two contexts: (1) relations among advanced industrial states and (2) relations between these states and poor countries.

---

[5]For an elaboration of this point, see Robert Gilpin, "The Politics of Transnational Economic Relations," in *Transnational Relations and World Politics*, ed. Robert Koehane and Joseph Nye (Cambridge, Mass.: Harvard University Press, 1971), pp. 57–59.

TRADE ISSUES AMONG
ADVANCED INDUSTRIAL STATES

Trade issues have played a central role in the political dialogue between less developed countries and rich states throughout the period since World War II. Only since the 1960s, however, have trade issues among non-Communist, advanced industrial states reemerged as particularly important political problems. Several factors have contributed to this turn of events after a period of some fifteen or twenty years following the creation of GATT, a period during which trade issues among these states were effectively depoliticized—that is, "discussed and resolved in their own realm . . . without intruding into high policy."[6]

As long as the United States had no economic peer in the non-Communist world and as long as the Cold War was perceived as the most salient problem in international politics, economic relations among Western states were not a predominant source of political tension. A shared perception of threat from the Communist world made advanced industrial states in the West relatively content to defer to Washington for security policy. The primacy of security concerns and the obvious dependence of Western states upon the United States in this area inhibited them from adopting trade, investment, and monetary policies wholly at odds with American interests. In any event, as long as other Western states were critically in need of American capital and production to reestablish their economic health, there was little incentive to challenge directly the postwar economic order that provided both. For its part, the United States was quite willing to tolerate departures by Western European states and Japan from GATT and IMF norms of nondiscrimination in foreign trade and monetary policies as long as these states remained crucial Cold War allies and as long as they were unable to pose a serious threat to American economic interests at home and abroad. These conditions prevailed in substantial measure until the late 1950s. They were conducive to an essentially constructive, though not always harmonious, approach to trade, investment, and monetary relations among advanced industrial states outside the Communist world.

As limited détente between the superpowers gradually superseded their intense Cold War postures, intra-Western conflicts of interest previously subordinated to the dictates of alliance cohesion began to emerge. Conflicts arose over appropriate security policy and the desirability of continued dependence upon the United States in this domain. Also, during the 1960s Japan and Western Europe became strong enough economically to act in accordance with new political and economic interests that they defined apart from the United States. A substantial reduction in the per-

<hr>

[6]Richard Cooper, "Trade Policy is Foreign Policy," *Foreign Policy*, No. 9 (Winter 1972–73), 19.

ception of threat from the Communist world made advanced industrial states in the West less prone to subordinate their particular interests to those of the United States in an effort to preserve Western unity. Whereas earlier all these states were desperately in need of American capital and exports, by the 1960s they were large exporters in their own right and had accumulated excess dollars as foreign exchange reserves. Thus, they were less dependent upon the United States and, indeed, were able to compete effectively against an increasing number of American goods in the U.S. market, their home markets, and around the world. U.S. automakers, steelmakers, and producers of consumer electric goods used to dominate world markets. During the 1970s, European, and especially Japanese manufacturers of these types of products were threatening the viability of some of the very largest American firms in their home market—for example, Chrysler and leading integrated steelmakers such as Bethlehem and U.S. Steel. Now that the Europeans and Japanese were strong enough to pose a serious threat to American economic interests, less competitive American industries and organized labor mounted increased pressure for protection. As a result of these changes in the domestic and international environment, the United States became much less willing than it was previously to tolerate departures by European states and Japan from GATT and IMF norms for national trade and monetary policies, such as discriminatory regional trade ties and the maintenance of significant barriers to imports and investments from the United States. For their part, the advanced industrial states in the West pointed to protectionist American policies (such as demands for "voluntary" export controls on the part of others, import surcharges, currency devaluations, and a reluctance to undertake internal measures appropriate to manage its chronic balance-of-payments deficits) as evidence of American departures from GATT and IMF principles.

In short, the Cold War détente and the economic resurgence of Western Europe and Japan combined to place a severe strain on cohesion among major Western states. The United States continues to be the largest national economy in the world. But, as the data on shares of world production, exports, and foreign exchange indicate (Figures 2-1, 2-2, 2-3), the United States finds itself in a much less commanding position relative to its major economic partners than was the case during the creation and formative years of GATT and the IMF. The present international political and economic problems among Western states are in a fundamental sense a result of this profound structural alteration in the international economy. These new economic realities will make it much more difficult for the United States to place its formative stamp on new global political-economic relations.

Rather than attempting to survey all the major trade issues confronting advanced industrial states, let us examine a number of behavioral traits and political and institutional characteristics that are likely to persist and, thus, to condition efforts to expand trade in the 1980s. Monetary and

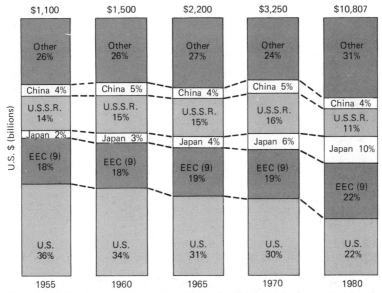

	$1,100	$1,500	$2,200	$3,250	$10,807
Other	26%	26%	27%	24%	31%
China	4%	5%	4%	5%	4%
U.S.S.R.	14%	15%	15%	16%	11%
Japan	2%	3%	4%	6%	10%
EEC (9)	18%	18%	19%	19%	22%
U.S.	36%	34%	31%	30%	22%
	1955	1960	1965	1970	1980

U.S. $ (billions)

FIGURE 2-1 National Production as a Percentage of Global GNP. **Sources:** Data for 1955–1970: *International Economic Report of the President, 1977* (Washington, D.C.: GPO, 1977), p. 138; data for 1980: *Economic Report of the President, 1981,* (Washington, D.C.: GPO, 1981), p. 353.

FIGURE 2-2 World Trade: Exports as a Percentage of World Exports. **Sources:** Data for 1955: *International Economic Report of the President, 1975* (Washington, D.C.: GPO, 1975), p. 131; data for 1960–1970: *International Economic Report of the President, 1977,* (Washington, D.C.: GPO, 1977), p. 148; data for 1980; *Economic Report of the President, 1981,* (Washington, D.C.: GPO, 1981), p. 351.

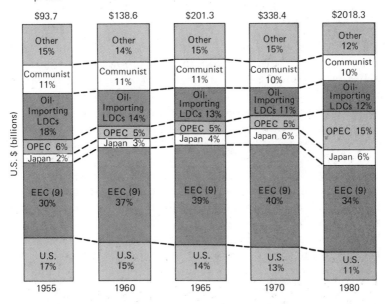

	$93.7	$138.6	$201.3	$338.4	$2018.3
Other	15%	14%	15%	15%	12%
Communist	11%	11%	11%	10%	10%
Oil-Importing LDCs	18%	14%	13%	11%	12%
OPEC	6%	5%	5%	5%	15%
Japan	2%	3%	4%	6%	6%
EEC (9)	30%	37%	39%	40%	34%
U.S.	17%	15%	14%	13%	11%
	1955	1960	1965	1970	1980

U.S. $ (billions)

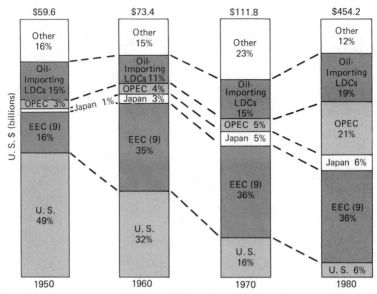

FIGURE 2-3 International Reserves as a Percentage of World Total. **Sources:** Data for 1950–1970: International Monetary Fund, *Annual Report, 1977* (Washington, D.C.: IMF, 1977); data for 1980: *Economic Report of the President, 1981,* (Washington, D.C.: GPO, 1981), p. 352.

investment relations have so much importance in their own right that they will be examined separately in subsequent chapters, but it is important to remember in any discussion of trade issues that all these phenomena are intertwined inextricably.

Neomercantilism

One characteristic feature of the advanced industrial states' trade policies throughout the postwar period, notwithstanding GATT, has been the persistence of a neomercantilist orientation. This orientation manifests itself in numerous ways and is the source of some major trade conflicts of contemporary importance. Neomercantilism is a policy whereby a state seeks to maintain a balance-of-trade surplus and to promote domestic production and employment by reducing imports, stimulating home production, and promoting exports.[7] The attractions of this policy for any single state are obvious. But, by the very nature of trade balances, a state can gain a trade surplus only when other states run a trade deficit. It is evident, therefore, that all states cannot successfully implement neomercantilist policies simultaneously.

Similarly, promoting domestic production at the expense of imports necessarily forces foreign producers to absorb production and employment losses. States that feel themselves victim to others' neomercantilist policies

[7]Harold Malmgren, "Coming Trade Wars?" *Foreign Policy*, No. 1 (Winter 1970–71), 120.

are seldom passive about it. Pursuit of such policies creates the conditions for trade wars that threaten all states' prosperity. Nonetheless, the United States and its major economic partners are all pursuing policies and making demands upon one another in international trade negotiations of a neo-mercantilist variety.

Neomercantilist policies have been an integral part of Japan's remarkable economic resurgence. Since 1960, Japan's share of world exports has doubled (from 3 percent to 6 percent)[8] by virtue of a very aggressive business-government partnership that increased capital investments in key industrial sectors, enhanced labor productivity, and promoted exports with lower profit margins than most private Western firms find it possible to sustain. By 1970, Japanese exports were expanding at a rate of 20 percent per year. Japan was able to generate a trade surplus and to protect domestic production by maintaining an undervalued yen and a large variety of import and foreign investment restrictions designed to make it extremely difficult for American and European firms to penetrate the expanding Japanese market. By the early 1970s, these aspects of Japan's foreign economic policy were all contributing to a severe strain in political relations between Japan and other advanced industrial states of the West.

These economic measures were resented particularly in the United States, which had contributed substantially to Japan's postwar reconstruction and had maintained fewer restraints than Europe had on imports from Japan. The United States, in a word, bore the brunt of Japan's export boom. Notwithstanding efforts by the Japanese to remove a number of quota and other import barriers, its trade surplus in 1977 soared to $15 billion ($8.5 billion with the United States alone). During the same year the United States ran a record trade deficit of $27 billion. These developments were blamed on Japan's continued practice of neomercantilism. The United States undertook a strong diplomatic offensive designed to reduce dramatically the Japanese trade surplus with the Americans, which led to a severe strain in overall U.S.-Japanese relations during 1977 and 1978.[9] Nevertheless, U.S. trade deficits with Japan continued to run between $8 billion and $11 billion per year between 1978 and 1980. The issue took on renewed urgency in 1981 and 1982 after the U.S. trade deficit with Japan surged to over $15 billion.

These trade deficits with Japan raised strong protectionist sentiment in America, particularly from economic sectors impacted by import surges. In 1980, for example, American automobile manufacturers incurred unprecedented losses of over $4 billion. More than 200,000 workers in the industry were laid off. Chrysler was able to survive the early years of the 1980s only with the help of over $1 billion in federally guaranteed loans. During this disastrous year for the American auto industry, Japan passed

[8]See Figure 2-2.
[9]For example see *The New York Times*, December 15, 1977, p. 69.

the United States as the world's leading auto manufacturer, and Japanese imports captured over 21 percent of the American car market. The United Auto Workers and the Ford Motor Company attempted unsuccessfully to force a reduction in Japanese auto exports to the United States in 1980. However, during 1981 extraordinary pressure was exerted on Japan to "voluntarily" reduce the level of its auto exports to America. The Japanese deeply resented this pressure, since they were being asked to bear the burden of Detroit's incapacity to meet Americans' demand for small, fuel-efficient cars of high quality. Had the Japanese not curtailed auto exports, bills introduced in the U.S. Congress would have confined their auto exports to even lower levels. America's willingness to offer the largest, most open market to imports in the world is being severely tested in the 1980s by developments such as these. The postwar liberal trade order will be jeopardized unless protectionist sentiments in the United States are contained and unless Japanese exporters display greater sensitivity to the disruptive effects produced by surges of their U.S. market penetration in key economic sectors.

The EEC, like Japan, has adopted a neomercantilist trade stance, particularly in its Common Agricultural Policy (CAP). The CAP has been described as "the ultimate in mercantilism: decrease in imports, stimulation of home production to substitute for imports, and increase in exports."[10] The CAP protects and stimulates high-cost domestic agricultural production within the Common Market by placing variable duties on all agricultural imports so that domestic production cannot be undersold. In the absence of production controls, the policy has generated agricultural surpluses in Europe that are priced too high to compete in world agricultural markets. The revenues derived from the agricultural import duties are thus used to subsidize Common Market agricultural exports to international markets that the Europeans would otherwise be unable to penetrate. For example, in 1978 French wheat growers got at least $4.25 a bushel for their crops, yet a European trading firm exported French wheat at only $3.50 a bushel to Brazil. Agricultural export sales below production costs are made possible by an EEC export subsidy to European traders of $3.35 a bushel financed by the import levies on agricultural sales to the EEC.[11] The CAP has emerged as a major issue of dispute between the EEC and the United States, which is anxious to maximize its export potential in agricultural products in Europe and elsewhere.[12]

Despite its posture as the world's leading proponent of free trade, the United States, too, has adopted neomercantilist trade policies. When foreign

[10]Malmgren, "Coming Trade Wars?" p. 121.

[11]Kathleen Patterson, "Keeping Them Happy Down on the Farm," *Foreign Policy*, No. 36 (Fall 1979), 64.

[12]As in the case of Japan, the memory of Marshall aid to Europe produces added American resentment of contemporary protectionism by Europe.

imports of steel and textiles began to pose a serious challenge to domestic producers in the 1960s, the American response was to reduce these imports and stimulate relatively inefficient national production by applying vigorous pressure on foreign states and their industrial producers to impose "voluntary" export controls on their sale of these products in the American market. When in 1971 the value of American imports exceeded its exports for the first time during the twentieth century, the United States imposed a temporary 10 percent import surcharge and ultimately negotiated a devaluation of the dollar at the expense of its major trading partners. More recently, the United States has imposed import quotas on specialty steels and has negotiated orderly marketing agreements or voluntary export restraints involving reductions in exports of shoes, color television sets, and automobiles by particularly successful foreign suppliers to the American market. These "voluntary" restraints by exporters to the United States were adopted as preferable to the alternative of even more restrictive trade measures that would certainly have been legislated by Congress, leaving little negotiating room for the exporter. These initiatives were designed to stimulate domestic industry, promote domestic employment, reduce imports, and increase American exports—another classic example of neomercantilist trade policy. The United States insisted that these policies were necessitated by the mercantilist policies of Europe and Japan—in particular, the CAP, which produced a dramatic decline in certain American agricultural exports to the EEC; Europe's barriers to Japanese exports, which made the United States bear the brunt of the rapid growth of Japanese exports of manufactured goods; the EEC's construction of regional preference arrangements that discriminated in favor of trade with numerous Mediterranean and African states; and Japanese barriers to American imports and investment. Even if this is true, however, such a response by the world's leading advocate of free trade is symptomatic of the pervasive appeal of mercantilist policies.

The leading trade powers alone account for over half of world trade. They all employ neomercantilist policies to some degree, and each justifies its own departures from GATT norms in this regard by pointing to the similar policies conducted by the others. This approach to trade policy could easily lead to trade wars and severe political cleavages among the leading economies, particularly during periods of stagnation or decline in the global economy such as those that began in 1974 and 1979. Even in the context of a buoyant global economy, negotiations over the growth of Japanese steel, automobile, and textile exports to the United States, for example, have been bitter and protracted affairs that have soured overall political and security relations between these allies.

Inflation

Neomercantilism is a trade policy designed primarily to protect national producers and maintain domestic employment to the detriment of competitive foreign producers and laborers. It also contributes to inflation by reducing the supply of goods in domestic markets and removing foreign competition to domestic producers. The severe inflation confronting all major industrial states in the 1970s and 1980s has increased interest in using trade policy to protect domestic consumers from price rises. This use of trade policy leads to measures that are quite the opposite of mercantilism, but if carried to extremes these measures can be just as threatening to growth in world trade and production. In particular, trade policy can be used to combat inflation by *lowering* import barriers to make available greater supplies of goods to consumers and to threaten domestic producers that raise prices with a loss of their share of the market to imports. President Carter, for example, reduced barriers to beef imports in 1978 to help offset domestic shortages that generated a 35 percent increase in beef prices earlier in the year. Similarly, in the face of severe import pressure on American steel production in 1977, the Carter administration opted to permit continued steel imports (above a specified "trigger" price) rather than to impose quotas as domestic producers preferred. This choice was adopted, in part, so that lower-priced steel imports would serve to discipline domestic producers contemplating inflationary price increases with the threat of a further loss of their market shares to Japanese and European suppliers.

If the process stopped at this point, trade policy designed primarily to maximize consumer interests might provide a constructive antidote to mercantilist policies. However, the process has not always stopped there. Advanced industrial states have experimented with export controls for the purpose of cutting off foreign demand on nationally produced products and thus increasing supplies available for domestic consumption. In 1973 the United States invoked temporary controls on wheat, soybeans, metal scrap, and timber toward this end.[13] Its major trading partners, particularly Japan, are heavily dependent on the United States for these vital needs. Indeed, shortly after the imposition of export controls on soybeans, U.S. Treasury Secretary Shultz visited Japan. While there, he was a guest at a seventeen-course Japanese dinner in which every dish contained some soybean ingredient. "I got the message," he said.[14] Ironically, Japan itself later imposed unilateral export restrictions on fertilizer and petroleum-based intermediate goods to cope with its own inflation problems. Such trade policies carry with them great potential for global trade disruptions and political conflict.

[13]A domestic wage and price freeze was in effect at the time to combat inflation. Had there been no export controls, further domestic shortages would have resulted from additional agricultural production being exported abroad where higher prices could be obtained. Also it should be noted that we are addressing the issue of export embargos for the express purpose of affecting domestic price levels, *not* export embargos for political reasons such as those directed at the Soviet Union in 1980.

[14]Mary Locke and Hans Binnedijk, "GATT Talks Begin," *European Community*, No. 170 (November 1973), 16.

TABLE 2-1   Inflation and Unemployment in Selected Advanced Industrial Nations

	Average Annual Increase in Consumer Prices (%)		Average Level of Unemployment (%)	
	1960–1972[a]	1973–1980[b]	1960–1972[c]	1973–1980[b]
United States	2.9%	9.4%	4.9%	6.5%
Average of Canada, Japan, France, West Germany, Italy, and United Kingdom	4.2%	11.1%	2.6%	4.4%

[a] Calculated from *International Economic Report of the President, 1977* (Washington, D.C.: GPO, 1977), p. 9.

[b] Data for 1977–1980 are from *Economic Report of the President, 1981* (Washington, D.C.: GPO; 1981), pp. 354–55.

[c] Calculated from *Economic Report of the President, 1978* (Washington, D.C.: GPO, 1978), p. 379.

Not long ago, the prospect seemed remote that all the major industrial states of the West would simultaneously find themselves in varying degrees confronting economic stagnation and chronic inflation. Yet this has happened. In recent years, virtually all advanced industrial states have experienced unemployment levels and rates of inflation well above those of the 1960s and early 1970s—see Table 2-1. These structural conditions present in the global economy are conducive to the development by the major economic powers of national trade policies employing *both* import barriers to protect jobs and export controls to lower prices. Increased political hostility is the likely result of either policy.

Protectionist Domestic Political Forces

These structural conditions give rise to strong domestic political pressures on the part of producers, organized labor, and consumers for their governments to erect various trade barriers. Domestic political considerations make constructive trade alternatives difficult to achieve, no matter how enlightened statesmen might wish to be in their attempts to avoid a resurgence of economic nationalism. Whereas the economies of advanced industrial states may in the aggregate be better off in the absence of protectionist trade policies, those particular interests hurt by liberal trade policies (such as textile, steel, and automobile manufacturers in the United States) bring extraordinary protectionist pressure to bear on their governments. For example, during the presidential campaign of 1968, Nixon's Southern strategy dictated a firm pledge to protect the Southern textile industry from strong Japanese import competition. This campaign commitment was honored by President Nixon and underlaid his administration's hard and bitter negotiations with Japan to curtail sharply Japanese exports of textile goods to the United States.

After the conclusion of the Kennedy Round of GATT negotiations in 1967, Congress was bombarded with a host of minor and major bills calling for trade protection. Demands were made for import restrictions on a wide variety of products, liberalized procedures for claiming injury from imports, more vigorous and prompt relief from imports that are dumped or subsidized, and more extensive financial aid to firms, regions, and workers disadvantaged by import competition. The most salient of these legislative initiatives were the Trade Act of 1970 (the Mills Bill) and the Foreign Trade and Investment Act of 1972 (the Burke-Hartke Bill). The Burke-Hartke Bill, for example, called for a sweeping imposition of import quotas to confine present and future imports to that share of the American market for which they accounted during the 1965-1969 period. Only strong pressure from the executive branch prevented either the Mills or Burke-Hartke bills from coming to a vote in Congress. Passage of either bill would have provoked strong retaliation from our major trade partners.

The Nixon administration initiated legislation committing America to new multilateral trade negotiations in GATT (the Tokyo Round), notwithstanding evidence of substantial domestic opposition to further reductions in trade barriers. The legislation was, however, more sensitive to protectionist sentiment than were previous authorizations for trade negotiations. The Trade Act of 1974 passed by Congress made it easier for industries to obtain a finding of import injury from the government. Relief, in the form of either new import barriers or adjustment assistance to firms and workers, no longer requires that injury from imports be linked to earlier trade concessions by the United States. Also, relief can be obtained when imports are found to be "a substantial cause" of serious injury, rather than "the major cause," as under previous trade law.

As these congressional and executive actions indicate, domestic political support for liberal trade policy has declined markedly in the United States since the late 1960s. Most significantly, organized labor has moved from its keystone position among domestic interests supporting free trade to a highly protectionist position. The AFL/CIO, for example, placed its full weight behind the neomercantilist Burke-Hartke Bill. Speaking in 1977, George Meany addressed the subject of trade policy in the following terms:

> Foreign trade is the guerrilla warfare of economics—and right now the United States is being ambushed. . . . Free trade is a joke and myth. And a government trade policy predicated on old ideas of free trade is worse than a joke—it is a prescription for disaster. The answer is fair trade, do unto others as they do to us—barrier for barrier—closed door for closed door.[15]

It should be noted that organized labor as a whole, and the AFL/CIO in particular, overrepresents those segments of the American labor force

[15]*The New York Times*, December 9, 1977, p. 5. ©1977 by the New York Times Company. Reprinted by Permission.

in traditional manufacturing industries that are most threatened by imports. Most underrepresented are workers in the services sector and high-technology industries that gain from liberal trade policies. For example, "workers in the service industries account for almost 70 percent of the total labor force, but only about 40 percent of the membership of the AFL/CIO. Traditional manufacturing industries such as textiles and steel, make up almost three times as great a share of AFL/CIO membership as they do of the total labor force."[16] These facts help to explain why organized labor has become so avidly protectionist in the past decade. Its memberhip is bearing the brunt of the structural adjustment being forced on the American economy by the increased competitiveness of traditional manufacuring industries located abroad. Note in this regard that, only two years after the American automobile industry was threatened severely by Japanese imports in 1979, the United Auto Workers (long-time advocates of free trade) moved toward reintegration with the AFL/CIO and its protectionist stance on trade.

The erosion in domestic political support that can be mobilized for liberal trade policies makes it considerably more difficult for the United States to promote liberal trade in the coming years than at any time since World War II. Yet, the U.S. economy as a whole continues to have a tremendous stake in an open international trade order. Approximately one out of every six U.S. jobs in manufacturing and one out of every three acres of U.S. farmland are producing for export abroad.

It is also important to realize there are strong internal political pressures that make it difficult for America's major trading partners to move toward more liberal trade policies. For example, a goal of the United States in its trade relations with the European Common Market has been to secure a major alteration in the community's Common Agricultural Policy in favor of reliance upon cheaper American agricultural supplies.[17] But such a move by the EEC would fly in the face of strong domestic pressure by European farmers for protection, and it would go to the heart of a political agreement holding the Common Market together. The CAP was the quid pro quo that France, as the Common Market's leading agricultural producer, secured for its willingness to open itself up to more efficient industrial producers within the EEC, such as West Germany. Many observers feel there could be no Common Market without the CAP. This is a prime example of how political pressures *within* the EEC are likely to frustrate the growth of trade and development of smoother political relations *between* Europe and the United States.

[16]Fred Bergsten, *Toward a New International Economic Order: Selected Papers of C. Fred Bergsten, 1972–1974,* (Lexington, Mass.: Lexington Books, 1975), p. 475. See also ibid., pp. 476–478, for more specific data on this issue.

[17]Ironically, by unilaterally initiating its embargo on grain exports in 1973 to fight inflation the United States gave the EEC its strongest argument *against* relying upon cheaper American agricultural imports for its food needs.

The Crises in Multilateral Institutions

The internal and external forces prompting protectionist trade policies in the major industrial states indicates the need for strong multilateral action to prevent further deterioration in contemporary global trade relations. To this end, the seventh (Tokyo) round of multilateral trade negotiations was initiated under GATT's auspices in 1973. From the beginning of these negotiations, concluded in 1979, stagnation in economic growth, combined with massive trade imbalances due to oil price increases, different rates of inflation, and fluctuating exchange rates, have increased pressures on states to adopt protectionist trade policies. Throughout the talks, unlike the previous negotiating rounds, the driving force for a successful conclusion was less a conviction that further reductions in trade barriers will assure dramatic new gains in trade flows and economic growth than a fear that failure to maintain the momentum toward a more liberal, nondiscriminatory trade order would unleash a highly destructive series of protectionist moves.

The challenge facing states in the Tokyo Round, and for the near future, is that the General Agreement on Tariffs and Trade is unable to contribute much more to world trade growth merely by performing the tasks it has done so well in the past. It succeeded admirably in reducing the level of tariff protection for industrial trade among its member states. These tariffs are now sufficiently low that nontariff barriers such as government procurement regulations, quota restrictions, and health and environment control standards are relatively more important than are tariffs as barriers to trade. Hence, advanced industrial states are entering a period of diminishing returns from mutual tariff reductions on industrial goods. Domestic pressures for protectionism stimulated by any further tariff cuts are likely to be intense, yet, because tariff levels are already low for most industrial goods, the growth in world trade from further tariff cuts on these products is likely to be less dramatic than in the past.

Major efforts to stimulate trade among Western nations must now be focused on the complex issues of agricultural and raw materials trade, nontariff barriers to trade, and more uniform agreement about "fair" practices in export promotion and industrial subsidies. Ways must be found to manage overcapacity and structural shifts in important sectors of the global economy such as textiles, steel manufacturing, consumer electronics, automobiles and shipbuilding, areas that threaten to precipitate trade wars. Increasing scrutiny is required over trade conducted as intracorporate transfers by multinational firms. Traditional instruments of trade policy were designed to deal with "arms-length" transactions between companies, not with internal company transactions across national boundaries. Yet, approximately 25 percent of America's exports consist of sales of U.S. parent companies to their foreign subsidiaries. In a word, the outstanding trade issues among the major economic powers in the West are concentrated in precisely those policy areas in which nations have shown the least interest in agreeing to international oversight by GATT, or in those policy areas that GATT was never designed to tackle. What seems to be required, therefore, is the negotiation of a widely accepted, enforceable system of new rules for these new issues, somewhat like those already developed by GATT for tariffs on industrial goods. Such a system would be designed to encourage nondiscriminatory trade expansion through international supervision of national policies on nontariff barriers, export and industrial subsidies, and agricultural and commodity trade.

Rudimentary first steps toward these ends were actually taken by GATT members in the Tokyo Round. In addition to further tariff reductions, the negotiations produced a number of multilateral codes outlining procedures for managing nontariff barriers distorting world trade. The practices covered in the codes include domestic subsidies for production and exports; various national health, safety, and environmental standards that affect international trade flows; government procurement practices that discriminate against imports; import licensing procedures that unnecessarily complicate and inhibit trade; and discriminatory custom valuation practices. These multilateral codes remain largely untested, but they represent movement toward a new emphasis in GATT. They signal the fact that the advanced industrial states recognize the trade-distorting effects of a wide variety of *domestic* policies and the need for international accountability in connection with them. Moreover, they signal the emergence of "fair" trade alongside "free" trade as a major challenge in the international trade order. Fair trade issues, such as production and export subsidies, are very contentious because they are based on different national concepts of the proper relationship between governments and private enterprise in market-oriented economies. Tremendous disparities among the advanced industrial states on such central aspects of their domestic political economic systems will make rapid progress in future international trade agreements very difficult. Such problems, for example, are at the heart of bitter conflict over steel production and trade in Europe, America, and Japan.

Several additional considerations make rapid progress on significant international trade reform particularly difficult at the present time. First, at the same time that existing GATT arrangements for the regulation of trade are recognized as being inadequate to cope with current trade problems, international mechanisms for handling monetary relations among states have also proved inadequate. The dollar devaluations of 1971 and 1973 marked the end of the Bretton Woods system. Thus, during the 1970s and 1980s the world faced not only the need for trade reform, but also the construction of a new international monetary order. These two challenges are related so closely that progress in both must occur for either to be truly successful. The world has not faced this situation since the 1940s. But, in early postwar negotiations on trade and monetary relations, the United States was in such a commanding economic and political position relative to its negotiating partners that it was able to secure agreements on trade (GATT) and monetary affairs (IMF) that were substantially in accord with American preferences. The present negotiations find Europe and Japan as major economic powers alongside the United States, even if the United States is still the strongest single economic power in the world. Thus, the United States cannot expect to emerge from contemporary and future trade and monetary negotiations with agreements that conform perfectly with American preferences. More important, this current distribution of economic and political power among advanced industrial states is likely to make a truly significant final agreement very difficult to achieve at all. The Europeans and the Japanese are now strong enough to challenge American leadership in the construction of a new economic order, but at the same time they are too weak and divided to replace U.S. leadership in the global political economy. This situation makes the challenge of constructing new trade and monetary orders more formidable to the United States and the world than the challenges of the 1940s.

The existence of these various pressures for the reemergence of economic nationalism among advanced industrial states has led to the fear that the future may bring an international trade order characterized by highly competitive regional trade blocs led by the United States, the EEC, and Japan.[18] The prospects for such a development are enhanced by the fact that multilateral institutions (such as GATT, the Organization for Economic Cooperation and Development, and the International Monetary Fund), long serving as guardians of the principle of nondiscrimination in international economic exchange, seem increasingly less able to produce conformity with this goal. Indeed, they as often appear to legitimize new forms of protectionism by advanced industrial states as to administer an open trade order.[19] Of course, this disarray in multilateral institutions is a reflection of an erosion of concensus among the leading industrial states on the norms that should govern the international trade order.

The harmonization of trade policies among advanced industrial states will be a formidable task indeed. These nations must cope simultaneously with neomercantilism, global inflation, domestic pressures for protectionism, escalating costs of petroleum, alterations in the relative economic strength of states, and the emergence of new problems in international economic relations with which existing international economic institutions are ill equipped to deal. These factors constitute general parameters that condition any efforts to construct a new global trade order. Their existence

[18]For empirical evidence of the existence of such trends already, see D. Calleo and B. Rowland, *America and the World Political Economy* (Bloomington: Indiana University Press, 1973), pp. 123–24. See also Ernest H. Preeg, *Economic Blocs and U.S. Foreign Policy*, National Planning Association Report No. 135 (Washington, D.C.: NPA, 1974).

[19]See Susan Strange, "The Management of Surplus Capacity: Or How Does Theory Stand Up to Protectionism 1970s Style?" *International Organization*, 33, no. 3 (Summer 1979), 330. Strange focuses her attention on textile, steel, and shipbuilding production and trade. Developments in the automobile sector and many others would also conform to her observations.

need not prevent progress toward that goal, however. These forces are clearly evident to decision makers within all advanced industrial states. At least in a general way, all recognize the danger that excessive economic nationalism poses for the maintenance, much less the growth, of their national prosperities. The acute oil crisis of 1973 and 1974 reinforced the fact that their national economies are increasingly interdependent. It amply demonstrated that even the largest powers are incapable of externalizing their economic problems by means of unilateral actions harmful to others. Thus, the salience of the threats to global economic prosperity posed by aggressive trade policies insensitive to the needs of others may provide the momentum necessary for constructive multilateral efforts to establish a new, more resilient framework for the promotion of orderly trade and monetary relations. Indeed, the habits of multilateral consultations and the mechanisms for economic organizations made a major contribution to international economic peacekeeping during the 1970s. Virtually all states were buffeted by a series of international economic shocks unprecedented since World War II—grain shortages, oil price increases, high rates of inflation, and economic stagnation. Even with their imperfections, the present international economic institutions succeeded well enough in these crises to help prevent nations from slipping back to the beggar-thy-neighbor policies of the 1930s.

TRADE AND LESS DEVELOPED COUNTRIES

Export earnings account for 75 percent of less developed countries' foreign exchange resources, clearly dwarfing foreign aid, commercial borrowing, and private investment as alternative sources of foreign exchange. It is not surprising that trade issues have long figured prominently in the political dialogue between less developed states and the advanced industrial states with which they conduct three-fourths of their trade. In particular, less developed countries share a profound sense of frustration with the international trade order developed after World War II. This frustration stems from a number of substantive trade practices and institutional characteristics of GATT that, in their view, combine to inhibit the development of their economies and relegate them to a secondary status in the global economy.

Less developed countries are particularly sensitive to the tariff structures of most advanced industrial states. As we noted earlier, successive rounds of negotiations under GATT's auspices have reduced the average level of tariffs on dutiable manufactured and semimanufactured products to less than 10 percent. But the manufactured and semimanufactured products of particular export interest to less developed countries (such as textiles and semiprocessed metal or wood products) typically face tariff levels of two to four times this average, and tariffs on these items have frequently been ignored altogether in GATT negotiations. In addition, agricultural commodities, which account for the bulk of less developed countries' exports, face a variety of trade barriers—quantitative restrictions; tariff, health, and environmental regulations; and so forth—that are designed to protect the agricultural sector in many advanced industrial states, such as the EEC and the United States.

These explicit barriers to less developed countries' exports are supplemented by more subtle aspects of tariff structures in advanced industrial states. For example, tariff protection typically increases by stages of production, thereby presenting greater barriers, say, to processed mineral resources than to raw materials in their unprocessed state. Accordingly, effective tariff protection is actually at much higher levels than nominal tariff rates would indicate.[20] Tariff rates are also typically higher for the more easily produced consumer goods than for capital goods.

These cascading tariff structures and other trade policies of advanced industrial states impose particularly severe barriers to goods that less developed countries are most capable of producing for export—agricultural goods, semiprocessed commodities, and labor-intensive consumer goods.[21] Capital goods and industrial products that face the lowest tariff barriers in world trade are traditionally the exports of rich states.

Less developed countries also complain that, when they are capable of penetrating these barriers, advanced industrial states, responding to domestic political pressures, erect new ones to protect inefficient domestic producers. In this regard, less developed countries refer frequently to the increased protectionism imposed by advanced industrial states in textiles, clothing, footwear, steel, and assembly of electronic consumer goods; economic sectors in which less developed countries are coming to possess a competitive advantage and that are suffering a decline in mature economies.

Less developed countries argue, further, that certain institutional characteristics of GATT contributed to the emergence of these trade practices and made it difficult for them to secure trade reforms commensurate with their needs. The most-favored-nation principle is one of the problems they see in GATT, notwithstanding the fact that its existence has meant that tariff reductions negotiated among advanced industrial states have lowered trade barriers to exports of less developed countries as well. Their main objection to the MFN principle is that it prevented rich states from

---

[20]To illustrate this fact, let us assume that copper ore faces no tariff protection whereas refined copper faces a tariff of 10 percent. Let us also assume that refining a unit of copper ore raises its value from 75 cents to $1. The 10 percent tariff (10 cents) on the refined copper applies to the $1 price, not just to the 25 cents of value added by the refining process. Thus, the *effective protection* on refined copper is 40 percent (the 10 cent tariff divided by the 25 cent value added by refining), not the 10 percent nominal tariff rate.

[21]For an excellent discussion of the obstacles to less developed countries' exports, see Harry Johnson, *Economic Policies Toward Less Developed Countries* (Washington, D.C.: The Brookings Institution, 1967), Chap. III.

granting preferential treatment to less developed countries' exports of manufactured goods as a spur to their development efforts.

> There are no industrial products of importance that are not produced for export by some developed country. Therefore, no country can now eliminate tariffs on manufactured goods for the benefit of the developing industries of poorer countries without simultaneously opening its markets to unrestrained competition from developed countries [because of the MFN principle]. It is this problem that has given rise to the demands of less developed countries that the most-favored-nation clause [of GATT] be suspended in their behalf.[22]

The bargaining principle of reciprocity underlying all tariff reduction negotiations is another characteristic of GATT long criticized by less developed countries. Poor states feel that they are placed at a disadvantage by the necessity to offer rich states an equivalent tariff concession for every tariff reduction they receive from them. They argue that reciprocity is equitable when applied to negotiations among states at approximately the same stage of economic development, but in negotiations between industrialized and less developed states, reciprocity (as with the MFN principle and the whole philosophy of the existing world trade order, for that matter) is a call for equal competition among fundamentally unequal economic units. Supporters of less developed countries argue that the reciprocity principle has made it difficult for these states to participate actively in GATT negotiations, and this in turn helps to account for the fact that tariffs remain high on industrial products of particular export interest to them:

> The developing countries of course had had no bargaining power, politically or economically. The rule of reciprocity has required them to give a matching concession, but clearly they are not in a position to give any. While over the past fifteen years, tariffs on industrial products of interest to industrial nations have been gradually brought down, those on products of interest to developing countries have remained at a high level.[23]

Less developed countries' criticism of the MFN principle and reciprocity are symptomatic of a more general charge they level at the GATT. They view it as a club created by advanced industrial states and managed in accordance with their primary interests. The norms guiding trade policy, the nature of trade negotiations, and the principal dimensions of progress in expanding world trade all reflect this fact. In the view of less developed states, these characteristics of GATT account for the continued existence of major barriers they face in their exports of agricultural products, mineral

---

[22]John W. Evans, "The General Agreement on Tariffs and Trade," in *The Global Partnership*, ed. R. Gardner and M. Millikan (New York: Praeger, 1968), pp. 92–93.

[23]Ambassador K. B. Lall of India, cited in John Evans, "The General Agreement on Tariffs and Trade," p. 76. Evans goes on to argue, however, that rich states have in fact extended tariff reductions to less developed countries without demanding equivalent concessions.

resources, semimanufactures, and industrial goods they are capable of producing. In substantial measure it accounts, in their view, for the decline of the less developed countries' share of world exports from 31.9 percent in 1950 to less than 20 percent in 1970.[24]

There is no shortage of either alternative conceptualizations of the basic trade challenges facing less developed countries or of policy prescriptions purporting to deal with these challenges. Not surprisingly, the proponents of liberal economic thought and the representatives of radical thought suggest starkly different courses of action on the part of various states to meet the trade needs of less developed countries. Let us examine these briefly, as well as the prescriptions of Raul Prebisch, the noted Argentinian economist and international politician, who more than any other person has provided coherence for the Third World's demands of rich states in trade and financial matters since World War II.

The Liberal Economic Explanation and Prescription

From the perspective of liberal economic thought, the basic problem facing less developed countries is the extent to which national trade policies of rich and poor states continue to depart from the ideal of free trade. Policy prescriptions focus upon the need for all states to return to the underlying spirit of GATT. This requires that both rich and poor states abandon their policy of negotiating waivers from conformity with free trade principles to protect relatively inefficient domestic production. Having created GATT and provided its leadership, advanced industrial states should bring their actual trade policies into line with their liberal trade rhetoric. They are called upon to remove the remaining barriers to trade among themselves and, especially, those particularly high barriers facing the goods that less developed countries produce for export. For their part, less developed countries are called upon to liberalize their own national trade policies, which, based on the protection of infant industries, are often more protectionist than those of advanced industrial states. Liberal economists feel that less developed countries can facilitate the modernization process by exposing their domestic producers to external competition through the encouragement of trade and foreign investment. If rich and poor states were to follow these policies, the argument runs, global production would be maximized and trade could make a maximum contribution to the development of poor states.[25]

---

[24]By 1980 developing countries' exports increased to 27 percent of the world total, but the OPEC states account for the lion's share of the growth. See Figure 2-2.

[25]For a discussion along these lines, see Harry Johnson, *Economic Policies Toward Less Developed Countries*, pp. 47, 130. See also Richard Cooper, "Third World Tariff Tangle," *Foreign Policy*, No. 4 (Fall 1971), 35–50.

There are substantial questions concerning the political efficacy of policy prescriptions for trade and development advanced by liberal economists. This is the case even for decision makers who are basically committed to the tenets of free trade, because (1) all organized interests within their societies do not embrace free trade as a concept, and (2) those who do tend to abandon the concept when, in the short run, it adversely affects their particular jobs, industry, region, or nation. Inefficient producers that would be hurt by the removal of existing trade barriers, whether within rich or poor states, will mount strong political opposition to policy prescriptions for further trade liberalization, notwithstanding the impact that their action will have on the national economy or the global economy. They will repeatedly marshal the argument that the national economy will benefit from continued protection of its relatively inefficient enterprises, since jobs are thereby preserved at home and the nation is able to enjoy the security of maintaining an indigenous productive capacity in the affected economic sector.

We have seen how the complexity of the issues and the nature of domestic opposition to free trade will make it difficult for advanced industrial states to make great strides toward further liberalization of trade policies during the coming years. This will be the case particularly if the Western economies continue to be plagued by stagnant growth rates and high levels of unemployment. In addition, less developed countries will find liberalization of national trade policies of the sort prescribed here very difficult to achieve. Less developed countries typically feel unable to compete on an equal footing with producers of advanced industrial states within their own economies, much less in international markets. The apprehensions of the less developed states must be overcome if they are to implement the policies prescribed by liberal economists. This is unlikely to occur on a broad scale since exposing one's economy to competition through trade and foreign investment is seen by important political elements within countries throughout the Third World as leading inevitably to foreign penetration and further loss of control over their economic and political destinies. Whatever the aggregate economic results, any leader of a less developed country who today embraces liberal economic policy prescriptions does so at the risk of generating substantial domestic political opposition by economic and political nationalists who are acutely sensitive to past injustices stemming from various forms of control that advanced industrial states have exercised over less developed countries.

As we noted before, liberal trade creates a dilemma of trade-offs between the gains that may well obtain for the economy as a whole in terms of efficiency and growth and the burdens of adjustment to import competition that are imposed upon particular segments of a national economy. It is well and good to argue that the overall economy of a rich or poor state is better off if it surrenders traditional types of production to more efficient foreign producers and shifts into new types of production for which it enjoys a competitive advantage. But, unfortunately, the particular workers, firms, and regions that are displaced economically by import competition seldom possess the skills, capital, and infrastructure to provide the new types of production consistent with liberal trade imperatives. Awareness of these facts typically motivates those elements of society that bear the burdens of adjustment to free trade to bring extraordinary political pressure on public authorities to inhibit structural shifts in the economy. The existence of these attitudes and political pressures in both rich and poor states suggests that the world is unlikely to move more than a little way toward the implementation of liberal economic solutions to the trade and development problems of less developed countries.

The Prebisch Explanation and Prescription

In his writings as an economist and through his activities as head of the Economic Commission for Latin America and later the United Nations Conference on Trade and Development, Raul Prebisch has mobilized considerable political support from less developed countries for an alternative conceptualization of these states' trade difficulties. Liberal economists attribute less developed countries' trade problems to the unwillingness of rich and poor states to adopt national trade policies consistent with the principles of a liberal trade order embodied in the General Agreement on Tariffs and Trade. Prebisch agrees that less developed states would be better off if barriers to their exports were removed, by rich states in particular; however, the actual implementation of free trade would not get to the heart of their trade and development problem. Prebisch argues that, even in a world of free trade, the benefits will be reaped disproportionately by advanced industrial states as a consequence of structural differences between countries at different stages of development.

The structural problem of central importance to less developed countries, according to Prebisch, is a long-term decline in the terms of trade for the exchange of commodities for industrial products; that is, the value of primary products has declined relative to the value of manufactured products in world trade. Since less developed countries typically are large exporters of primary products (such products constitute roughly 75 percent of their exports) and must import most industrial goods, they find themselves having to export ever larger amounts of primary products to earn the foreign exchange necessary to purchase the same volume of manufactured imports from year to year.

A number of factors are cited to account for the decline in the terms of trade between less developed states and advanced industrial states. Crucial among them, according to Prebisch, is the fact that productivity advances in advanced industrial states lead to wage and other input cost increases that keep prices constant or rising. In contrast, in less developed countries productivity advances do not lead to wage increases and/or constant prices because of disguised unemployment and weak labor organizations. Instead, they lead to price declines that are passed on to the consumers—located predominantly in rich states.[26]

Additional factors involve the relatively lower income elasticity of the demand for primary products, as compared with manufactures. This means, for example, that forces operate to dampen increases in demand for primary products as income increases: food expenditure as a percentage of income declines, and primary products as a percentage of total factor inputs needed to produce industrial goods decline. These forces, along with the development of synthetic substitutes, serve to depress demand and prices for primary products in world trade relative to manufactured goods, for which demand and expenditures increase as a proportion of income as income increases.

All these factors are seen by Prebisch and most other advocates for less developed countries as evidence of a structural bias in world trade that relegates producers of primary products to a permanent second-class status in the global economy, even if all barriers to free trade were to be removed.[27] Of course, numerous restrictions on trade continue to exist in fact, and as we have seen they make it particularly difficult for less developed countries to transform themselves from exporters of primary products to exporters of manufactured and semiprocessed goods as a means of overcoming the problem posed by the terms of trade.

This conceptualization of the manner in which less developed countries are denied their fair share of trade benefits is quite at odds with classical liberal economic theory. Not surprisingly, Prebisch and his followers find the liberal policy prescription for free trade a deficient solution to the trade and development problems of poor states. Instead, they call for comprehensive reforms of the international economic order designed to eradicate the structural inequalities that produce disproportionate gains from trade for rich states and to compensate poor states for any remaining inequalities. Such a program would require advanced industrial states to facilitate the

---

[26]See Albert O. Hirschman, "Ideologies of Economic Development in Latin America," in *Latin American Issues* (New York: Twentieth Century Fund, 1961), pp. 14–15. Hirschman provides a concise overall summary of Prebisch's economic philosophy.

[27]The dramatic price increases of commodities during the early 1970s raised considerable doubt about the persuasiveness of the terms of trade thesis. Nevertheless, adherents of the thesis would argue that in the same period inflation led to price increases in their imports of manufactured products as well. Moreover, with a recession in the Western states during the mid-1970s, prices in international commodity markets once again fell more than did prices of industrial goods in world markets. In short, advocates of the terms of trade thesis are unlikely to see anything in the relative prices of commodities and industrial products during the 1970s that would convince them to alter their orientation or their demands.

expansion of less developed countries' exports of manufactured and semi-manufactured goods. It would also include numerous commodity agreements covering primary product exports of particular importance to less developed countries. These agreements between major exporters and importers would be designed to ensure access to the markets of rich states as well as to stabilize world market prices for specific commodities at levels assuring poor states both a larger income and smaller annual fluctuations in revenues. To the extent that such agreements in commodity and industrial trade fail to arrest the decline in the terms of trade between less developed and industrial states, Prebisch insists that a compensatory finance scheme be established by which industrial states would return capital to less developed countries in the form of grants or low-interest loans. This capital flow should be in amounts at least equal to the "excess" in revenues industrial states receive as a consequence of any further declines in the terms of trade.

Prebisch argues that trade reforms cannot and should not be accomplished primarily by reciprocal tariff cuts of the GATT variety between rich and poor states. Rather, he summons the rich states unilaterally to extend preferential treatment to less developed countries for their exports of manufactures and semimanufactures. Such a move would help to arrest the decline in the terms of trade between center and periphery states while facilitating industrialization crucial to the latter's rapid development.[28]

Quite obviously, Prebisch and his advocates do not want a return to the spirit underlying GATT. Indeed, they want to create a new economic order—one that recognizes the special needs of less developed countries and that affords them a greater share of the benefits from the conduct of trade than could be expected even in a world of free trade. Trade in accordance with GATT principles is viewed as a means of exploiting poor states and denying them the opportunity of industrializing rather than as a means of enhancing the welfare of all states. Consistent with this orientation, less developed countries pushed hard for the establishment of the United Nations Conference on Trade and Development (UNCTAD) in 1964, with Raul Prebisch as its first secretary-general. UNCTAD is the institutional expression of Prebisch's conceptualization of the global economy and the less developed states' role in it. It was created to challenge GATT both philosophically and institutionally as the central multilateral arena for world trade relations.[29]

---

[28]For a more complete account of Prebisch's economic analysis and policy prescription, see *Towards a New Trade Policy for Development*, report by the Secretary-General of the United Nations Conference on Trade and Development (Raul Prebisch), E/CONF. 46/3 (New York: United Nations, 1964).

[29]For a comprehensive description and assessment of UNCTAD as an institution from an advocate's viewpoint, see Branislav Gosovic, *UNCTAD: Conflict and Compromise* (Leiden: A. W. Sitjhoff-Leiden, 1972). See also R. S. Walters, "International Organizations and Political Communication," *International Organization*, 25, no. 4 (Autumn 1971), 818–35.

Through UNCTAD and other bilateral and multilateral channels, the less developed countries have sought to secure a variety of structural reforms of world trade. In certain respects, they have been notably successful.

The Generalized System Of Preferences In the early 1970s the less developed countries were successful in negotiating a Generalized System of Preferences (GSP) with advanced industrial states. This system was designed to stimulate exports of manufactured goods from less developed countries. The advanced industrial states agreed to eliminate tariffs for ten years on manufactured and semimanufactured goods exported by less developed countries. These tariff concessions were applicable only to less developed countries' trade, seeking to stimulate their industrialization and to improve the competitiveness of their exports relative to the production of similar goods in more advanced economies.

The GSP constitutes a departure from the most-favored-nation principle and the practice of reciprocity underlying GATT—the poor states were not asked to offer tariff concessions in return for those granted by the advanced industrial states. The advanced industrial states have placed a variety of limitations on their GSP programs to minimize domestic economic disruptions and protectionist demands. European states, for example, impose quota ceilings on goods imported from less developed countries under the GSP. The United States excludes imports of textiles and shoes under the GSP, and initially it did not offer its GSP program to those less developed countries participating in producer cartels, such as OPEC.

Not surprisingly, less developed countries are continuing to press the advanced industrial states to remove these and other constraints that undermine the Generalized System of Preferences. Rich states are moving gradually to expand their programs. But, at present, the GSP is most significant as a symbol of the advanced industrial states' willingness to depart from cherished principles of liberal trade philosophy (MFN and reciprocity) on behalf of less developed states under carefully defined and circumscribed conditions. It has not proved to be a major stimulus to industrial exports of less developed countries.

The Integrated Commodity Program Less developed countries have long been very concerned about the decline in the terms of trade between the prices of their commodities versus the prices of industrial goods. They are also confronted with massive fluctuations in commodity price levels that dramatically affect the foreign exchange earnings of less developed countries that rely heavily on exports of one or a few primary products. Since 1974 less developed states have pressed vigorously for implementation of UNCTAD's proposed Integrated Program for Commodities (IPC) to deal with these problems.

The IPC represents a bold departure from the isolated efforts in past years to control both the price fluctuations and the average price levels of commodities through agreements between major exporters and importers negotiated on a case-by-case basis. It involves a comprehensive effort to forge commodity agreements for eighteen primary products that account for approximately 75 percent of less developed countries' exports of agricultural and mineral commodities. Ten of these eighteen commodities have been identified as suitable for stockpiling[30] and, thus, lend themselves to the creation of buffer stocks as a means of influencing the market when it approaches the floor and ceiling prices established through individual commodity agreements.[31] The IPC calls for the creation of a common international fund (initially estimated to require $6 billion) through contributions from commodity importers and exporters. The Common Fund would presumably make it easier to finance any buffer stock arrangements that might emerge as a component of a commodity agreement negotiated under the auspices of the IPC. In addition, the IPC envisions the adoption of various measures (such as tariff structure changes, technology transfers, and investment and tax incentives) to enable less developed country commodity producers to process more of their own raw materials.

At the Nairobi session of UNCTAD in 1976, target dates were established for the convening of a negotiating conference to create the Common Fund and to establish a series of meetings to culminate in the negotiation of commodity agreements for the eighteen IPC products. The less developed countries and advanced industrial nations have engaged in a protracted series of negotiations since 1976, but they are far from reaching agreement on the implementation of the set of eighteen commodity agreements.

The major Western powers, and the United States in particular, remain highly skeptical of the Integrated Program for Commodities, although they have participated in the negotiations in recognition of the importance attached to them by all less developed countries and by the OPEC states. American officials remain convinced that only in rare circumstances should negotiated commodity agreements replace traditional market mechanisms governing commodity trade. To the extent that commodity agreements are explored, the United States still prefers to do it on a case-by-case basis. American officials are wary of universal formulations, such as the IPC emphasis on buffer stocks, which they do not think will work as hoped for by the less developed countries. The aim of any commodity agreement entered into by the United States is likely to be stabilization of fluctuations

[30]The commodities are cocoa, coffee, copper, cotton and cotton yarns, hard fibers and products, jute and jute products, rubber, sugar, tea, and tin. A buffer stock facility is a stockpile of a commodity managed under the auspices of an international commodity agreement. The stockpile is used for the purpose of controlling prices of that commodity traded in world markets.

[31]When approaching the floor price, the buffer stock manager would enter the market to purchase the product and strengthen prices; when approaching the ceiling price, the buffer stock manager would enter the market to sell quantities of the product to reduce prices.

in price levels, not an increase of the price level above market trends for the product. That would increase inflationary pressure and discourage inefficient producers from diversification. American analysts, moreover, view as a fallacy the notion that less developed countries as a group actually benefit from a comprehensive program of commodity agreements stabilizing and raising the prices of primary products in world markets. Many advanced industrial states including the United States, Canada, Australia, and South Africa are major commodity exporters, and less developed states import many primary products. Less developed states accounted for only 33 percent of the world's nonfuel mineral exports in 1974, and they possess approximately 45 percent of the world's known reserves of nonfuel minerals.[32] Thus, the effects of the IPC will be complex and will not necessarily reduce the gap between rich and poor states. "In most cases, selected industrial countries would benefit as much or more from price increases in nonfuel minerals than would the less developed countries."[33]

For reasons such as these, the prospects of *comprehensive* implementation of UNCTAD's Integrated Commodity Program are slim. On the other hand, the mere participation of the United States and all other advanced industrial states in IPC negotiations since 1975 represents a major change in their behavior. Concrete agreement was reached in March 1979 to create and finance a Common Fund with two "windows." A "first window" with resources of $400 million will be used to finance buffer stocks in support of commodity agreements negotiated as part of the IPC. A "second window" with planned assets of $350 million will be used to help finance commodity research and development, market promotion, and certain aspects of diversification.[34]

Compensatory Financing   A third component of Prebisch's philosophy involves financial transfers from advanced industrial states to less developed countries through grants or low-interest loans to make up for shortfalls in the export earnings of less developed countries that arise for reasons substantially beyond their control. These may result from a decline in the terms of trade, crop failures in agricultural raw materials, or decreased demand for raw materials exported from less developed countries because of recessions in advanced industrial nations. This compensatory finance would supplement, not replace, traditional forms of bilateral and multilateral economic assistance to poor nations. Compensatory finance is a means of dealing with the *effects* of shortfalls in export earnings, notwithstanding

[32]Dennis Pirages, *The New Context for International Relations: Global Ecopolitics* (North Scituate, Mass.: Duxbury Press, 1978), p. 170.

[33]Ibid.

[34]"UNCTAD V Ends Session in Manila," United Nations, TAD/INF/1079, (Geneva, Switzerland, June 5, 1979), pp. 3 and 4. These resources are still far short of the $6 billion initially proposed for the Common Fund.

reforms such as the Generalized System of Preferences and the Integrated Program for Commodities designed to deal with the *causes* of the shortfalls. The goal of compensatory finance is to guarantee export earnings, not to administer commodity prices. As such, it is more popular than commodity agreements in countries such as the United States that are reluctant to interfere with market mechanisms presently governing commodity trade.

Two compensatory finance schemes are presently in operation. The International Monetary Fund (IMF) introduced a compensatory finance facility in 1963, which was expanded and whose terms governing access were liberalized in 1976. It is available to all IMF members, although it is designed primarily for the less developed states. It can be used when a country finds itself with a balance-of-payments deficit due to reductions in its overall export earnings for reasons substantially beyond its control. From the period January 1976 through April 1981, approximately fifty countries received $4.4 billion from the IMF through this program.[35] This compensatory finance was used largely to cover export earnings shortfalls experienced by less developed states when commodity prices plunged in 1975 due to the recession in advanced industrial states.

A second compensatory financing scheme, STABEX, was initiated in 1975 as a component of the Lomé Convention governing economic relations between the European Economic Community and forty-six (now fifty-three) African, Caribbean, and Pacific (ACP) countries. The STABEX scheme involves the extension of grants or interest-free loans to ACP states when their export earnings from any of nineteen primary products specified in the Lomé Convention fall more than 7.5 percent below the average export receipts for the previous three years in trade with the European Economic Community. The STABEX facility was limited to approximately $80–90 million per year for the period 1976–1980. Its assistance is extended on easier terms than the compensatory finance through the IMF facility, but the STABEX scheme applies only to specific products in trade between a limited number of countries and the European Economic Community. Moreover, the IMF facility permits far larger financial transfers than does the STABEX scheme.[36]

The less developed countries are understandably disappointed in the present international trade system and are frustrated over the limited progress in reforming the world trade order. Nevertheless, there has been a

---

[35]"Fund Activity," *Finance and Development*, 16, no. 3 (September 1979), 5 and *Annual Report 1981* (Washington, D.C.: International Monetary Fund, 1981), p. 84. See also, Louis Goreaux, "The Use of Compensatory Financing," *Finance and Development*, 14, no. 3 (September 1977), 21.

[36]For an excellent, brief summary of these compensatory finance facilities as well as of the Generalized System of Preferences and the Integrated Program for Commodities, see Guy Erb, *Negotiations on Two Fronts: Manufactures and Commodities*, Development Paper No. 25, (Washington, D.C.: Overseas Development Council, March 1978). See also, Louis Goreaux, "The Use of Compensatory Financing."

fundamental alteration of the principles underlying trade between less developed states and the Western powers. To these accomplishments should be added the explicit recognition given throughout the Tokyo Round that the GATT principals of nondiscrimination and reciprocity would be relaxed on behalf of less developed countries.[37] The ideas that Prebisch popularized and politicized constitute the agenda for contemporary commercial relations between rich and poor states in a variety of negotiating forums. That, itself, is a substantial accomplishment on behalf of less developed countries, even if resource transfers through these trade reforms are far less than initial expectations or current needs.

Further progress toward implementation of Prebisch's concept of an international trade order that benefits less developed countries is, nevertheless, likely to be very slow. The policy prescriptions outlined by Prebisch and his followers to benefit poor states place the burden of international structural reform primarily on the shoulders of advanced industrial states. In advanced industrial states relevant decision makers typically think in terms of liberal economic principles. Liberal economists view the critical assumptions of Prebisch's economic theory (such as the terms of trade arguments) with great skepticism.[38] Thus, successful implementation of the Prebisch program to meet the trade and development problems of poor states depends upon unilateral concessions by advanced industrial states, whose decision makers are not predisposed to accept the philosophical underpinning that gives rise to demands for these concessions.

Differences in economic philosophy are only part of the problem. More important is the lack of a sense of community among center and

[37]See Stephen Krasner, "The Tokyo Round," *International Studies Quarterly*, 23, no.4 (December 1979), 524.

[38]Classical liberal economists are skeptical of the terms of trade arguments advanced by Prebisch and others. They note that the magnitude, and indeed the direction, of the terms of trade between primary products and manufactured goods vary greatly from commodity to commodity, depending upon the base years chosen from which to measure price trends. Basing calculations on prices prevailing in the early 1950s or early 1970s, for example, will reveal sharp declines in the terms of trade for commodity exporters because those base periods reflect extraordinarily high commodity prices relative to those for industrial goods. The choice of other years as a base period would yield very different results. Also, while commodity exports have virtually the same characteristics today as they did years ago, manufactured goods embody significant qualitative improvements over the years. The properties of natural rubber, for instance are the same today as they were in the 1950s, but automobile tires may get four times the mileage as they did in the 1950s. Therefore, it may be appropriate that prices for rubber (or other primary products) have not increased as rapidly as for tires (or other manufactured products).

Nothwithstanding the controversy over the terms of trade among economists, most advocates for less developed countries believe the Prebisch position to be valid. It constitutes the assumptional base underlying virtually all their political and economic assessments of world trade.

For a summary of views attacking Prebisch's terms of trade arguments see A. S. Friedeberg, *The United Nations Conference on Trade and Development* (Rotterdam: Rotterdam University Press, 1970), pp. 46–61.

periphery states that is strong enough to trigger a substantial redistribution of income through commodity agreements, aid programs, preference agreements, and the like that are adequate to meet the development needs of poor states. At the heart of any effective income redistribution program is a prior sense of political and social community. Prebisch's program for a comprehensive structural reform in the global economy depends upon a sense of community *between* rich and poor states that is every bit as strong as that existing *within* advanced industrial states with a long tradition of national unity. This sense of community between rich and poor states simply does not exist at present.

Evidence of this fact, and still another obstacle to implementing Prebisch's policy, is the domestic opposition within the major advanced industrial states to unilateral concessions on the order of those demanded by Prebisch. Protectionist forces within all advanced industrial states are likely to prevent a resource transfer to poor states from ever approaching the scale contemplated by Prebisch and less developed countries in their demands for a generalized system of preferences, an integrated program for commodities, and expanded compensatory finance. This is particularly true when advanced industrial states suffer from slow economic growth, high unemployment, and inflation.

The political obstacles to the implementation of Prebisch's proposals are not confined to advanced industrial states. Less developed states, for example, must act together in pressing demands for structural reforms in the international economic order that are consistent with Prebisch's philosophy. Since commodity agreements, tariff preferences, aid programs, and other means of transferring resources to less developed countries do not benefit each of them equally, there is increasing difficulty in maintaining political cohesion among periphery states in their negotiations with center states. In the absence of a united front by less developed countries, it is unlikely that advanced industrial states will find it necessary to extend concessions along these lines.

The Radical Explanation and Prescription

The radical view of the trade and development problems faced by poor states has some things in common with Prebisch's orientation, but in other respects it differs sharply. Radical analysts in rich and poor states share with Prebisch the conviction that the free trade prescription in the liberal economic tradition will not generate modernization and economic development in less developed countries. They embrace Prebisch's argument about the decline in the terms of trade and view the conduct of trade between Western states and less developed countries in accordance with GATT principles as an exploitative relationship.

In spite of these similarities with the Prebisch conceptualization of the global economy, the radical view goes well beyond Prebisch in its assessment of how profoundly the structural arrangements *among* and *within* states are at odds with the developmental possibilities and capacity for autonomy of poor states. Consequently, radicals differ greatly with Prebisch on what solutions are appropriate to achieve the basic political and economic interests of states in the periphery of the global economy.

Prebisch views inequities in international economic relations between rich and poor states as having evolved gradually out of certain structural characteristics of exchanges between states at different stages of economic development. As we have seen, his prescription to remove these inequities focuses upon comprehensive reform of the norms governing international economic relations. In essence, this means reliance upon policy changes by advanced industrial states designed to redistribute income to less developed countries. Prebisch feels that this can be accomplished through multilateral negotiations between less developed countries and advanced industrial states if the former maintain a unified position in applying sustained political pressure for precisely defined alterations in the conduct of trade and other forms of international economic exchange. Since 1964, UNCTAD and the United Nations have been the locus of this effort.

Radicals see the poverty of poor states as a consequence of a capitalist (imperialist) international political economy in which periphery states are held subordinate politically and economically to Western states. The global political economy based on the norms of liberal economic philosophy is very effective in assuring center states access to cheap raw materials and cheap labor as well as new markets for capital investments and exports. These characteristics of the international political economy are the key to understanding both the poverty of the Third World and the prosperity of Western countries, the United States in particular. The development of center states and the underdevelopment of periphery states are both "outcomes of the same historical process: the global expansion of capitalism."[39]

Western states are able to continue this exploitative relationship with less developed countries because of their control of the key international institutions that establish norms for international transfers of goods and capital. In addition, these governments buttress the leadership position of a small economic and political elite (client class), present in most poor states, whose source of domestic power derives from the maintenance of close external ties with the political and economic elites of advanced industrial (capitalist) states. This client class is viewed by radicals as a junior partner to elites in center states. Such a class benefits handsomely from its position

---

[39]Suzanne Bodenheimer, "Dependency and Imperialism: The Roots of Latin American Underdevelopment," in *Readings in U.S. Imperialism*, ed. K. T. Fann and D. Hodges (Boston: Porter Sargent, 1971), p. 160.

in the international capitalist system, even though the country it dominates may remain economically underdeveloped.

Given these perceptions, it is easy to understand the radicals' criticism of both the liberal economists' and Prebisch's prescriptions for dealing with the trade and development problems of poor states. The liberal prescription of free movement of goods and capital among states is to the radicals merely a blatant effort by advanced industrial states to penetrate and further de-nationalize the political and economic systems of less developed countries. Prebisch's prescriptions appear very naïve to radical thinkers. Western states are not going to redistribute income to poor states to remedy inequalities in the benefits derived in international economic exchange. To do so would mean an end to the exploitative relationships that they created (consciously or unconsciously) and upon which their continued prosperity depends. In radical thought, multilateral negotiations of the sort Prebisch suggests hold no promise. The international economic institutions that define the post–World War II economic order (GATT, IMF, IBRD) are firmly controlled by Western (capitalist) states. Indeed, these agencies constitute the machinery through which rich states exploit less developed countries. Radicals also see little progress resulting from negotiations in an international institution such as UNCTAD, even though it ostensibly represents the interests of poor states. Not only will Western states refuse to agree to any critical reforms demanded by less developed countries in such a forum, but also, since the leaders of most less developed countries depend so thoroughly on Western ties for their economic and political survival, they will not even pose demands that would threaten the dominant position of advanced industrial states in the global economy.

For poor states to secure autonomy of economic and political action or to escape from the economic exploitation that has condemned them to poverty, they must interrupt the existing linkages between center and periphery states. Among the radicals there is general agreement that this can be accomplished only by replacing capitalism with a socialist political-economic order. New Left advocates in the United States tend to focus their attention on the need for the emergence of socialism in the United States and in other center states. Only then will the rich states be predisposed toward a redistribution of income to less developed countries and the erection of a new, nonexploitative global economic order based on socialist principles of exchange. Moreover, the external support critical for continued control by present-day political and economic elites in less developed countries would be withdrawn by socialist governments in rich states. Hence, from this perspective the emergence of socialism in Western states would be necessary and sufficient to remove the primary local and international obstacles to the development of poor states. *Dependencia* theorists in Latin America, on the other hand, tend to focus their attention on socialist revolutions in periphery states, revolutions that would remove present domestic political-economic elites and clear the way for an interruption of the existing ties between poor states and the capitalist global economy that produces their poverty. Hence, the radical solution to the trade and development problems of poor states is revolution in the center states and/or in the periphery states of the global economy. It is dramatically different from the classic liberal or Prebisch approaches, which, though different from each other, are alike in that they call upon rich states merely to alter their foreign economic policies and to implement relatively modest reforms in trade and the larger economic order.[40]

A number of questions arise regarding the political efficacy of the radicals' policy prescriptions. The program of the New Left in the United States depends essentially on the transformation of the United States and other Western states from capitalist to socialist systems. There is very little evidence to suggest that such a transformation is likely to occur, at least in the near future. But even if it were likely to occur, careful scrutiny would have to be given to the categorical assertion that less developed countries will be incomparably better off in dealing with a socialist West and a socialist United States than with the same states under capitalist systems. Whether Western states are socialist or capitalist, less developed countries will be engaged in economic exchanges with economic and military giants. Throughout history, the largest economic and military powers have defined their relationships with lesser powers in a manner that lesser powers typically view as exploitative. This situation is likely to repeat itself even in a world of socialist states.[41] Soviet relations with the Peoples Democracies of Eastern Europe provide some evidence on this point.

The emphasis of the *dependencia* theorists upon socialist revolutions in the periphery states raises another basic problem. In most instances, if a state, or states, in the periphery of the global economy achieves a socialist revolution, its need for foreign capital, technology, and markets will still exist. Unless the advanced industrial states also abandon capitalism, the new socialist state, or states, in the periphery will still have to operate within a capitalist global economy. Even if the character of its linkages with the international economy is altered drastically by a socialist revolution at home, the state in the periphery will in all probability find that the alternative to dependency is not autonomy; rather, at best it will be a new form of interdependence, one that still sets severe constraints on domestic economic and political programs.

[40]For examples of the radical perspective on trade, see Arghiri Emmanuel, *Unequal Exchange: A Study of the Imperialism of Trade* (New York: Monthly Review Press, 1972); and Harry Magdoff, *The Age of Imperialism* (New York: Monthly Review Press, 1969).
[41]This discussion of the radical interpretation of global economic relations between rich and poor states has purposefully been couched in terms larger than the trade issue. The basic dynamics described here can be applied to other forms of economic exchange besides trade, such as aid, private investment, and monetary relations.

Summary

The profound differences among the liberal, Prebisch, and radical interpretations of the contemporary trade and economic challenges facing less developed states are summarized in Figure 2-4. Each school of thought identifies a different fundamental obstacle inhibiting the economic performance of poor states. Each school of thought, accordingly, identifies a different focal point for concerted action appropriate to alter the condition of less developed states.

Liberal analysts and decision makers attribute the source of poor states' problems in trade to departures in the foreign economic policies of rich and poor states from the liberal economic principles embodied in the GATT and IMF statutes. They are likely to place primary emphasis on bringing the foreign economic policies of less developed and advanced industrial states into conformity with liberal trade principles that, in their view, serve appropriately as the norms for economic relations in the post–World War II era. Doing so will mean acceptance of some structural shifts in the domestic economies of both poor and rich states.

Prebisch and his followers attribute the primary sources of the poor states' trade problems to inequities of the market system and of liberal principles governing foreign economic exchange. They are likely to place primary emphasis on redefining these liberal norms governing international economic exchange to give particular advantages to less developed states relative to advanced industrial states. For example, they would like to see UNCTAD's philosophy replace the GATT philosophy as the linchpin of the international trade order. The burden of adjusting to new norms governing world trade would necessarily fall primarily on the advanced industrial states whose foreign economic policies toward poor states must change dramatically. Implementing these reforms would mean some structural shifts in the domestic economies of rich and poor states, as well as some alteration of the foreign economic policies of less developed states.

Radical analysts take a more holistic approach to problem definition and proposed reforms than do liberal analysts or Prebisch. All activities at the domestic and international levels are interrelated inextricably. Radical doctrine insists that nothing can be left the same if the development prospects of poor states are to improve markedly. These analysts place primary emphasis on a radical alteration of the domestic economic and social structures of all advanced industrial and less developed countries. Capitalism must be replaced by socialism. This domestic transformation would necessarily produce drastic shifts, as well, in the foreign economic policies of rich and poor states and in the norms governing international economic exchange.

Existing Terms of and Norms
for International Economic
Transactions

Trade
Aid
Direct Investment
Commercial Lending

Domestic Economic and Social Structure of AISs	Foreign Economic Policy of AISs		Foreign Economic Policy of LDCs	Domestic Economic and Social Structure of LDCs

Analytical Approach	Primary Problems and Efforts at Reform	Secondary Problems and Efforts at Reform	Marginal Problems and Efforts at Reform
Liberal	Foreign economic policies of LDCs Foreign economic policies of AISs	Domestic economic and social structures of LDCs Domestic economic and social structures of AISs	Existing terms of and norms for international economic transactions
Prebisch	Terms of and norms for international economic transactions Foreign economic policies of AISs	Foreign economic policies of LDCs	Domestic economic and social structures of AISs Domestic economic and social structures of LDCs
Radical	Domestic economic and social structures of LDCs Domestic economic and social structures of AISs	Terms of and norms for international economic transactions Foreign economic policies of LDCs Foreign economic policies of AISs	

FIGURE 2-4 Emphases for Reform in Trade and Other Economic Relations Between Advanced Industrial States (AISs) and Less Developed Countries (LDCs).

CONCLUSION

We have attempted to outline the way in which prescriptions for reforms in trade between states in the center and states in the periphery of the global economy follow logically from the assumptions that liberals, Prebisch, and radicals make about the nature of international economic exchange. Serious questions arise concerning the prospects for conducting trade completely in accord with the desires of advocates of each school of thought. The questions raised about each approach need not be seen as a cause of despair. No serious analyst truly expects global economic and political relations as complex as trade to lend themselves to solutions that are totally consistent with a single school of thought, particularly in an era when even the most powerful state in the world finds it increasingly difficult to mobilize international and domestic support for policies consistent with the school of thought it has long championed. Rather, the questions we have raised point to the need for decision makers and analysts of the various persuasions discussed to recognize the political, attitudinal, and structural realities that make their policy proposals difficult to implement. More fundamentally, these questions point to the need for decision makers and analysts to reexamine the basic assumptions that generate logically compelling, yet often unworkable, policy prescriptions.

To the extent that this reexamination of assumptions occurs, particularly within governments, workable solutions to the trade and development problems facing less developed countries may be generated. If it does not occur, political discourse among states at different levels of economic development will continue to produce conflicts as to which is the most appropriate, if unattainable, utopia within which to conduct economic exchange.

In spite of these considerable obstacles to the trade prospects of less developed countries, certain contemporary developments afford these states an opportunity to enhance their bargaining position in the global economy. First, the trade and monetary issues dividing advanced industrial states are so profound that, quite aside from the problems of less developed countries, protracted negotiations are underway to implement important new trade and monetary reforms. Authorities on less developed countries have pointed out that, through unified action, they could be in a position to take advantage of divisions among rich states to assure that some of their own demands in monetary, trade, and aid affairs be met.

> The process of monetary reform ... will require near unanimity if it is to succeed in reestablishing stability and flexibility. It is an issue on which the rich countries are deeply divided; but the poor countries stand in broad agreement. It is therefore a situation in which the poor, very unusually, should be able to act in concert to ensure their reasonable demands are met.
> Those demands are not limited to the field of monetary reforms in general.

... They include in rough order of magnitude, a new deal on agricultural exports, the adoption of GSP (the General System of Preferences for less-developed countries) by Canada and the United States, a revision by the EEC and Japan of their schemes of GSP, and a more rapid approach to the Second Development Decade aid targets.[42]

Earlier in the post-World War II era, the negotiating strength of the United States and the unity of advanced industrial states on trade, monetary issues, and other political issues precluded serious consideration of this type of bargaining by less developed countries.

A second development that should enhance the bargaining position of poor states is the recent appearance of resource shortages as a primary concern in global economic relations. Until recently, the central focus of international trade deliberations had been the securing of access by producers to the markets of consuming nations.[43] The oil embargo imposed by Arab states and acute global shortages of grain, fishmeal, soybeans, and fertilizer during 1973 and 1974 have made the issue of assured access by consumers to supplies of raw materials as important as the traditional focus of trade negotiations since World War II. Since less developed countries are major sources of some raw materials that are periodically in short supply, they hold an unprededented bargaining position with advanced industrial states. Although not all less developed countries stand to benefit directly from current shortages in particular raw materials, there is evidence that pivotal less developed states, such as those in OPEC, may use their bargaining leverage to focus attention on the economic grievances of less developed states. Such was the case in the special United Nations General Assembly sessions in 1974 and 1975 on problems of raw materials, development, and economic cooperation. And it was repeated in the twenty-seven-state Paris Conference on International Economic Cooperation, which between December 1975 and June 1977 constituted the central arena for the North-South dialogue on the construction of a new international economic order. Without OPEC's insistence, this conference would not have taken up the broader demands of the Third World; it would have focused exclusively on the relations between the oil-exporting states and the Western powers. Here again, divisions among the Western states over access to raw materials and over other economic issues enhance the prospects for success by less developed countries in securing some of their reasonable economic demands of long standing.[44]

[42]Charles Elliot, *Fair Chance for All* (New York: United Nations, 1973), p. 63.

[43]This line of reasoning is developed nicely by James P. Grant, "The Fuel, Food, and Fertilizer Crises and the New Political Economics of Resource Scarcities," statement before the Subcommittee of the House Foreign Affairs Committee on Foreign Economic Policy, May 8, 1974, p. 7.

[44]In Chapter 7 we will focus on various specific strategies by which less developed countries might enhance their share of benefits from international economic exchange.

To cite these developments is not to suggest that states in the periphery of the global economy now occupy the decisive position in the construction of a new economic order. But it is true that alterations in the political and economic relations among rich states, combined with the emergence of new economic problems that cannot be managed within existing institutional arrangements, give less developed countries opportunities not available to them in the past. The last comprehensive attempt to alter basic trade and monetary relations took place when the decolonization drive was in its infancy; at that time, the interests of newly emergent states received scant attention. Now, states in the Third World are at least in a position to make themselves heard.

CHAPTER THREE
THE GLOBAL MONETARY ORDER
Interdependence and Dominance

The political-economic links among states through international economic relations as well as the links between domestic and foreign economic policy are nowhere more evident than in balance-of-payments adjustments and the conduct of international monetary relations. Balance-of-payments policies and international monetary relations involve highly technical economic decisions that carry with them extremely important domestic and foreign political implications. We will discuss the technical aspects of these relations only in the depth required to appreciate some of the political connotations of international financial interdependencies.

BALANCE-OF-PAYMENTS
ADJUSTMENT ALTERNATIVES

A country's balance of payments consists of a comparison of the sum of all payments the state and its residents made to foreigners with the total of all receipts obtained by the state and its residents during the same year. Any expenditures or movement of finances abroad contributes to a country's payments deficit. Any purchases by foreigners or movement of finances into the country contributes to a payments surplus. Most states seek to achieve a balance-of-payments surplus or equilibrium (financial outflows equal to inflows). Components of a country's balance-of-payments position include the gamut of public and private financial transactions across national boundaries—trade (exports and imports), services (shipping, insurance, banking fees, consulting, etc.), direct foreign investment, portfolio investment (stocks, bonds, etc.), tourism, and government expenditures abroad (military personnel and bases, diplomatic personnel and support, economic and military aid, etc.).

Countries that persistently find themselves with a significant payments imbalance must find ways to restore a position of financial equilibrium. Those with payments surpluses feel fewer pressures for adjustment as they are, after all, in the enviable position of earning more than they spend in international economic transactions. Typically, deficit countries are under much more urgent pressure to adjust their payments position, because they seldom enjoy the luxury of being able to "live beyond their means" for years on end.

There are three basic types of mechanisms available to states for adjusting their deficit payments position: internal adjustment measures, external adjustment measures, and access to liquidity (loans or financial reserves). The adjustment mechanism, or combination of mechanisms, chosen has important political-economic impacts at home and abroad.

Internal adjustment measures include any policies designed to decrease a country's purchases abroad by reducing domestic and foreign expenditures of the state and its residents. This might involve such policies as raising interest rates and taxes to reduce the level of spending by businesses and individuals, as well as reducing government expenditures by curtailing publicly financed programs at home and abroad. These "deflationary" policies place less disposable income in the hands of individuals, businesses, and government agencies for domestic and foreign purchases. As a result, a country's balance of payments should, theoretically, improve through a reduction in its imports, foreign investment, travel abroad, foreign aid, military and diplomatic presence abroad, and the like. All variety of expenditures contributing to a country's payments deficit should contract.

Obviously, internal measures are adopted at considerable economic and political costs to the country (or elements of society within it). Deflation closes businesses and throws people out of work. Cutting government programs means sacrificing certain domestic and foreign policy goals. Should a nation sacrifice social policy by reducing unemployment compensation, social security payments, and aid to education? Should a nation sacrifice security by reducing defense expenditures, foreign economic and military aid, and military, economic, and political presence abroad? The choices are difficult. Restoration of a balance-of-payments equilibrium is seen typically as an economic problem. But the determination of where to cut and upon whom the impact of the cut falls are political decisions at the core.

Internal measures place the burdens of adjustment primarily upon the citizens, business enterprises, and the government of the state adopting them. This is not to say, however, that such measures are without impacts abroad. Deflation in the United States, for example, reduces economic growth and production in states abroad by virtue of America's importance as a market in world commerce. A reduction of American defense expenditures and foreign aid affects not only our own security, but the security and development of numerous states around the world.

External adjustment measures are designed explicitly to restore equilibrium to a country with payments deficits by altering directly the terms of exchange for foreign economic transactions. New tariffs or quotas might be introduced to limit imports. Tax incentives might be extended to domestic firms expanding their exports. Financial controls may be applied to reduce the outward flow of direct and portfolio investments. Companies with foreign operations might be encouraged to accelerate the repatriation of profits from their foreign subsidiaries. A country might devalue its currency—reduce the value of its currency relative to foreign currencies. This discourages purchases of foreign goods, services, and capital because everything abroad will cost more to its citizens. It simultaneously encourages foreigners to purchase goods, services, and capital in the country devaluing, because all will be cheaper to foreigners. Policies such as these have the effect of reducing financial outflows and increasing financial inflows to the nation confronted with balance-of-payments deficits.

External measures place the burdens of adjustment primarily upon citizens, enterprises, and governments abroad rather than upon the country seeking to restore its balance of payments to equilibrium. However, these measures are likely to increase domestic inflation and favor inefficient domestic producers at the expense of more internationally competitive enterprises at home and abroad. External adjustment measures disrupt international economic exchange and, characteristically, invite retaliation from states whose domestic and foreign economic interests are harmed.

States with access to financial assets (liquidity) in the form of gold holdings, accumulated reserves of foreign exchange from past balance-of-payments surpluses, or in a position to secure loans from international banks or other states can finance their payments deficits without resort to stringent internal or external adjustment measures. Very few states are in a position to handle a chronic deficit position for a sustained period in this manner. They rapidly exhaust their accumulated international financial reserves as well as their credit worthiness from major lending institutions. Financing balance-of-payments deficits through liquidity is usually suitable only in the short run. Chronic payments deficits must be dealt with through some combination of internal and external adjustments.

The relationship among the three alternative methods has been illustrated most clearly by Richard Cooper through the device of a triangle
(see Figure 3-1), the points of the triangle representing internal measures,
external measures, and access to liberal liquidity. Most analysts and decision
makers want states to "avoid extreme forms of each of the three categories
of action."[1] Statesmen and analysts differ, however, over where they would
prefer to see states with a balance-of-payments deficit positioned in terms
of trade-offs among the three methods of adjustment available. Bankers
and finance ministers insist typically upon the need for discipline and rely
upon external and internal adjustment measures to eliminate the root causes
of a state's payments deficits. They desire to see states located away from
the liberal liquidity position in the triangle—in other words, strict economic
constraints should be placed on states seeking to finance their payments
deficits.[2]

Liberal economic analysts and decision makers insist upon avoiding
policies that interrupt the free flow of goods, capital, and services across
national boundaries. They desire to see states located away from the external measures position in the triangle. Radical economic analysts and
decision makers insist upon states' prerogatives to pursue autonomous paths
to development with social-economic policies assuring full employment and
equity in income distribution. Not wanting to sacrifice these goals to achieve
balance-of-payments equilibrium, they desire to see states located away from
the internal measures position in the triangle. Decision makers of states
enjoying balance-of-payments surpluses are prone to argue that states in
deficit should rely primarily upon internal measures and assume the primary burdens of adjustment themselves. Decision makers of states confronting payments deficits, not surprisingly, are prone to argue for access
to liberal liquidity with minimal conditions and rely upon external measures
designed to force creditors and states with payments surpluses to share the
burdens of adjustment with them.

In addition to identifying various schools of thought, the diagram
also enables us to appreciate distinctions among the policy positions of
various states over time. For example, with its massive financial reserves
generated from oil exports, Saudi Arabia would be able to operate very
near the liquidity corner of the triangle if it were to face balance-of-payments deficits in the future. For reasons we shall see shortly, the United
States has enjoyed a unique capacity since World War II to operate near
the liquidity extreme while remaining in a chronic payments deficit posture.
During the 1930s virtually all nations were operating near the external
measures position in the triangle while pursuing beggar-thy-neighbor foreign economic policies. During the 1920s, Britain operated near the internal

[1]Richard Cooper, *The Economics of Interdependence* (New York: McGraw-Hill, 1968),
p. 19.
    [2]Ibid.

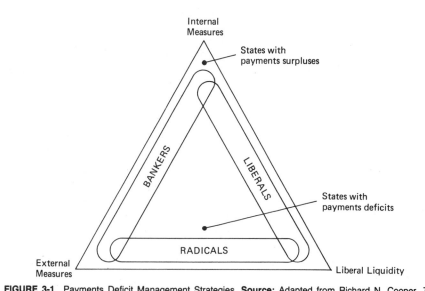

FIGURE 3-1 Payments Deficit Management Strategies. **Source:** Adapted from Richard N. Cooper, *The Economics of Interdependence* (New York: McGraw-Hill, 1968), p.18.

measures extreme of the triangle—unemployment rates of over 10 percent were accepted for years to restore the pound sterling to its 1913 value and maintain it in relation to gold.[3]

THE BRETTON WOODS INTERNATIONAL MONETARY ORDER

Just as Western statesmen developed an international trade order after World War II with the creation of GATT, they institutionalized an international monetary order through the creation of the International Monetary Fund (IMF) at Bretton Woods, New Hampshire in 1944. The liberal trade and monetary systems embodied in the two institutions under American leadership are closely related. A liberal international economic order requires the free flow of capital as well as goods. International trade cannot flourish in the presence of severe restrictions on international financial flows. If countries with payments deficits resort systematically to external measures of adjustment, for example, the liberal trade order envisaged in GATT would collapse. Accordingly, the framers of the IMF attempted to create a postwar international monetary order that would avoid the excessive economic nationalism of the 1930s.

The IMF provides loans to its member states to tide them over *temporary* balance-of-payments deficit problems. These loans provide an alter-

[3]Ibid., p. 26.

native to states imposing draconic internal or external adjustment measures that would disrupt their domestic economies, raise barriers to international trade, and invite retaliation by injured foreign economic interests. For states with *structural* rather than temporary payments problems, the IMF makes loans conditional upon the borrower's undertaking internal adjustment measures appropriate to restore it to a balance-of-payments equilibrium. These loans help to soften the impact of deflationary policies typically required in such circumstances, and at the same time are meant to enable states to retain liberal foreign economic policies.

In terms of the diagram of payments adjustment alternatives, the IMF was designed to move states away from the external measures location in the triangle (where most countries were positioned after the war) and toward a location closer to the internal measures position, through the incentive provided by IMF loans. The financing available through the IMF is more an inducement for adopting internal adjustment measures (always discomforting to a state) than a solution in and of itself for a payments deficit problem. Strict limits on borrowing from the IMF prevent extensive, persistent reliance upon its resources by member states with chronic payments deficits.

The IMF's capital pool now amounts to $75 billion (up from $8.8 billion in 1944). Its capital is raised from contributions by its member states (now 138) in accordance with quotas assigned on the basis of countries' relative economic capabilities (as reflected in such indicators as size of GNP, volume of trade, and reserves holdings). The U.S. quota, for example, is approximately $15 billion. Traditionally, quotas have been paid into the IMF in the form of gold (25 percent of quota) and the member state's national currency (75 percent of quota). States are permitted to borrow foreign currencies from the IMF for the purpose of settling their international accounts in amounts up to 125 percent of their quota. The conditions imposed upon a nation borrowing from the IMF become increasingly stringent as that nation approaches the limits of its borrowing capacity. The IMF insists that countries seeking loans adopt internal (and sometimes external) measures under multilateral (IMF) supervision sufficient to restore it to a stable balance of payments equilibrium. The conditions giving rise to a nation's deficit position are to be corrected so it will not be necessary to reapproach the fund repeatedly in future years.

Voting power in the IMF is weighted roughly in proportion to nations' quotas. As the largest contributor to the IMF the United States presently exercises just under 20 percent of the votes in IMF decision making. Quotas and voting power are adjusted through periodic reviews of the fund's capital needs and of alterations in the relative economic positions of its member states.

In addition to these liquidity (financing) and adjustment provisions of the IMF, the Bretton Woods monetary system envisioned a regime of easy convertibility among the currencies of states at stable exchange rates.

As the dominant nation in the international economic system following World War II, the U.S. dollar became the centerpiece of the international monetary order. The dollar was valued at $35 per ounce of gold, and the United States committed itself to exchange its gold upon request for dollars held by central banks abroad at this stable exchange rate. Other countries joining the IMF, in turn, valued their currency at an appropriate exchange rate vis-à-vis the dollar. Members agreed to alter the exchange rate of their currency only when absolutely necessary to correct a fundamental disequilibrium in their balance of payments—and, even then, only upon prior consultation with other states through the IMF. It was felt that liberal international trade could thrive only if stable exchange rates enabled importers and exporters to make commitments for future trade transactions at predictable prices. Conversion of one national currency into another at predictable exchange rates was to be a routine matter.

The international monetary order evolved in a manner somewhat differently from the original concept that emerged at the Bretton Woods Conference. The International Monetary Fund was little used during the first one and one half decades of its existence. The major European powers and Japan found that the requirements of post-war reconstruction necessitated maintenance of stringent controls on their currency and foreign trade. They did not make their currencies widely convertible until 1958. Exchange rate alterations proved to be traumatic politically and economically under the Bretton Woods system. Devaluations were taken as indications of weakness and economic failure by states and, thus, were resisted. Exchange rates became more rigid than the founders of the IMF had anticipated. When states, nevertheless, were compelled to devalue their currencies, it was usually done without consultation with the IMF, because negotiations prior to the fact invited heavy speculation against the weakening currency in international money markets. Also, developments in connection with the U.S. dollar took monetary relations in unanticipated directions with tremendous political and economic consequences. The IMF evolved to accommodate these developments and has emerged in the 1970s and 1980s as perhaps the key international economic institution—but a very different one from that created in 1944, as we shall see.

THE CHANGING ROLE
OF THE DOLLAR IN INTERNATIONAL
MONETARY RELATIONS

Most international economic transactions, such as trade, investment, loans, and travel, involve the exchange of goods, services, land, and labor for some form of monetary compensation. Internationally acceptable currencies are, therefore, required to conduct virtually any large-scale economic exchange across national boundaries. Such currencies (e.g., the U.S. dollar,

British pound, German mark, French franc, Japanese yen, and Swiss franc) perform several basic functions in the international monetary system. We will focus on the dollar as the most important of the international currencies in the post-World War II era.

First, the dollar as an international currency serves as a medium of exchange. It is an acceptable form of payment to providers of goods and services in a wide array of countries. The dollar is used widely to finance trade and other economic relations between parties that do not even involve the United States; Italy, for example, may be asked to pay for its oil imports from Saudi Arabia with dollars, because dollars are more useful than are lira to the Saudi Arabians in their other foreign transactions. About 25 percent of world trade is financed in dollars, whereas the United States accounts for only a little over 10 percent of world trade. International currencies, unlike the currencies of most states, have purchasing power outside their own nation. This is so because they are easily convertible into other international currencies or gold, and their value in relation to other international currencies or gold remains comparatively stable.

Second, international currencies (and the dollar in particular) serve as a store of value, a reserve asset, that states can save for future purchases throughout the world. As long as there is general confidence that the dollar is widely acceptable as a medium of exchange with stable value, it is held willingly as a reserve asset by other states. Under the Bretton Woods system, the American promise to convert dollars held abroad into gold upon request made the dollar a reserve asset "as good as gold."

Finally, the dollar as an international currency serves as a unit of account—a widely understood standard by which to price international transactions. Thus, in international economic transactions, the prices or value of goods and services are frequently quoted in dollars, even if the exchange is not necessarily conducted in dollars. A recipient of foreign aid from the Soviet Union, for example, might announce the value of its economic aid package in dollars, even though the aid itself is disbursed in rubles. This occurs because the dollar is understood much more broadly as a unit of account in international economic relations than is the ruble. Within specific states, prices are denominated in their national currencies, but by and large, where international transactions are involved, the domestic currency price is translated and defined in terms of an international currency such as the dollar.

While the pound, the mark, the yen, and a few other currencies also perform these three functions, the dollar since World War II has become the top international currency. It is relied upon to finance a greater variety of international economic transactions by a far greater number of states than is any other currency. The dollar, like the British pound in an earlier era, achieved top currency status by virtue of the dominant political and economic position in the international system the United States enjoyed after the war. Over a prolonged period of time, the dollar's role as top currency has had profound implications for the United States and for the international political economy.[4]

The top currency state has unparalled opportunities for expanding its economic, political, and military presence abroad. Countries in need of foreign exchange are particularly interested in forging relations with the top currency state because they bring the most universally accepted medium of exchange within grasp. Following World War II, for example, all variety of states clamored for exports to the United States, direct foreign investments from U.S. firms, American economic and military aid, and agreements for U.S. military base rights, among other things. They sought these things because they shared political-economic-security interests with America and also because such relations generate dollars for states with critical shortages of internationally acceptable currencies and reserves. Moreover, the universal utility of the top international currency as a medium of exchange gives the top currency nation the unique privilege of enjoying international support, or at least tolerance, for running persistent balance-of-payments deficits without having to adopt significant adjustment measures to restore a payments equilibrium. Deficits for the top currency state pump money into the international economy that can be used by other countries for international transactions. Thus, the top currency nation can enhance its economic-political-military posture abroad at levels of expenditures that exceed its international earnings for years on end—no other nation in the international system can behave in such a fashion. Charles de Gaulle pointed to this fact with frustration as America's "exorbitant privilege."

If the dominant state in the international system consciously seeks to pursue a policy of expansion and penetration abroad, having the top international currency immeasurably facilitates implementation of the policy. If the dominant state manifests no explicitly expansionist designs, having the top international currency will almost certainly draw it into an internationalist posture with vital political-economic stakes throughout the globe. Charges of self-aggrandizement and imperialism would seem to be an inevitable concomitant of occupying the top currency status in the international economy.

Years of occupying top currency status also make a country's decision makers prone to equate their state's national economic interests with the interests of the international economic system. An attack on the dollar is viewed instinctively by Americans as an attack on international economic stability. Given the roles played by the dollar in international economic exchange, this viewpoint is understandable. On the other hand, it fails to accord any legitimacy to other states' concerns that their own national eco-

---

[4]The discussion that follows on the implication of top currency status is based primarily upon the work of Susan Strange. See her illuminating piece, "The Politics of International Currencies," *World Politics*, 23, no. 2 (January 1971), 215–31.

nomic interests are not always served best by American concepts of appropriate international monetary policy. It also fails to take account of the unique political and economic advantages that accrue to the United States by virtue of its top currency status—and the resentment this generates among states that must operate on a different and more strict standard of balance-of-payments discipline. The viewpoint leaves other countries with little legitimate basis, in the eyes of the top currency state, for challenging the dominant state's prescriptions for foreign monetary relations.

Susan Strange refers to this viewpoint as the "top currency syndrome." She has seen it manifested in the behavior of both Britain and the United States:

> The Top Currency state seems inclined to develop a strong political/economic ideology that asserts (a) that [its] domestic and international interests are coincident if not identical, and (b) that a prime aim of the state should be to persuade others that their national economic interests coincide with the maximum development and extension of the international economy. The Top Currency state characteristically does all it can to propagate this ideology and to use it to enlist the support of others for whatever measures of international cooperation and support it thinks are needed to protect, defend, and stabilize the international economic system . . . the opinions of foreigners who put national economic interest before the general welfare are regarded as simply unregenerate and perverse. Indeed, a high moral tone quickly creeps in, and what I would describe as the Top Currency syndrome is distinguished by an obstinate and to others inevitably an objectionable, tendency to self-righteousness.[5]

The syndrome helps us to understand the basis for profound political-economic clashes between the United States and other countries as the international monetary order has evolved since World War II.

Top currency status imposes great burdens on a state while affording it unique political-economic opportunities. As the major reserve asset and international medium of exchange, there are tremendous international and domestic pressures to maintain a stable value for the currency—even when altering its exchange rate might seem appropriate for the nation's economic competitiveness and payments equilibrium. Other states can undergo exchange rate alterations without generating the international turmoil that inevitably follows when the same policy is adopted by the top currency state. In short, the top currency state is denied (at least in a monetary system based upon fixed exchange rates) a useful economic policy instrument available to virtually all other states. The top currency state faces an additional burden since its currency is the vehicle for the bulk of international economic transactions—any financial shock or major imbalance emerging anywhere in the international economy affects the top currency state directly. It is extremely vulnerable to the transmission of economic shocks from abroad, notwithstanding its substantial economic capabilities.

[5]Ibid., p. 229.

With these general characteristics of top currency status in mind, let us examine the dollar's performance and its impact upon international monetary relations since World War II.

The Dollar Ascendant

From 1947 to 1960 the United States, with the enthusiastic support of its major economic and political partners, managed the international monetary system through a calculated effort to run balance-of-payments deficits. The United States continued to export more goods than it imported, but it regularly spent more each year than it earned through trade— primarily as a result of foreign military and economic assistance (such as the Marshall Plan), expenditures connected with developing and maintaining bases abroad, and an expansion of direct foreign investment by American firms.

The persistent American balance-of-payments deficits were welcomed internationally during this period for a variety of reasons. In 1947 the United States held 70 percent of the world's total official monetary gold stocks upon which nations relied principally at that time for their international reserve position. This was viewed by all international economic experts as a maldistribution of international reserves. By running balance-of-payments deficits, the United States permitted other countries to acquire dollars that they could either hold onto or convert to gold from the United States at $35 an ounce. Most countries chose the former since dollars were so useful as a medium of exchange for all variety of international economic transactions, since dollars could be converted to gold at any time, and since dollars could earn interest (unlike gold) while being retained as reserves. As new quantities of gold could not be produced to keep pace with the overall liquidity needs of a rapidly expanding international economy, dollars sent abroad through U.S. payments deficits provided the primary source for the necessary expansion and redistribution of international reserves. America's deficits were regarded as a temporary, controllable phenomenon. They were a result of a policy choice by the United States with which its post-World War II allies concurred. Moreover, an export surplus each year underlined the inherent strength and international competitiveness of the American economy. There was a sustained demand for dollars in the international economy. The deficits in no way cast doubt upon the vitality of the American economy or the strength of the dollar as an international currency.

Of course, these deficits were also financing the establishment of a massive foreign presence by the United States through private investment, economic aid, and the maintenance of a system of military bases abroad. This posed few problems in U.S. relations with its major partners because they felt that their own economic, political, and security interests were served by these American actions. If American deficits were to cease, the allies reasoned, their own interests would be hurt.

For all these reasons there was broad international support for the United States' continuation of its balance-of-payments deficits through the 1950s. During this period the dollar established itself clearly as the linchpin of the international monetary system.

The Dollar in Question

International acceptance of persistent American balance-of-payments deficits and unbounded confidence in the dollar as an international currency gradually gave way to opposition and doubt during the 1960s. U.S. payments deficits had been widely acceptable abroad as long as (1) U.S. foreign policy and expenditures abroad were regarded as consistent with other countries' own sense of their political, economic, and security interests and (2) there was general confidence in the strength of the American economy and the ultimate capacity of the United States to control its payments position. Confidence in the dollar as an international currency remained firm as long as it remained clear that dollars held abroad would be converted to gold upon request at $35 an ounce. Over the course of the 1960s serious questions arose in connection with all of these points, with potent effects on the functioning of the international monetary system and the dollar's role in it.

As the United States continued to run balance-of-payments deficits over the years and foreign governments willingly held onto dollars generated in this fashion, the amount of official dollar holdings abroad gradually approached, and then exceeded, the value of total American gold reserves. The foundation of the dollar's role as a reserve asset under the Bretton Woods monetary system was the American commitment to convert official dollar holdings abroad into gold upon request. Over the course of the 1960s it became clear that the United States was incapable of honoring *en masse* its gold conversion obligations. By 1971 official dollar holdings abroad exceeded U.S. gold stocks by 300 percent.

During this period the "dollar overhang" problem was kept within manageable proportions by several forces. The American economy continued to remain internationally competitive, as evidenced by yearly export surpluses. International confidence in American economic strength was firm. Also, the United States successfully prevailed upon its major economic partners to continue to hold dollars without exercising their right of conversion to gold in the interest of international monetary and economic stability. The international monetary system by the 1960s revolved around the dollar as a medium of exchange and international reserve unit. In 1965, for example, foreign exchange (mostly dollars) comprised $24 billion of the world's total reserves of $71 billion.[6] Whose interests would be served by an international stampede to convert dollars to gold? Such behavior on

---

[6]International Monetary Fund, *1971 Annual Report* (Washington, D.C.: IMF, 1971), p. 19.

a massive scale would undermine the value of the dollar—not only harming the United States but also eroding the value of one-third of the world's total international reserves. Realization of this fact led most states to refrain from exchanging their dollars for gold on a large scale, but the problem of the dollar overhang continued to worsen. Everyone, including U.S. officials, realized that international monetary and economic interests were no longer served by America's persistent balance-of-payments deficits. There was a widespread belief that the United States should bring its balance of payments back into equilibrium. Failure to restore the U.S. balance of payments to equilibrium would result sooner or later in a gold and dollar crisis.

Pressure for ending its deficits and altering the political-economic prerogatives enjoyed by the United States as the top currency state came from another quarter during the 1960s—Charles de Gaulle. De Gaulle's challenge was explicitly political, in contrast to the largely economic challenge of the dollar overhang.

As long as America's major political allies and economic partners saw fundamental congruence between their own interests and American foreign policy, there was relatively little criticism of U.S. deficits. American deficits permitted a more vigorous pursuit of foreign political, economic, and security goals of importance to Europeans as well as to Americans than would have been possible with U.S. payments discipline. When de Gaulle defined French interests in a way that diverged from U.S. policies, he also attacked the United States for its payments deficits and sought to convert dollars into gold in an attempt to force an alteration of America's international posture.

French interests and American foreign policy were increasingly at odds during the late 1950s and 1960s. The United States opposed French-British occupation of the Suez Canal in 1956 and forced an embarrassing retreat. France also developed considerable doubts about the reliability of American nuclear guarantees. Beginning in the late 1950s, de Gaulle opened a severe conflict within the Western alliance over the issue of a greater French voice in Western strategic policy and, later, over the development of French nuclear capability independent of American or NATO controls. During the course of the 1960s, de Gaulle drew away from America's pro-Israeli position in the Middle East conflict and opposed U.S. policies in Vietnam. Along another dimension of policy, the French became wary of the massive influx of direct foreign investment by U.S.-based multinational firms operating in Europe. The French and European economies appeared to be threatened with progressive denationalization and subjugation to U.S. corporate giants.[7] For these as well as other reasons, de Gaulle no longer saw French interests as congruent with America's international security and foreign economic policies.

[7]See Chapter 4.

De Gaulle correctly linked America's capacity to pursue such an active international posture with its top currency status. The scope of American international involvement was enhanced by its capacity to run persistent balance-of-payments deficits without having to make internal or external adjustments to bring them under control. This constituted the "exorbitant privilege" of the United States as the top currency state. Its payments deficits expanded other nations' international reserves, permitting it to elude the pressures of living within its means. Alone among states, America could finance its foreign activities virtually through printing money.

This exorbitant privilege and a virtually limitless international expansion of U.S. political and economic influence could be curtailed if countries refused to hold those dollars pumped abroad through U.S. payments deficits. By holding dollars, other countries were underwriting America's foreign policy. If the United States were forced to finance its payments deficits through gold conversion, it would exhaust its reserves rapidly and be required, like other states, to restore a balance-of-payments equilibrium. The inevitable result would be an erosion of American public and private expenditures abroad—hence, a decline in U.S. international political and economic influence. De Gaulle demanded gold conversion for dollars held by France, and he launched a largely unsuccessful international campaign to have other countries do the same. Through attacking the dollar, de Gaulle was attempting to erode American hegemony.

The United States responded to de Gaulle's attack on the dollar in exactly the manner Susan Strange refers to as the "top currency syndrome." The French position was regarded in Washington as an attack not primarily on the dollar and U.S. foreign policy but, rather, a perverse assault upon global monetary and economic stability, which depended upon the strength of the dollar during the 1960s. The United States prevailed in this struggle with de Gaulle because most nations sought to avoid bringing the dollar overhang problem to a head and because few Western states were as disaffected with American leadership as was de Gaulle.

This episode illustrates forcefully the pursuit of national objectives through the instrument of international monetary policy. The economic-legal questions of dollar conversion to gold during the 1960s turned essentially on America's retaining top currency status and international political-economic hegemony.

The dollar overhang and the French challenge indicated that international political and economic conditions were changing rapidly during the 1960s. New conditions and new opposition would not permit the United States to run payments deficits without incurring substantial political and international economic costs. Yet a dilemma emerged. If the United States were to bring its deficits under control, the primary source of growth in world financial reserves would be eliminated and the international economy would be threatened with a shortage of liquidity. On the other hand, if

U.S. deficits continued, the increasing excess of dollars abroad relative to U.S. gold stocks would produce a gold and dollar crisis.[8]

The international economy requires an adequate supply of financial reserves (liquidity) in the form of gold or international currencies. Shortages of reserves reduce global demand for the purchase of goods and services through international trade, serving to inhibit the growth of economic production in all nations. Continued growth of the global economy and the economic health of most states require an expansion of liquidity adequate to meet the increasing financial needs of expanding international economic transactions. By the 1960s, as we have seen, it became apparent that the United States should eliminate its payments deficits. But how would an expanding global economy's liquidity needs be met? Gold was simply not being mined in amounts sufficient to meet the liquidity requirements of the international economy and private gold consumption.

Monetary officials in 1969 agreed to the formation of a new, multilaterally controlled international reserve asset to be disbursed and administered in accordance with global economic needs under the auspices of the International Monetary Fund. The new reserve assets were called special drawing rights (SDRs). National financial authorities agreed to accept SDRs in addition to gold or international currencies to settle official financial accounts among their central banks. SDRs would be created by the IMF to supplement gold, dollars, and other international currencies during periods when the latter were not expanding sufficiently to satisfy the liquidity needs of the global economy. Approximately $9 billion worth of SDRs were created between 1969 and 1972 and disbursed to countries within the IMF in proportion to their IMF quotas.

The creation of SDRs as a reserve asset seemed to offer the solution to several problems confronting the international monetary system in the 1960s. The U.S. could now eliminate its payments deficits without precipitating an international liquidity shortage. The SDR plan offered the prospect of liquidity expansion appropriate to the financial requirements of the international economy. Neither the mining of gold nor the creation of dollar reserve assets through U.S. payments deficits were related directly to the requirements of international monetary relations. And of importance, unlike the dollar or any other international currency, SDRs conferred no special political or economic privilege to a particular state. That was essential in their acceptability to finance officials throughout the world.

The 1960s ended with the dollar's role in the international monetary order being brought into question on economic and political grounds. Widespread confidence in the strength of the American economy and the in-

---

[8]This came to be called the "Triffin dilemma." Robert Triffin first identified the dilemma in the late 1950s. See his *Gold and the Dollar Crisis* (New Haven, Conn.: Yale University Press, 1961), pp. 3–14.

novative step of creating special drawing rights preserved the Bretton Woods system and delayed the ultimate challenge to the dollar as the top currency. As it turned out, the delay was brief.

The Dollar in Decline

The United States ran a disastrous balance-of-payments deficit in 1971. Compared with "modest" deficits of $1.9-3.8 billion over the previous five years, the 1971 deficit soared to $10.6 billion.[9]

The most alarming aspect of the 1971 deficit, in addition to its size was the fact that U.S. imports exceeded exports for the first time in the twentieth century. Most analysts attributed the emergence of the trade deficit to inflation unleashed in the late 1960s, when financing the war in Vietnam and uncurtailed domestic expenditures produced huge budget deficits in the United States. The pace of inflation, combined with an overvalued dollar relative to the German mark and Japanese yen, cut deeply into the ability of the U.S. economy to retain its overall international competitiveness.

Confidence in the dollar as an international currency had rested upon widespread confidence in the strength of the American economy as evidenced by its export surpluses. The 1971 deficit was alarming not only because its magnitude suggested America's inability to maintain control over its payments position, but also because the 1971 trade deficit raised doubts about the vitality and strength of the U.S. economy. Against the backdrop of increasing international concern about the dollar in the 1960s, these developments threatened to unleash international monetary chaos. Confidence in the dollar was collapsing.

Rather than waiting for an international stampede to convert dollars held abroad into gold—an obligation that the United States clearly could not honor—the Nixon administration took the initiative in August 1971. The United States insisted that its major economic partners enjoying payment surpluses should assume a major share of the burdens of adjustment required to restore the United States to payments equilibrium, in return for past American actions on their behalf. These actions included postwar U.S. aid to Europe and Japan, as well as massive defense expenditures incurred by the United States assumed to enhance the security of its major allies. In addition, among the major economies only the United States had maintained the value of its currency since World War II, thereby contributing stability to the international monetary order. Plainly, these factors had contributed to U.S. payments deficits and had benefited America's allies. Therefore, the United States sought to force the strong European and Japanese economies to assume a major share of the burdens associated with ending U.S. deficits. In so doing the United States was abandoning

[9]*International Economic Report of the President,* (Washington, D.C.: GPO, March 1975), p. 137.

its traditional position that the deficit country should bear the burdens of adjustment to restore payments equilibrium.

The United States insisted that the Japanese yen and German mark be revalued upward to assist the American trade balance; this would have the same effect as a dollar devaluation, except that its impact would be concentrated on those economies contributing the most to America's trade deficit in 1971. As a bargaining chip to promote the currency realignment, the United States imposed an across-the-board 10 percent surcharge on all imports. And to stanch the anticipated stampede of foreign central banks to convert their dollars into gold, the United States abruptly abrogated its commitment of twenty-five years to exchange gold for dollars. Finally, the United States called for intensive international negotiation on trade and monetary affairs, hoping to restore order and to strengthen the U.S. payments and trade position. These unilateral moves in August 1971 marked the demise of the Bretton Woods monetary order created in 1944 and opened a new era of increasingly volatile international monetary relations.

These actions provide a classic example of a strong state's relying heavily upon external adjustment measures to cope with its payments deficits. The Smithsonian Agreement in December 1971, involving the leading Western economies, formalized commitments to implement the basic elements of the unilateral U.S. demands for monetary and trade reform. The dollar was devalued approximately 10 percent relative to the mark, the yen, and gold. The United States rescinded its 10 percent surcharge on imports. Intensive efforts were started to reach multilateral agreement on new rules to ensure international monetary stability in the post-Bretton Woods era. In the meantime, states holding dollars as reserves, in response to earlier American appeals to refrain from converting them to gold, were stuck with the dollars—now worth less in settling their international accounts. Gold conversion was a relic of the past. An extraordinary display of American economic power, this would be the swansong of America's postwar, unilateral dominance over the international monetary system.

These events during 1971, followed by a second dollar devaluation two years later, signaled an end to fixed exchange rates among the major national currencies. Since that time, the values of the dollar and other major currencies have fluctuated in response to international supply and demand as well as to shifts in international confidence in the economic vitality of the country. While the dollar enjoyed periods of strength as well as periods of weakness over the course of the 1970s, it had declined 19 percent against ten other major currencies by 1977.[10]

These fluctuations in the value of the dollar are basically associated with the degree of domestic and international confidence in the strength of the American economy and the effectiveness of its economic policies.

---

[10]The dollar declined 54 percent against the Swiss franc, 42 percent against the mark, and 33 percent against the yen between 1970 and 1977. Robert Triffin, "The International Role of the Dollar", *Foreign Affairs*, 57, no. 2 (Winter 1978–79), 275.

Balance-of-payments deficits, particularly when accompanied by large trade deficits created by runaway oil imports and/or serious erosion of U.S. competitiveness in manufactured goods production are likely to lower the value of the dollar (that was the case in 1978 under the Carter administration, for example). The dollar is likely to stabilize or gain value when domestic and international observers are impressed by public policies that they feel can control inflation, increase the competitiveness of American industry, reduce the volume of U.S. oil imports, and defend the value of the dollar through active U.S. intervention in international currency markets (as in 1981, for example, with high interest rates and optimism about President Reagan's new economic recovery program). The dollar has run an uncertain course since the mid-1970s in respect to these challenges.

Despite its more precarious position, the dollar has retained its top currency status in the international economy. It has done so by default. No other economy is large enough for its currency to serve as a medium of exchange for such a large volume of international transactions. The dollar in 1979 still accounted for approximately 80 percent of the world's international reserves held in the form of foreign exchange. The German mark over the course of the 1970s emerged as the second most important international currency, displacing the British pound. Yet the mark ranks a distant second, accounting for only about 11 percent of the foreign exchange being held as international reserves.

States have become increasingly less sanguine about the role of the dollar as a reserve asset and as a unit of account. To the extent that opportunities exist, states are prone to diversify their financial reserves among various international currencies and gold rather than to hold them entirely in dollars. Fee structures for international services (such as airline travel) and international prices for raw materials are increasingly being expressed in terms of SDRs rather than dollars. SDRs are valued in terms of a "basket" of the five major national currencies and, therefore, remain quite stable even in the face of altered exchange rates.

The dollar may remain the top currency in the international economy, but with fewer political and economic advantages accruing to America. The United States no longer enjoys the exorbitant privilege of immunity from balance-of-payments deficits. Rather than being accepted as a welcome addition to other states' reserve positions, large U.S. payments deficits are now viewed as a sign of America's political and economic mismanagement that produces a decline in the dollar's value. Unlike the period prior to 1971, there are now explicit linkages of U.S. payment deficits, the purchasing power of the dollar, domestic economic well-being and America's capacity to sustain indefinitely its international military, political, and economic posture. Like other states, America must now adopt internal and external adjustment measures to control its payments position. It can no longer manage its deficits successfully through printing still more dollars and pumping them abroad.

In coming to grips with its own payments deficits and ensuring a degree of stability in the international monetary order, the United States must now bear a greater share of the burdens of adjustment than that which it now accepts as "normal" by virtue of its past top currency status. America is finding important foreign and domestic policies imposed upon it by the imperatives of its international payments position.

For a time, top currency status is accompanied by extraordinary opportunities for extending a state's political, military, and economic influence abroad. In the case of Britain and the United States, however, prolonged exploitation of top currency status also has produced currency overvaluation, acute balance-of-payments deficits, and unemployment. The United States may well be entering a period in which increasing political and economic costs receive greater attention than do the benefits of retaining top currency status.[11]

THE POST–BRETTON WOODS
INTERNATIONAL MONETARY SYSTEM

International monetary relations now differ in important respects from the Bretton Woods system, which revolved around a strong dollar. They are less orderly, less predictable. Even so, some basic characteristics of the contemporary international monetary system are clear.

There has been a dramatic expansion of international liquidity in the international monetary system over the past decade. International reserves rose from $128 billion in 1970 to $738 billion in May 1980.[12] The quantity of gold held as international reserves remained virtually steady across this period, but increases in the market price of gold have raised the total value of these reserve assets. Continued U.S. payment deficits during the 1970s were responsible for a massive increase in the volume of international reserves held in the form of foreign exchange during the period.[13]

In addition to increases in official holdings of international reserves, there was an explosion of private bank lending to governments during the 1970s, primarily through growth of the Eurocurrency market. Eurocurrencies, mostly dollars, are currencies deposited in and loaned by banks outside the country of those currencies. For example, dollars managed by foreign

[11]For such a view and an explanation of the reluctance of Germany, Switzerland, or a common European effort to replace the dollar and assume the burdens associated with top currency status, see ibid., p. 284.

[12]The 1970 figure is from the International Monetary Fund, *1979 Annual Report* (Washington, D.C.: IMF, 1979), p. 47. Gold reserves valued at London market prices, SDRs converted to dollars at 1 SDR = $1.00. The 1980 figure from International Monetary Fund, *1980 Annual Report*, (Washington, D.C.: IMF, 1980), p. 59. Gold reserves valued at London market prices, SDRs converted to dollars at 1 SDR = $1.30.

[13]As noted previously, dollars account for approximately 80 percent of international reserves held in the form of international currencies (foreign exchange).

banks in Europe or European branches of U.S. banks are referred to as Eurodollars. German marks and Swiss francs held in banks outside Germany and Switzerland are referred to as Euromarks and Eurofrancs, respectively. The Eurocurrency market began in the late 1950s and has grown rapidly since then because banks trading in currencies outside their country of origin can escape the regulatory practices of national monetary authorities (such as minimal reserve requirements, interest rate limitations, and exchange controls). They are able to offer higher rates of interest to depositors and lower rates of interest to borrowers than those prevailing in domestic money markets,[14] thus attracting immense deposits and large borrowers from all over the globe. The Eurocurrency market grew from $85 billion to $600 billion between 1971 and 1979.[15] Advanced industrial states and less developed countries borrowed extensively in Eurocurrency markets to finance staggering current account deficits caused by oil price hikes and runaway inflation during the 1970s. The market played a central role in recycling "petrodollars" from OPEC states to oil-importing nations (rich and poor) with payments deficits—particularly in the years immediately following the abrupt oil price increases in 1973 and 1979.

The combination of massive increases in the value of gold, large U.S. payments deficits, and the availability of large amounts of credit in the Eurocurrency market enabled many states to finance their payments deficits without confronting the politically sensitive and economically painful discipline of implementing internal or external adjustment measures. This undoubtedly stimulated international trade and production during the 1970s, but it also postponed adjustment of serious payments imbalances that will be all the more difficult to implement in the 1980s. This tremendous expansion in international liquidity, moreover, has constituted an important source of global inflation.

The international economic community is now casting about for ways in which to enhance the role of special drawing rights in an effort to diminish the central position of the dollar in global monetary relations. The dollar's fluctuating value makes it much less attractive then formerly as a reserve asset. U.S. payments deficits continue to generate new international reserves at a rate far in excess of the global economy's financial requirements. These sources of global monetary instability and inflation will continue as long as the dollar remains the centerpiece of the international monetary system.

The prominence of SDRs has been heightened by the IMF decision to resume disbursements of an additional 12 billion SDRs ($19.6 billion)

[14]Morgan Guaranty Trust, *World Financial Markets* (New York: Morgan, January 1979), p. 13.

[15]Morgan Guaranty Trust, *World Financial Markets* (New York: Morgan, August 1980), p. 9.

over the period 1979–1981. This was the first new allocation of SDRs since the initial 9 billion SDRs were created a decade earlier. An attempt is being made by international monetary authorities to enlarge the role of SDRs in the overall composition of international reserves—particularly in relation to dollar holdings of foreign exchange.

Efforts along these lines, in addition to the 1979–1981 SDR allocations, involve active consideration of creating a voluntary "substitution account" that would permit governments to convert their dollar reserves into SDR reserves. Implementation of an SDR allocation for this purpose would "mop up" that portion of dollar reserves states now hold reluctantly. Presumably, this would restore more order to international monetary relations that have revolved around a dollar enjoying less and less confidence. It is clear that there is widespread interest in designing an international monetary order in which no national currency serves as a central reserve asset. A further reduction in the dollar's functions as the top international currency are clearly in the offing to the degree that these difficult multilateral steps can proceed gradually.

The role of gold has also been altered in the post-Bretton Woods international monetary system. After the link between the value of the dollar and gold was severed in the early 1970s, monetary authorities sought to "demonetize" gold by letting it trade at market prices like most other commodities. The United States and the IMF actually auctioned off part of their gold holdings in the late 1970s.

The price of gold has fluctuated under the post-Bretton Woods arrangement. Ordinarily, its value has increased dramatically during periods of greatest concern about the stability of international currencies, such as the dollar's decline in 1978. Gold prices also rise during periods of grave concern about political stability in the Middle East—there are massive financial surpluses in that area that move toward gold whenever political instability threatens to interrupt domestic and foreign money markets. This was the case with the revolution in Iran, the Soviet invasion of Afghanistan, and the Iraq-Iran war during 1979 and 1980. In general, the movement of gold prices serves as a barometer of confidence in the international monetary system; the lower the confidence, the higher the jumps in gold prices. Massive jumps in gold prices during 1979 and 1980 arrested efforts by the United States and the IMF to demonetize gold and reduce their holdings of the precious metal.

The international monetary system is in an era of transition. The turmoil since 1971 makes international monetary relations under the Bretton Woods system look tranquil and coherent by comparison. While monetary relations still revolve around the dollar, there is increasing doubt that the dollar or any national currency can or should continue to occupy such an important role in the international economy. SDRs are being positioned to assume a more central role in international monetary relations.[16] They are a multilaterally controlled reserve asset, with a more stable value than any international currency, that can be created in accordance with monetary authorities' sense of the requirements of the international economy. SDRs confer no special political-economic privileges to any state. If progress toward the enhancement of SDRs' importance continue, the United States will have to adjust its foreign and domestic policies to the imperatives of its balance-of-payments position in ways that it could have avoided when the dollar dominated the international economy. At the same time, however, America will be able to shed the increasingly onerous burdens of maintaining the dollar's top currency status in the world economy.

The international monetary system is likely to become more highly politicized as U.S. dominance gives way to truly multilateral direction of international financial policy because of the absence of a consensus among important states on norms to guide their monetary relations. Yet, during this difficult transition period, the international monetary system has weathered the most traumatic international economic shocks since the 1930s more successfully than most observers would have predicted.

DEVELOPING STATES
AND MONETARY RELATIONS

Thus far, we have examined the nature of international monetary problems and their relationships to domestic and international politics by focusing on advanced industrial states, particularly the United States. Developing countries encounter a number of particularly serious difficulties in their attempts to interact with and adapt to the international monetary order. We need to consider briefly how the monetary problems of the advanced industrial states adversely affect the developing countries. Center state concerns about balance-of-payments deficits frequently result in policies that are detrimental to the interests of developing countries. To reduce a deficit, advanced industrial states may seek to erect barriers (external measures)

---

[16]Particularly if SDRs are unable to assume this enhanced role in international monetary relations, we can probably expect to see groups of states with closely linked economies developing their own alternatives to an unstable dollar as the key international reserve asset and unit of account. Thus, under Germany's leadership the Common Market states in Europe agreed in 1979 to create a European monetary system with exchange rates among the member states being maintained within quite narrow limits. Together they would create a new international currency called European currency units (ECUs), which would serve as an alternative to the dollar as a reserve asset.

Failure of international agreement upon a new, universally accepted international asset could well lead to a fragmentation of the world economy, with some states orbiting around the dollar, others orbiting around European currency units, and still others orbiting around the Japanese yen. In any event, we should expect to see joint or fragmented efforts to reduce the centrality of the U.S. dollar in future international monetary relations.

against the import of goods from other countries. When they do this, the burdens fall heavily on the developing countries, since they often depend upon the export of a few products. The 10 percent American surcharge imposed in 1971 was particularly harmful to less developed countries that relied upon exports to the United States for much of their foreign currency needs. Moreover, as we examined in Chapter 2, tariffs or quotas on sem-imanufactured goods, which often compete with economically marginal but politically powerful industries in advanced states, inhibit less developed countries' diversification and industrialization efforts. Both the textile and the shoe industries in the United States have actively sought and received protection from foreign competition.

Other center state policies might involve the establishment of restrictions on capital outflows for investment purposes. To the extent that a less developed country desires such capital to further industrialization, to tap natural resources, or to obtain needed capital and technology, it will perceive these restrictions as harmful. Similarly, balance-of-payments problems in center states may lead them to reduce foreign aid expenditures or to require that such funds be used to purchase goods from the donor country; either strategy is costly to developing countries. Thus, in trying to correct balance-of-payments deficits, advanced industrial states may adopt policies that are detrimental to the interests of the developing countries. There are few remedies for these states, since they are often innocent bystanders to conflicts among and within the advanced industrial states.

Balance-of-payments adjustment problems and liquidity concerns are as important to developing countries as they are to center states. Indeed, most less developed countries have traditionally been confronted with chronic payments deficits and extraordinary liquidity needs. Fluctuation in the prices received for their commodity exports and extended periods of decline in their terms of trade lead to shortages and unpredictable foreign exchange earnings through exports. Yet their ambitious development programs require a sustained, high level of imports. It has become increasingly difficult for most less developed countries to finance the gap between their export receipts and import bills through reliance upon international reserves and development assistance from foreign governments and public international lending institutions such as the World Bank.

The International Monetary Fund was, of course, created for the purpose of providing loans to its member states facing payments deficits. Less developed countries have frequently relied upon the IMF, but they feel that IMF policies frequently ignore economic and political realities and place unwarranted burdens upon the less developed countries. Thus, they rely upon the fund only as a last resort.

In particular, less developed countries object to strict limits on the size of loans they can obtain from the IMF. Countries are normally limited to borrowing 125 percent of their quota, with longer-term stand-by agreements negotiated with the IMF sometimes permitting states to double or triple that figure. Since quotas are calculated upon states' overall economic size and capabilities, however, less developed countries typically have relatively small quotas—and, thus, small borrowing capacities in the IMF.

Also problematic are the economic policies typically imposed by the IMF upon less developed countries as conditions for access to substantial IMF loan packages. The IMF has been inclined to impose severe economic austerity programs upon less developed countries with serious payments deficits. These programs include stringent curtailment of public expenditures, restrictive fiscal and monetary policies, devaluation of the nation's currency, and removal of restrictions on the free flow of trade and foreign investment.

Less developed countries argue that the political and economic impacts of this standard IMF prescription are often catastrophic. Currency devaluation is often as likely to increase inflation and worsen a less developed country's balance of payments as it is to reduce its payments deficit. A large proportion of their imports, such as energy and intermediate and heavy industrial goods, are vital to the functioning of the domestic economy, so the volume of a less developed country's imports can seldom be reduced without undermining their economy. Devaluation, rather than reducing imports, merely increases the size of a less developed country's import bill by raising the cost of all foreign goods. Also, most primary products (the chief exports of poor states) exhibit a price inelasticity of demand—that is, lower prices made available to foreign consumers by devaluation will not lead to a proportionate increase in the volume of purchases. The demand for coffee, for example, does not increase much when the price drops. The dilemma is that currency devaluation by less developed countries neither increases export revenues nor reduces import expenditures in the manner expected by the IMF and liberal economic theory.

The deflationary policies imposed by the IMF often produce traumatic political upheavals in less developed countries, referred to as "IMF riot." Domestic chaos has confronted regimes in Turkey, Peru, Portugal, and Egypt during the 1970s in the wake of these governments' acceptance and implementation of austerity packages required for access to IMF loans. Over 700 people died in Egyptian riots prompted by IMF-imposed elimination of government food subsidies in 1976. Some countries such as Tanzania and Jamaica have found the conditions attached to IMF lending so objectionable economically, politically, and ideologically that they have broken off negotiations for desperately needed foreign loans. While most less developed countries have not gone this far, they all find the intrusion of the IMF upon their domestic and foreign policies excessively meddlesome.[17]

[17]We have seen at the outset of this chapter that the IMF feels that these internal and external adjustments, if painful, are necessary to eliminate the root causes that create payments deficits and lead states to approach the Fund for loans.

Even though the conditions that the IMF attaches to its loans are resented by less developed countries and the magnitude of IMF loans is limited by their relatively small quotas, most less developed countries with severe payments problems wind up agreeing to an IMF loan package. This occurs not only because they need access to IMF resources, but also because they find it impossible to obtain private bank loans and bilateral development assistance elsewhere until other creditors are assured by a less developed country's agreement with the IMF that they are good credit risks. In short, the IMF is not only a lender of last resort, but the international economic community's legitimizer of a state's credit worthiness for all variety of public and private sources of foreign capital.

Not surprisingly, less developed countries have long pressed for access to larger amounts of resources from the IMF on easier terms (lower interest rates, longer repayment periods, fewer conditions attached to their domestic and foreign economic policies). Over the past one and one half decades, the IMF has responded by creating and expanding a number of special facilities of particular relevance to less developed country needs. These include:

Compensatory Finance Facility: For loans to states with payments deficits from shortfalls in export earnings due to price fluctuations and other circumstances beyond the control of a state. Between 1977 and 1979 $3 billion in loans were disbursed to forty-nine states through this facility. (This facility is discussed further in Chapter 2.)

Buffer Stock Facility: For loans to states contributing to buffer stock arrangements as part of international commodity agreements negotiated between producer and consumer states. (See Chapter 2 for a discussion of these arrangements.)

Oil Facility: For loans to states facing payments deficits due to massive increases in the prices they had to pay for oil imports after 1973. This facility was financed at $9 billion in 1974–1975.

Supplementary Financing (Witteveen) Facility: For supplemental loans to the most needy less developed countries that have already borrowed heavily from the IMF and may be approaching their borrowing limit. This facility was financed at $10 billion in 1977.

Trust Fund: For subsidizing (lowering) interest rates on IMF loans to the poorest less developed countries. This fund was raised by IMF sales of gold totaling $4.6 billion between 1976 and 1980.

Beyond these specialized, supplementary facilities, less developed countries have sought to increase their access to Fund resources through enlargement of their quotas and implementation of a proposal to link new SDR allocations to increased development assistance for less developed countries. A decision was reached in the IMF to increase all states' quotas 50 percent above those prevailing in 1978. This expanded the resources of the Fund to $75 billion (59 billion SDRs) in the early 1980s. Less developed countries will be able to borrow more as their quotas, like everyone else's, were increased by 50 percent. Less developed countries as a group, however, still accounted for only about 30 percent of total IMF quotas in 1980. It was also agreed in 1980, however, that borrowing limits would be expanded from 125 percent of a state's quota to 200 percent for one year, or 600 percent for three years. This should significantly expand IMF loans to less developed countries facing severe payments deficits.

The less developed countries have been far more frustrated in their efforts to link special drawing rights to their development aspirations. SDRs are created in accordance with international liquidity needs and are disbursed to members of the IMF in proportion to their quotas. Thus, less developed countries receive only approximately 30 percent of any new SDR allocations. For years less developed countries have pressed for a variety of proposals that would distribute new SDR allocations primarily to poor states—either directly or through an international lending agency such as IBRD. Because of the less developed countries' great need for imports, the newly granted reserves would finance increased purchases from the advanced states; these purchases would in turn contribute to the development objectives of the developing countries. Greater liquidity would be provided in the world monetary system, but instead of SDR reserves sitting more or less idle in OPEC states and rich countries with balance-of-payments surpluses, they would be working to provide needed goods and services in the poor countries—goods and services that would be obtained largely from oil exporters and the advanced industrial states of the West. SDRs would, in essence, be allocated to less developed countries with the expectation that they would be recycled to the advanced industrial states and oil exporters.[18]

Decision makers in advanced industrial states have remained very cool to such proposals. If SDRs are to have the possibility of emerging as the principal international reserve asset replacing existing international currencies, the international financial community must have complete confidence that SDR creation will be governed exclusively by liquidity requirements of the world economy viewed as a whole. Should SDRs be transformed into a new type of development assistance through these link proposals, less developed countries would be expected to demand new SDR allocations in large quantitites to meet their development aspirations. Yet there would frequently be occasions when further reserve creation would clearly be inappropriate in terms of liquidity requirements of the global economic system. In short, the SDR link would enhance the prospect of exacerbating global inflation by creating excessive amounts of liquidity, and it would politicize the SDRs in a fashion that could undermine their potential for emerging as the centerpiece for the international monetary system. Such fears were confirmed in 1980 when the finance ministers of twenty-four

[18]For a brief overview of SDR link ideas see "SDRs and Development, $10 billion for Whom?" *Foreign Policy*, No. 8 (Fall 1972), 102–28.

less developed countries called for the creation of an additional 56 billion SDRs ($73 billion) over the period 1980–1986. Western monetary officials feared this would be highly inflationary.[19]

The complaints of less developed countries about the IMF extend beyond the limits upon and terms attached to their borrowing. They seek a more potent role in the IMF's decision-making process. The Fund relies upon a weighted voting arrangement reflective of countries' quotas. Although less developed states comprise three-fourths of the IMF membership, they hold only about one-third of the votes. The United States alone has 19.8 percent of the votes in the IMF, and the five largest Western states together account for 40 percent of the votes in the Fund. Until well into the 1960s, moreover, the most important international monetary deliberations and decisions took place in the Group of Ten—a body meeting under the auspices of the Organization for Economic Cooperation and Development in Paris that performed a kind of executive function for the entire international monetary order, including the IMF. The Group of Ten was comprised of only the most important advanced industrial states, and less developed countries were seldom even consulted about deliberations conducted there.

Over the years the less developed countries have fought to enhance their voting power in the IMF and to move international monetary decision making into forums, including the IMF, where their power could be felt. As a result of their pressure, in combination with other events, a Group of Twenty was created under the auspices of the IMF with significant less developed country participation as the locus for key international monetary deliberations.[20] Less developed countries have also sought to politicize monetary questions and to enhance their bargaining position by raising monetary policy in UNCTAD and other U.N. institutions where they enjoy a voting majority.

The Debt of Less Developed Countries and International Monetary Challenges in the 1980s

Steadily frustrated by the IMF and the conduct of international monetary relations, the less developed countries were confronted with the need to finance rapidly expanding payments deficits following the sharp increase in the prices of their oil, food, and industrial goods imports after 1973. The current account deficits of non-oil-exporting less developed countries are shown in Table 3-1. Lacking access to foreign loans, these countries

---

[19]*The New York Times*, September 9, 1980, p. D8.

[20]Of course, this has not eliminated ad hoc consultation among the advanced industrial states under the OECD and other auspices on international monetary relations of common concern to them.

TABLE 3-1 Current Account Deficits of Non-Oil-Exporting Less Developed Countries, 1973–1980 (in billions of U.S. dollars).

1973	1974	1975	1976	1977	1978	1979	1980[a]
−11.5	−36.9	−45.9	−32.9	−28.6	−35.8	−52.9	−70

[a]IMF staff projection.

Source: International Monetary Fund, *Finance and Development*, 17, no. 3 (September 1980), 7.

would be required to curtail their imports and their development sharply—to their detriment and that of the advanced industrial states with large export markets in the Third World.

The poorest less developed countries had to borrow heavily from the IMF through both regular credit and supplementary lending facilities outlined previously. The more rapidly industrializing less developed states, by contrast, were able to borrow extensively from private banks operating primarily in Eurocurrency markets. These banks played a key role in recycling OPEC financial surpluses to non-oil-exporting less developed countries after the massive oil price hikes of 1973 and 1979.[21] The external debt of less developed countries in Africa, Asia, and Latin America (excluding oil exporters) skyrocketed from $48 billion in 1970 to over $301 billion in 1980.[22] Significantly, private borrowing accounted for 43 percent of the less developed country's outstanding foreign public debt of all less developed countries in 1980, compared with only 12 percent in 1970.[23]

As the international economy entered the 1980s, the non-oil-exporting less developed countries faced greater external financial needs than ever before. Their oil import bills had more than doubled over those of 1978 because of OPEC price increases, and the advanced industrial states were in a recession that dampened the less developed countries' export opportunities. Current account deficits approaching $70 billion a year were confronting them as well as heavy debt-servicing obligations stemming from loans obtained over the course of the 1970s. Private banks were wary of significant further increases in the proportion of their loan portfolios accounted for by less developed countries with eroding credit worthiness. Between 1974 and 1978, the number of less developed countries either unable to meet their debt repayments on time or seeking to reschedule

[21]For a concise summary of this process, see Charles Lipson, "The Organization of Third World Debt," paper delivered at the American Political Science Association Convention, Washington, D.C., August 1980.

[22]International Bank for Reconstruction and Development, *World Development Report, 1981* (Washington, D.C.: IBRD, 1981), 57.

[23]Ibid.

their debt rose from three to eighteen.[24] It was clear that the IMF and other public lending institutions (bilateral and multilateral) would have to assume a larger proportion of the risks and the new debts non-oil-exporting less developed countries would require in the 1980s.

These challenges imply an enhanced role for the IMF, yet an altered and more highly politicized one. The IMF is likely to be pushed toward accepting greater responsibility for managing Third World debt and in recycling financial surpluses from OPEC states to the oil-importing less developed countries. Less developed countries that relied heavily on private bank loans to finance their deficits throughout the 1970s will find these banks less willing to reschedule repayments of existing debts or to issue new loans without firm assurances from the IMF of the borrowers' future credit worthiness. This will require greater IMF scrutiny over the economic policies of newly industrializing states—such as Brazil, the Philippines, South Korea, and Argentina—than they were willing to submit to in the 1970s. Moreover, as fewer less developed countries are able to rely as heavily as they used to on private bank loans to finance their deficits, more resources will have to be provided to them directly through IMF programs. The 1980s should be characterized by a significant expansion of the IMF's importance in its capacities as both a legitimizer of states' credit worthiness for all variety of private and public financial programs and as a lender in its own right.

For the IMF to assume this larger role, it must expand substantially its resources for lending to less developed countries with payments problems. In large measure, these new resources must come from OPEC states (notably, Saudi Arabia, Kuwait, and the United Arab Emirates) accumulating immense financial surpluses—over $100 billion per year in the early 1980s. Increasing IMF dependence on OPEC states with financial surpluses will open the institution to new political pressures on issues of importance to these major creditors. For example, in 1980 Saudi Arabia linked its contribution to a new IMF facility to help finance less developed countries' debts with the granting of observer status to the PLO (Palestine Liberation Organization) in the annual meeting of the IMF.[25]

The IMF's enhanced role in the debt financing of less developed countries will clearly produce some major challenges and likely changes in its policies. The economic vitality of advanced industrial states, the economic development of oil-importing less developed countries, and the financial interests of international banks all require further lending to less developed countries in substantial amounts. There will be pressures from each of these sources, as well as from OPEC states courting Third World solidarity, for the IMF to increase the value of its lending to less developed

[24]IMF, *1979 Annual Report*, p. 24.

[25]The PLO was refused observer status, and Saudi Arabia refused to contribute to the IMF facility.

countries and to reduce the stringency of the conditions it imposes upon those less developed country borrowers from the Fund. This is the only way in which less developed countries are likely to be both capable of and willing to incur new debts in amounts needed to avoid their economic collapse. Severe international political and economic repercussions would inevitably follow.

The IMF is moving into a new era, from one dominated by Western (especially U.S.) interests to one in which key OPEC states must be accommodated. During the course of this transition, stalemates are likely to occur between American and OPEC interests that will prevent the IMF from raising capital both vital to the less developed countries and to the stability of the global economy.

THE RADICAL VIEW OF THE IMF

The conditions attached to IMF loans that require deflationary domestic economic policies, reduction of public expenditures (often designed to reduce income inequalities within society), and liberalization of international trade and investment policies expose the IMF to harsh criticism from radical analysts and decision makers. The acceptance of IMF policies sharply limits the options of less developed countries. They may be required to abandon socialist policies designed to reduce domestic income inequalities, or to protect local production from displacement by foreign imports or direct foreign investment, or to sever existing links with the international capitalist economy. The Fund, in the radical view, imposes capitalist domestic and foreign economic policies on borrowing states, thereby ensuring the dominance of the advanced market economies over the developing countries. The IMF's reliance upon traditional liberal economic advice, its rejection of noncapitalist policies, and its attempts to bind borrowing states to the current political-economic system (through their vulnerability and indebtedness) are all seen as evidence that the Fund serves as the handmaiden of dominant capitalist states. Harry Magdoff charges that "the very conditions which produce the necessity to borrow money are continuously reimposed by the pressures to pay back the loan and to pay the interest on these loans."[26] Another radical critic of the IMF writes that "IMF missions descend like vultures in the wake of right-wing coups in countries such as ˙Ghana, Indonesia, and Brazil."[27] Moreover, "the discipline imposed by the IMF has often eliminated the need for direct military intervention in order to preserve a climate friendly towards foreign investment."[28]

[26]Harry Magdoff, *The Age of Imperialism* (New York: Monthly Review Press, 1966), p. 98.

[27]Cheryl Payer, "The Perpetuation of Dependence: The IMF and the Third World," *Monthly Review,* 23, no. 4 (September 1971), 37.

[28]Ibid., p. 38.

The influence of the IMF is not limited to its ability to impose conservative policies on developing countries that seek to borrow from the Fund. Equally important, according to radical thought, is the central role the IMF occupies in the entire public and private credit system at the international level. If a deficit developing country seeks to obtain funds from the IMF but refuses the latter's advice or is otherwise denied a loan, then most of the other major sources of credit (including multinational institutions such as the World Bank, regional development organizations, bilateral government-to-government loans, and private sources of credit) also refuse to loan money to that country. The IMF acts somewhat as a central credit agency, then, setting the standard by which other sources of funds may be obtained. The radicals claim that it is no coincidence that President Allende of Chile was unable to find any loans after the IMF rejected his request for funds because of his unwillingness to accept IMF conditions. And they point out that in the wake of the military coup in September 1973 the IMF did indeed provide funds to a now more pliable Chile; what is more, this was followed by loans from other sources, both public and private.[29] In sum, the IMF is perceived by some to be the linchpin of the entire international monetary and economic order, which is designed to perpetuate capitalism and the subservience of developing states to the advanced industrial states. Cheryl Payer argues in this regard that:

> The [international loan] system can be compared point by point with peonage on an individual scale. In the peonage, or debt slavery, system the worker is unable to use his nominal freedom to leave the service of his employer, because the latter supplies him with credit (for overpriced goods in the company store) necessary to supplement his meager wages. The aim of the employer-creditor-merchant is neither to collect the debt once and for all, nor to starve the employee to death, but rather to keep the laborer permanently indentured through his debt to the employer. The worker cannot run away, for other employers and the state recognize the legality of his debt; nor has he any hope of earning his freedom with his low wage.
> Precisely the same system operates on the international level. Nominally independent countries find their debts, and their continuing inability to finance current needs out of imports [sic], keep them tied by a tight leash to their creditors. The IMF [and IBRD] orders them, in effect, to continue laboring on the plantations, while it refuses to finance their efforts to set up in business for themselves. For these reasons the term "international debt slavery" is a perfectly accurate one to describe the reality of their situation.[30]

[29]The same pattern applied in the case of Jamaica under leftist Prime Minister Michael Manley. His refusal to accept IMF terms of reduced public employment, budget cuts, and higher prices for desperately needed loans during 1980 led commercial banks to refuse extension of further credits until Jamaica resumed discussions with the Fund. Manley's electoral defeat by Edward Seaga, a staunch advocate of private enterprise, resulted in a prompt renegotiation of an IMF loan package and the resumption of private bank credits.

[30]Cheryl Payer, "The Perpetuation of Dependence: The IMF and the Third World," *Monthly Review*, 23, no. 4 (September 1971), 40.

SUMMARY

We saw in the previous chapter how liberals, radicals, and advocates for less developed countries in the Prebisch tradition differ in their analyses of key problems and policy prescriptions for enhancing the Third World's trade and development prospects. Similar patterns are present in their assessments of international monetary relations. Liberal economists, reflected in U.S. and IMF policy positions, stress the need for less developed countries to concentrate on internal adjustment measures while opening their economies to market forces in foreign trade and investment. Their prescriptions focus on the need for alterations in the domestic and foreign policies of states with payments deficits. Consistent with the Prebisch approach, less developed country analysts stress the need for changing the terms of, and norms for, international financial relations. They seek improved access to loans from the IMF and other sources as well as loans with fewer strings. In a word, they seek to reform the international monetary order. Radical analysts deplore the less developed countries linkage with advanced capitalist states—a linkage that increases their dependence through indebtedness and vulnerability to center states. The IMF, of course, lies at the center of less developed countries dependency, in their view. As in the case of trade, radical analysts argue for a transformation of Western states and less developed countries to socialist political-economic systems that would truly revolutionize existing international financial relations.

CHAPTER FOUR
THE MULTINATIONAL CORPORATION
Challenge to the International System

The multinational corporation is probably the most visible vehicle for the internationalization of the world economic system. As the economies of different nations have become increasingly linked and functionally integrated, the multinational corporation seems to have been the institution most able to adapt to a transnational style of operation. Indeed, multinational corporations are a major result of and a prime stimulus for furthering the number and complexity of transnational interactions and relationships.

A number of recent developments have focused attention on the multinational corporation as an international actor having important consequences for domestic as well as international politics and economics. For example, multinational corporations have been charged with the prime responsibility for the run on the dollar that resulted in its February 1973 devaluation. Moreover, the activities of multinational corporations have led to extensive investigations and studies by such diverse groups as the U.S. Senate, the United Nations, the International Labor Organization, and a large number of other governmental and nongovernmental agencies at national, regional, and international levels. Labor unions in the United States, Sweden, and the United Kingdom have charged their own multinationals with exporting jobs and have attempted to obtain government action to restrict the ease with which these corporations can invest abroad. In various host states, both United States and non-American multinational firms have been accused of economic imperialism, the fostering of intercountry competition, and the promulgation of insensitive and unsavory business practices. In sum, multinational corporations have become the most visible and the most attacked agents in the global economic system.

CHANGING PATTERNS
OF DIRECT FOREIGN INVESTMENT

Multinational corporations or their predecessors have existed for a long time. For instance, in the fifteenth century the Fuggers, headquartered in Augsburg, created and managed financial houses, trading concerns, mining operations, and processing plants in many parts of Europe.[1] Companies such as Singer, Heinz, Unilever, Nestlé, and a number of others have been active direct foreign investors for most of this century. However, the rapid expansion of direct foreign investment during the last three decades has done much to accelerate the internationalization of production. This has attracted increased attention to the impact of multinational firms on the world's economy and the economies of individual countries.

The total book value of all direct foreign investment was approximately $350 billion in 1979.[2] This reflects a 122 percent increase in the value of the worldwide stock of foreign direct investment from $158 billion in 1971.[3] Of the total amount of direct foreign investment in 1976, U.S. based multinational corporations accounted for 47.6 percent; European firms, 35.9 percent; Japanese, 6.7 percent; and Canadian, 3.9 percent.[4] The predominance of American multinationals has declined somewhat as the Europeans and Japanese have increased their international activity as a result both of their new economic and political stature in the world and of the devaluations of the American dollar during the 1970s.[5] Table 4-1 indicates the relative change in the international activity of selected source countries of multinational corporations.

[1]A. W. Clausen, "The Internationalized Corporation: An Executive's View," *The Annals,* 403 (September 1972), p. 21.

[2]In 1976, the book value of all direct foreign investment was $287 billion. United Nations, Economic and Social Council, Commission on Transnational Corporations *Transnational Corporations in World Development: A Re-examination,* (E/C. 10/38 (New York: United Nations, March 1978), p. 36.

[3]Ibid., p. 8.

[4]Ibid., p. 236.

[5]An emerging phenomenon is the rise and growth of Third World multinationals from South Korea, Mexico, Taiwan, Hong Kong, the Philippines, India, and Brazil.

TABLE 4-1   Trends in the Direct Investment Abroad of Selected Countries, Selected Years 1971–1976 (in percentages)

PARENT COUNTRY	1971	1976
United States	52.3%	47.6%
United Kingdom	15.0	11.2
Germany	4.6	6.9
Japan	2.8	6.7
Canada	4.1	3.9

Source: United Nations, Economic and Social Council, Commission on Transnational Corporations, *Transnational Corporations in World Development: A Re-examination,* E/C. 10/38 (New York: United Nations, March 1978), p. 236.

American multinational firms have a profound impact on the ways in which the United States is linked to the world economy. Data in Table 4-2 indicate the large size and rapid growth of American direct investment abroad since 1950. However, these figures represent the cumulative book value of U.S. direct foreign investment. On an annual basis, the affiliates of U.S. companies abroad had an income of $680 billion in 1977.[6] This compares with U.S. exports for that year of $120.8 billion.[7] In this same year, 4,715 U.S. companies and banks had more than 35,700 affiliates in other countries.

The direction and composition of American direct investment have changed dramatically. As Table 4-3 shows, by 1970 Europe had become the most important area for the operations of American multinational corporations; Latin America and the developing countries have become relatively less important. This same pattern is descriptive of foreign investment from all capital-exporting countries.

TABLE 4-2   Total Stock of Direct Foreign Investment of U.S. Multinational Corporations, Selected Years 1950–1980 (in billions of dollars)

	1950	1960	1970	1980
Direct foreign investment (Book value)	$11.8	$32.0	$78.1	$213.5

Sources: U.S. Congress, Senate Committee on Finance, *Implications of Multinational Firms for World Trade and Investment and for U.S. Trade and Labor,* 93rd Cong., 1st sess., 1973, p. 95; and U.S. Department of Commerce, *Survey of Current Business,* August 1981, pp. 21.

[6]U.S. Department of Commerce, *U.S. Direct Investment Abroad, 1977.* (Washington, D.C.: Bureau of Economic Analysis, April, 1981), p. 34.

[7]This figure excludes exports of goods under U.S. military agency sales contracts.

TABLE 4-3 Geographic Breakdown of U.S. Direct Investment Abroad, Selected Years 1950–1980 (in billions of dollars and percentages)

	1950		1960		1970		1980	
	Amount	% of Total	Amount	% of Total	Amount	% of Total	Amount	% of Total
Total developed areas	$ 5.7	48%	$19.6	61%	$53.2	68%	$157.1	74%
Canada	3.6	31	11.2	35	22.8	29	44.6	21
Europe	1.7	14	6.7	21	24.5	31	95.7	45
Others	0.4	3	1.7	5	5.9	8	16.8	8
Total less developed areas	4.4	37	10.9	34	21.3	27	52.7	25
Unallocated	1.7	14	1.5	5	3.6	5	3.7	2
Total	$11.8	99%	$32.0	100%	$78.1	100%	$213.5	100%

Sources: U.S. Congress, Senate Committee on Finance, *Implications of Multinational Firms for World Trade and Investment and for U.S. Trade and Labor,* 93rd Cong., 1st sess., 1973, p. 72. The 1980 figures are from the U.S. Department of Commerce, *Survey of Current Business,* August 1981, pp. 21-22.

At the same time, the devalued dollar and the more aggressive posture of non-American enterprises have led to a rapid inflow of foreign investment into the United States. From 1973 to 1980, foreign direct investment in the United States increased from $20.5 billion to $65.5 billion.[8] Already, there is more direct foreign investment in the United States than in any other country, except Canada. The leading sources of foreign direct investment in the United States, by country of origin, are the Netherlands, United Kingdom, Canada, Germany, Japan, and Switzerland respectively, and they account for almost 90 percent of the total.[9] Despite the extensive amounts of petrodollars earned by the thirteen members of the Organization of Petroleum Exporting Countries (OPEC), together they accounted for less than 1 percent of the total.[10] Given the large American market, it is reasonable to predict that eventually the United States will be the world's largest host as well as its largest source of foreign investment.

The composition of American investment abroad has also changed. During the 1960s and thereafter, American firms invested much more heavily in manufacturing facilities than in extractive operations. By 1980, 42 percent of American direct foreign investment was in manufacturing industries, compared with 35 percent in 1960. From 1960 to 1980, the share

[8]U.S. Department of Commerce, *Survey of Current Business,* August 1981, p. 41.
[9]Ibid., p. 47.
[10]Ibid.

of investment in extractive industries decreased from 43 percent to 25 percent, even though absolute investment in these activities more than tripled during that period. Investment in other sorts of economic activity, such as service industries and financial institutions, accounted for 33 percent of all American direct foreign investment by 1980.[11]

These figures convey several important points. First, American and non-American direct foreign investment and multinational corporations have expanded so rapidly within the last two decades that they now account for a major part of international economic activity. Furthermore, although they do have predecessors, their size and growth make them an essentially new international economic institution. Third, the patterns of international business activity are changing. Direct foreign investment, including that from the United States, is more likely to be a manufacturing or service industry located in other advanced industrial states than an extractive industry located in developing countries. Even within Latin America, a greater percentage of American direct investment is nonextractive in character.

THE NATURE OF MULTINATIONAL CORPORATIONS
AND DISTINCTIONS AMONG THEM

What is a multinational corporation? The definitions vary. Some are broad ("all firms—industrial, service, and financial—doing international business of all types, within a myriad of organizational structures"[12]); others are narrower, based on size, extensiveness of operation in foreign countries, type of business, and organizational structure and managerial orientation. The difficulty in arriving at a widely accepted definition is that various parties, such as government officials, international executives, and scholars, all have different interests and purposes in their analyses of multinational corporations. Consequently, their definitions vary. For instance, the Harvard Business School Multinational Enterprise Project is interested primarily in studying large international firms appearing in *Fortune's* 500 with each firm having operations in no fewer than six different countries.[13] However, government officials in a developing country may be faced with unemployment resulting from the closure of a subsidiary of a rather small foreign-owned firm with operating facilities in only two or three countries. In this case, the international character of the corporation is as real and as disconcerting as if the corporation were among the one hundred largest manufacturing firms and had facilities in many areas of the world.

---

[11]Ibid., p. 32.

[12]U.S. Congress, Senate Committee on Finance, *Implications of Multinational Firms for World Trade and Investment and for U.S. Trade and Labor*, 93rd Cong., 1st sess., 1973, p. 83.

[13]Ibid., p. 83.

Our objective is to examine the political implications, both national and international, of these firms as important actors in the international arena. Consequently, a broad rather than a narrow definition seems more appropriate for our purposes—although finer distinctions will be drawn shortly. Multinational corporations are those economic enterprises—manufacturing, extractive, service, and financial—that are headquartered in one country and that pursue business activities in one or more foreign countries. We are concerned with direct investment that is central to the business of the firm—not portfolio investment. Using these criteria, there are nearly 10,000 multinational corporations.

Although this definition is useful for incorporating the many variations found in this class of actors, it is too broad to allow more precise statements of relationship and analysis. For instance, questions regarding the impact of multinational corporations on host states or the importance of foreign operations to corporations cannot be answered in the general terms we used earlier. Instead, distinctions must be made among different types of multinational enterprises as they affect host states. To indicate the great diversity of multinational corporations, a number of important factors will be examined. The behavior, impact, and consequences of corporate activities will vary with the specific set of characteristics used to describe the enterprise.

Some multinational corporations are gigantic. Others are rather small. A U.S. Department of Commerce census in 1966 identified 3,400 American firms engaged in direct foreign investment and determined that these firms had a total of 23,000 foreign affiliates; however, a mere 298 of these firms accounted for 55 percent of the total assets and 66 percent of the sales of foreign affiliates of American companies.[14] Even though these figures are from 1966, they do suggest that, although there are many foreign subsidiaries that interact with host state governments, society, and culture, no more than several hundred of them—large and well-known firms—dominate American foreign investment activity. The size and consequent visibility of these American firms make them particularly important domestic and international economic actors. On the other hand, the many smaller and often less sophisticated firms may themselves act in a fashion that poisons the atmosphere for all foreign investment. In 1978 a small subsidiary of Raytheon in Belgium engaged in behavior that mobilized unions and governments in Europe to press the Organization for Economic Cooperation and Development (OECD) to monitor general corporate adherence to its guidelines for multinational corporations. Moreover, the guidelines were incorporated into the national laws of Belgium and several other countries.

[14]U.S. Department of Commerce, *Special Survey of U.S. Multinational Companies, 1970* (Springfield, Va.: National Technical Information Service, 1972), p.3.

The size of a corporation's international component relative to its overall operations is another important distinguishing characteristic. For some firms, such as Pfizer and IBM, international (non-U.S.) activities may account for nearly 50 percent or more of their sales or profits, but for many other corporations international operations constitute a minor part of their business. Generally, it is likely that those firms whose international activities are quite large and critical will seek actively to secure a favorable environment for these activities in host and parent states and at regional and international levels. Foreign investment is fundamental and important to their business success, but such investment may be of marginal concern to other companies involved less internationally. However, the rapid expansion of direct foreign investment indicates that increasing numbers of corporations are consciously attempting to broaden the scale and scope of their international operations.

A related factor serving to differentiate types of firms is the number of countries in which a firm's subsidiaries are located. The extent to which a specific firm's activities are located around the world may reflect its commitment to international business. It may also indicate a conscious effort to decentralize and thus make its international activities less vulnerable politically. Firms with subsidiaries in only a few countries may just be beginning their international efforts, or they may merely be doing business where critical natural resources can be found, or they may centralize production to serve business activities throughout the world. Simple conclusions cannot be drawn from the extent of a firm's activities throughout the world.

The nature of the corporation's business is a fourth type of distinction that must be made among multinational firms. A partial list of the different types of businesses conducted on an international scale is presented in Figure 4-1. There is frequently a significant difference between the behavior and impact of an extractive type of multinational corporation, that of a capital goods enterprise, and the activities of a consumer products manufacturing concern. From the perspective of the host state, the costs and benefits of each type of firm are quite different. For example, host states may tend to view direct foreign investment in extractive industries as more exploitative than investment in manufacturing.[15] On issues such as employment, technological transfers, taxes and other revenues, and balance-of-payments matters, a host state's evaluation of a foreign firm varies with the specific character of the firm. Even within the category of extractive industries, there are important differences in the relative bargaining strengths of firms in various industries, implying that there will be differences among the political and economic relations between host states and the multinationals.[16]

[15]See the discussion of nationalization in Chapter 7.
[16]Raymond Vernon, *Sovereignty at Bay* (New York: Basic Books, 1971) Ch. 2.

```
1. Extractive
     Petroleum (Exxon)
     Mining (Kennecott)
     Lumber (Weyerhaeuser)
2. Agriculture (Standard Brands)
3. Industrial
     Capital goods (Caterpillar Tractor)
     Intermediate goods (Ford)
     Consumer goods (Colgate-Palmolive)
4. Service
     Transportation (Greyhound)
     Public Utilities (GTE)
     Wholesaling and retailing (Sears)
     Tourism (Holiday Inns)
     Insurance (INA)
     Advertising (The Interpublic Group)
     Management services (McKinsey and Co.)
5. Financial Institutions
     Banking (Bank of America)
     Investing (International Basic Economy Corporation)
6. Conglomerate (IT&T)
Note: The companies in the parentheses are examples of the types of firms. However, many of these
firms engage in numerous kinds of business activities and, thus, might be found in several of these
categories.
```

FIGURE 4-1 Types of Business Activities Pursued by Multinational Corporations

Another characteristic distinguishing multinational corporations is the pattern of ownership linking the parent firm with its subsidiaries. Multinational corporations may have wholly owned subsidiaries or they may share ownership, to varying degrees, with joint venture partners of different types. Between 1961 and 1970, 56 percent of all new American foreign investment took the form of wholly owned subsidiaries or foreign branches.[17] Another 12 percent of new American investment involved a majority share for the American enterprise, and only 8 percent of the new investment was a minority investment. (Unfortunately, information was not available for 24 percent of the new investment during these years.) Japanese firms show a strikingly different pattern: only 29 percent of new investment involved total ownership, 34 percent entailed majority ownership, and 37 percent involved minority ownership.[18] These data suggest that American firms in general are less willing to accommodate the desires of host countries for participation in the ownership and control of American direct foreign investment. By such actions, American firms may stimulate host country regulations that require a certain amount of local participation.

[17]These figures were taken from a study by Booz, Allen, and Hamilton that was reported in "American Investment Abroad: Who's Going Where, How, and Why," *Business Abroad*, June 1971, p. 9.

[18]Gregory Clark, "Japanese Direct Investment Overseas," unpublished manuscript, 1971, Table II, as reported in Richard D. Robinson, "Beyond the Multinational Corporation," mimeographed, p. 1.

Similarly, the host country partner of a majority-or minority-owned investment may vary widely. Three of the more likely partners are private entrepreneurs, individual stockholders, and host government or quasi-governmental agencies. There are a number of other types of possible partners in joint venture arrangements, but the main point is that corporate practices and objectives as well as the response of host state government officials and other interest groups may differ with the specific nature of the joint venture relationship. For example, some corporations may feel that a joint venture with a host state government agency may reduce the chances of nationalization,[19] but the price may be constant governmental meddling.

Of the other factors that are useful in attempting to differentiate among types of multinational enterprises, two of the most important are organizational structure and managerial orientation. A number of schema have been developed by students of multinational corporations to describe these aspects of international firms, and although they differ in the terms they use, they are basically quite similar.[20] Several general types of organizational forms are examined in the paragraphs that follow, but it must be recognized that they are only archetypes; any specific firm is likely to incorporate attributes from more than one of these models.

The parent-dominant–subsidiary-subservient type of enterprise is organized in such a way as to ensure that its international activities enhance the efforts of the firm in its major market in the parent country. Organizationally, the international operations are subordinate to the objectives, standards, and actions of the domestic business of the headquarters. Similarly, management orientation is that of the parent company and parent country. As Howard Perlmutter[21] has termed it, management is *ethnocentric* regarding goals, frames of reference, perspectives, and nationality. The prevailing view in this type of organization is that what is good and appropriate for the parent firm is paramount, and the efforts of the foreign subsidiaries should support and supplement the business in the parent country. Probably a majority of the multinational corporations existing today resemble this parent-dominant type of enterprise. This is particularly true of the smaller and newer entries in the field of international business as well as some of the extractive industries. Also, this type of enterprise tends to emphasize the difference between the multinational corporation and the host state, for host state objectives, practices, and standards are clearly secondary to those developed by the parent company.

[19]A recent study has suggested that having a joint venture arrangement with a host government agency is not a safeguard against nationalization. Stephen J. Korbrin, "Foreign Enterprise and Forced Divestment in the LDCs," *International Organization*, 34 (Winter 1980), 65-80.

[20]See Howard V. Perlmutter, "The Tortuous Evolution of the Multinational Corporation," *Columbia Journal of World Business*, 3 (January–February 1969), 9–18.

[21]Ibid., 9-18.

A second type of multinational enterprise structure and orientation can be likened to an international holding company in which the various subsidiaries operate with a high degree of autonomy. In this, the subsidiary-independent form of organization, the parent company has very little to do with either the goal-setting or operational phases of the subsidiaries' business. Local managers, most likely citizens of the host country, determine their own objectives, standards, and ways of doing things with little interference from or reference to the headquarters. In this type of arrangement, clashes between host states and the international enterprise are less likely to occur, since the subsidiaries are very similar to local firms. The international nature of the subsidiary-independent type of corporation is primarily in the area of ownership, not in the area of control.

The third type of multinational organization, the integrated international enterprise, is quite different from the other two in that the parent company's operations as well as the subsidiaries' are incorporated into an overall managerial effort. The enterprise is organized in such a fashion as to advance regional or global objectives and activities; no particular nationality, whether parent or host country, prevails. Instead, corporate goals, corporate standards of performance, and corporate practices dominate. Decentralization of management occurs but only within the framework of an integrated, centrally directed effort aimed at maximizing broad-scale corporate objectives. In this organizational structure and management orientation, the potential for clashes with host state interests is great, but the source of such conflict comes from the truly international or anational character of the firm, not, as in the first archetype, from its foreign, ethnocentric character.

Increasingly, multinational enterprises are tending to take on the characteristics of this third type of organization. The more progressive and successful U.S. multinationals are consciously attempting to develop a worldwide approach to business, in terms of organization, management orientation, and the substance of their business activity. W. J. Barnholdt, vice president of Caterpillar Tractor Corporation, described this type of enterprise in a speech in the early 1970s:

> Caterpillar is owned by approximately 48,000 shareholders and our stock is traded on exchanges in the United States, France, England, Scotland, West Germany, Switzerland, and Belgium. We have 65,000 employees, 22 percent of whom work abroad. We are a multinational company, treating foreign operators as co-equal with domestic, in both structure and policy, willing to allocate resources without regard to national frontiers.
>
> We will one day become a transnational company—a multinational business managed and owned by people of different nationalities—through current programs aimed at developing more top managers of different national origins and greater ownership by investors outside the U.S. Thus, while we export from the U.S., our views as to transportation, markets, and product are worldwide. For example, there is no U.S.-made Caterpillar tractor. A Caterpillar

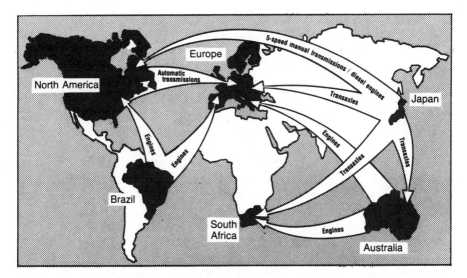

FIGURE 4-2 The J car's global assembly lines. **Source** WORLD BUSINESS WEEKLY, September 14, 1981, p. 22. Reprinted with permission of the Financial Times of London.

product—wherever it is built—is just that—a Caterpillar product—graphic evidence that people of different national origins and political interests can achieve common objectives.[22]

What this means is that the activities of the enterprise are integrated on a regional or global scale. This type of firm is particularly sensitive to political and economic developments in various states and in the global economy, and through its worldwide orientation it seeks to capitalize on international economic interdependencies. Thus, for instance, capital needed for new investment or expansion is secured wherever the most favorable terms exist. Similarly, marketing strategies are integrated and coordinated in such a fashion as to take advantage of spillover advertising and similar markets. Of course, to the extent feasible, production is also integrated.

The international nature of production is illustrated by a map that depicts General Motors' "J" car global assembly lines and product sourcing (Figure 4-2).

Although most multinational corporations are variants of one of the three archetypes discussed, other ideal types have been suggested. One proposes the existence of a supranational corporation that is truly non-national in that its ownership, board of directors, management, and orientation are not dominated by one nationality. Furthermore, such an enterprise would be chartered by, and pay taxes to, an international body

[22]Quoted in *U.S. Multinationals: The Dimming of America,* a report prepared for the AFL-CIO Maritime Trades Department, Executive Board Meeting, February 15-16, 1973, p. 12.

on the order of a GATT or an IMF established precisely for this purpose. This model is based on the assumption that international firms should be subject to international rules and regulations, a procedure, it is claimed, that would protect both host states and multinational corporations.

Richard Robinson describes another type of organization, the transnational association, that a number of Japanese firms have adopted.[23] It is not like the forms of foreign investment already described, but it is a mechanism, he thinks, that might allow transnational business activity without severely threatening the sovereignty of states. Under this structure, the headquarters has little or no equity investment in the "subsidiaries" located in various countries. Instead, the "subsidiaries" are locally owned and managed, but they receive extensive managerial and technological assistance from the headquarters. In addition, most or all of the production of the "subsidiaries" is sold contractually to the headquarters, which then serves in some cases as the assembler and, most important, as the international marketer and distributor for the association. The central headquarters still plays a dominant role in the integration of production and marketing, but its role as owner and as "subsidiary" manager is for the most part eliminated. Certainly, the implications for relations between the multinational corporation and the host state differ from those of other types of multinational firms.

The wide variation among multinational corporations has been demonstrated in this discussion. Differences in size, importance of international operations, type of business activity, ownership patterns, and organizational structure and managerial orientation result in different goals, actions, and responses from host states. Meaningful analysis of the impact of multinational corporations requires a precise understanding of the type of enterprise involved.

A final caveat needs to be made. The characteristics of different types of multinational corporations may appear in combination in a single corporation. For instance, the same firm may contain an extractive subsidiary that is wholly owned and that is treated in an ethnocentric fashion and a majority-owned subsidiary that is involved in the production of intermediate goods and that is linked closely with operations in other countries. Thus, it may be inappropriate to generalize from an overall pattern describing the enterprise as a whole to the specific cases of individual subsidiaries and vice versa. As a result, assessments or predictions about the nature of the relationships between the host country and the multinational corporation depend very much on the specific characteristics of the subsidiaries as well as of the corporation as a whole.

[23]Richard Robinson, "Beyond the Multinational Corporation," in *International Business-Government Affairs*, ed. John Fayerweather (Cambridge, Mass.: Ballinger, 1973), pp. 17–26.

MOTIVATIONS FOR CORPORATE
INTERNATIONAL EXPANSION

Both corporate apologists and radical critics agree that corporations expand internationally for sound economic and business reasons from the capitalist's self-interested point of view. Certainly these two groups differ as to the legitimacy of the capitalist perspective and, therefore, the impact of foreign investments. Despite this difference of opinion, both groups recognize a number of motivations for domestic firms to become international corporations. As we just indicated, however, distinctions need to be made among various types of multinational enterprises.

Extractive industries have traditionally been international in scope because they depend upon the location of fuel, mineral, or other raw material deposits. Consequently, even if domestic supplies exist, extractive firms must seek foreign sources of supply to supplement or substitute for domestic sites that are drying up or are too expensive to operate. Moreover, control over foreign resource supplies serves as a hedge against disruptions in supply or as a preemptive maneuver designed to deny existing or potential competitors access to the same source.

Manufacturing corporations establish foreign subsidiaries for quite different reasons. If the firm has obtained foreign markets through the export process, it is possible that increasing costs of production and transportation will lead the firm to serve these same markets more profitably through local manufacturing facilities. Establishing a local subsidiary also eases servicing problems and allows for greater adaptation of the product to local conditions and desires. The possibility of losing a market to either local or international competition also stimulates corporations to establish foreign subsidiaries, sometimes in anticipation of a future market's developing. Also investing in the parent country of an international competitor may cause the latter to redirect its energies away from international expansion to protect its home country market. Furthermore, tariff and other trade barriers raise the cost of exporting to the protected market, and local subsidiaries constitute an effective mechanism to circumvent these barriers and maintain or increase market share. The European Common Market's external tariff was a major reason for the explosive growth of U.S. direct foreign investment in Europe in the 1960s.

A quite different stimulus to establish manufacturing subsidiaries abroad is the practice by many states of offering substantial investment incentives that are designed explicitly to attract foreign investment to depressed areas. Indeed, 26% of the foreign affiliates of U.S. corporations received at least one incentive from the host country.[24] Tax holidays, cash grants, the training

[24]U.S. Department of Commerce, *U.S. Direct Investment Abroad, 1977*, p. 168.

of a local work force, and the provision of land and buildings are a few of the many ways by which host countries attempt to draw foreign investors. Often, actual cash grants are made to foreign investors. Canada, which is developing a more restrictive policy toward foreign investment, provided IBM with a $6 million nonrepayable grant for the purpose of establishing a large computer facility in a depressed area of Quebec. Volkswagen received a set of incentives amounting to $58 million from the government of Pennsylvania to establish its assembly facility near Pittsburgh. Such efforts are duplicated many times over by most of the countries of the world, and they serve to emphasize the fact that multinational corporations are often pulled into specific foreign investments by the actions of host governments. This image is quite different from that of the corporation thrusting itself upon an unwilling host state.

Furthermore, parent-country policies may foster the development of foreign subsidiaries. For example, the tax credit and deferral policies of the U.S. government stimulated massive investment abroad by American firms. In response to fuel and natural resource shortages, the Japanese government has urged Japanese firms to find new sources of supplies in other countries.

Of course, some manufacturing concerns become international because of the existence of a substantial and growing overseas market, which offers excellent earnings prospects. The huge expansion of American investment in manufacturing in Europe during the 1960s reflected, among other things, the wealth, size, and stability of the market available in an economically healthy Europe. The attractiveness of the reduced trade barriers and the large market offered by the European Economic Community were critical factors too. The establishment of the convertibility of European currencies further facilitated international economic transactions, including investment.

Additionally, the increasingly competitive and saturated market in the United States in certain industries led dynamic American firms to look to other countries as a place for new profit and growth opportunities, for the effective utilization of restive management talent in new and challenging areas, and for a method by which headquarters' overhead costs could be shared over a larger base. Raymond Vernon and his colleagues at Harvard summarize many of these motivations in the concept of the product cycle, wherein the firm facing a decline in its technological advantage in the parent country market essentially exports this advantage to foreign countries through the vehicle of foreign subsidiaries.[25]

These reasons for corporate international expansion do not suggest a conspiracy among capitalists to dominate the world. Rather, they suggest a rational response, from the capitalist perspective, to opportunities for the

[25]Raymond Vernon, *Sovereignty at Bay* (New York: Basic Books, 1971) pp. 65-77.

pursuit of business activities in other countries. Indeed, business executives as well as most radical critics would agree that the development of multinational corporations is a logical and rational step in the evolution of capitalism.[26] Indeed, some of the largest European-based multinationals are state owned fully or partially, indicating that the drive for foreign investment may be a phenomenon of business, not necessarily private capitalism.

The growth and development of the more highly integrated and managerially sophisticated multinational corporations are due to additional motivations. Business operations with a regional or global orientation can finance, produce, and market in a fashion that maximizes the ability of the firm to take advantage of different costs and investment climates around the world. New developments in communications and transportation systems and important improvements in management practices have greatly facilitated the task of managing these complex international enterprises. By integrating production, finance, and marketing corporations are able to service American and foreign markets without incurring the high cost of American production. For example, some American-based multinational firms have shifted production away from the well-organized labor force and the high production costs in the more developed countries to the developing countries. Much of the small appliance manufacturing of U.S. companies occurs in other countries, and black-and-white television sets are just not made in the United States. Similar developments are occurring in European and Japanese firms as they face rising labor and production costs in their home countries. Foreign manufacturing may be necessary to stay competitive on a worldwide basis. Interestingly, some of these firms are establishing investments in the United States to take advantage of lower labor costs and to avoid U.S. barriers to imports.

Corporations, banks, and other firms involved in service activities tend to expand overseas because of their need to provide services on an international scale to their multinational clients. U.S. banking, consulting, and advertising firms became international because their customers in the United States were multinational. Most assuredly, the reasoning goes, if one firm in a particular service sector failed to provide these necessary facilities and processes for its clients, competitors would do so on the international level and might, in that fashion, eventually capture the huge domestic business of serving such firms. Again, the logic and reasonableness of the growth of multinational enterprises are inescapable if the basic premises of capitalism are accepted.

Radical critics, while recognizing this logic, do not accept the premises of capitalism as an appropriate basis for organizing the economy and society, at either the national or international levels. Thus, although the growth of

[26]We have not examined, and will only mention here, the traditional Leninist argument that the expansion of foreign investment is the result of the need to find an outlet for surplus investment capital.

multinational corporations may logically follow from capitalism, radical critics focus on the disadvantages and evils of such firms, and of capitalism in general, for parent and host states as well as for the international system. They view the abolition of capitalism, either in parent states or in host states (according to *dependencia* theorists), as the only sure way in which to control multinational corporations. On the other hand, classical liberal theorists typically stress that the benefits of direct foreign investment outweigh some of its admittedly negative aspects. They feel that the problems associated with foreign investment can be alleviated or eliminated through more sensitive state and corporate policies.

THE IMPACT OF THE MULTINATIONAL CORPORATION: SOURCE OF CONFLICT OR AGENT OF GROWTH?

Various domestic groups and policymakers within both parent and host states are likely to react differently to multinational corporations. Those with a particularly strong ideological commitment will see either great benefit or great harm resulting from the actions of these enterprises; most, however, will observe a mixture of effects, and policy debates and policy prescriptions will thereby reflect a mélange of promotion and restriction. Different postures that might be adopted by host and parent governments or by regional and international organizations will be examined in the paragraphs that follow, but before doing so let us examine the complaints and praises stimulated by the existence of multinational enterprises.

Host States' Concerns

Countries, especially developing countries, that serve as hosts to extractive industries frequently charge the extractive subsidiary with "stealing" its precious natural resources—the petroleum, copper, bauxite, or whatever is deemed to be a national resource—and point to the significant profits that are being obtained from this source of national wealth by multinational enterprises. Furthermore, such firms often exist in enclave-type surroundings and have few meaningful links to the local economy. The product is exported; the management is foreign; the benefits accrue primarily to the foreign firm and foreign societies. Moreover, because of the importance of the natural resource, the foreign firm and the parent government are often thought to collaborate and sometimes interfere in order to protect the investment from local political and social disturbances. In sum, the allegation is that the large and wealthy foreign firm—supported by a powerful, and probably imperialistic, parent government—is exploiting a relatively weak, underdeveloped host state, which seeks to obtain a reasonable return on its natural resource while trying to maintain its national sovereignty and pride.

This somewhat exaggerated view of the negative aspects of international firms engaged in extractive operations is not nearly as appropriate for multinational manufacturing companies. Manufacturing firms, which are more extensive in advanced states than in developing countries, are much more integrated with host state societies and economies. In many cases, the extractive operation seems to be almost a wholly foreign enterprise with the exception of local workers and the location of the facility. Foreign-owned manufacturing subsidiaries, in contrast, become very much a part of the local scene. For example, they are likely to have local business supporters as well as domestic business enemies. Often, the products are consumed locally, a situation that is aided by massive advertising campaigns designed to increase consumer awareness and a predisposition toward the product. The plants tend to be located in the more heavily settled areas of the country, unlike the often isolated sites of extractive facilities. Generally speaking, manufacturing enterprises are more pervasive (though not necessarily more important) in the host state environment than are extractive operations. The charges leveled against such firms are particularly important because of the extent of international manufacturing, because of its rapid growth rate, and because of the acute concern that has been expressed in advanced industrial states as well as in the developing countries.

Many host states fear that the size and wealth of multinational corporations, whether extractive or manufacturing, will dominate their economies. One frequently sees lists that rank states according to GNP and size of central government budgets in relation to sales figures of the largest multinational corporations.[27] Leading firms have sales figures larger than the GNPs of most states, even some that are industrialized. Such comparisons are designed to indicate the huge power of multinational corporations. Aggregate data of this sort do support fears that multinational corporations have the size and stength to dominate weaker states. But, in reality, such lists are deceptive. There is often an erroneous implication that General Motors, for example, would marshal all its resources to influence or overwhelm a state like Belgium. Nonetheless, the fact that thirty-nine of the one hundred largest economic entities are private corporations—sixty-one are states—is indicative of the potential power and real importance of multinational corporations.

A more specific, and probably more realistic, concern is that, within a particular state, foreign investment may dominate the most profitable, the most technologically advanced, the most growth-oriented, and the economic trend-setting industries. Studies have shown that American multinationals tend to invest in the most profitable host state industries and then to be even more profitable than their local competitors. As a result, host states (even if highly industrialized) perceive that important segments of

---

[27]An example of such a list can be found in Louis Turner, *Invisible Empires*, (New York: Harcourt Brace Jovanovich, 1971), pp. 135-36.

their economy are increasingly subject to the control of multinational companies rather than national firms. Data to support this concern reveal that, in Germany in 1974, foreign firms controled 33 percent of the assets in chemicals, 48 percent in rubber, and 51 percent in electrical machinery.[28]

In addition, almost by definition, the control of multinational corporations resides in the hands of executives whose loyalties are to the foreign-based corporation and probably the parent country. Critical decisions are thought to be made at headquarters in foreign countries, which makes host country efforts to influence those decisions very difficult. The combination of foreign ownership and ultimately foreign management control leaves host country nationals feeling powerless to affect those decisions with substantial impact for the host state.

Host states at all levels of industrialization also fear that these circumstances will produce technological dependence upon the United States or other technologically active parent states, such as Japan. The charge is often made that the headquarters company and country will become technological innovators while the rest of the world becomes little more than technology consumers or technological colonies.[29] In the pharmaceutical, synthetic fiber, and chemical industries in Colombia, Constantine Vaitsos found that a mere 10 percent of the patent holders (all of which are multinational enterprises) own 60 percent of all patents in these industries.[30] When this situation occurs, there is a fear that host state industry will be stunted and that the multinational corporation will be able to extract enormous profits through license fees and royalties. This process is advanced by the centralization of research and development activity in the parent state of most multinational enterprises and by the brain drain in terms either of the emigration of scientists to the United States or of their working for local subsidiaries of foreign firms.

Continuing with the technology theme, it is often charged that multinational corporations charge exorbitant prices to host countries for technology that has already been developed and applied. Sometimes, it is alleged that these high prices are demanded for technology that is old and obsolete, but the company continues to reap profits at the expense of the host country. Another concern is that the technology transferred to the host country is "inappropriate." This usually means that the technology is too advanced, too expensive, and too capital intensive for a country that desperately needs to find jobs for large numbers of unemployed and would thus need labor-intensive investment instead of capital-intensive facilities.[31]

[28]United Nations, *Transnational Corporations in World Development*, p. 273.

[29]See Chapter 6 for a more comprehensive discussion of technological gaps in the international political economy.

[30]Constantine V. Vaitsos, "Patents Revisited," *The Journal of Development Studies*, 29 (1973), p. 12.

[31]The major issue of the transfer of technology will be discussed in greater length in Chapter 6.

All these factors combine to produce fears that multinational corporations will act in a fashion counter to what is perceived to be in the best interests of the host state. Failure to conform to national plans and the precedence of international or foreign business interests over national political, economic, and social interests are especially galling and are very noticeable when committed by foreign firms. For example, within a span of two weeks during 1962, French subidiaries of General Motors and Remington Rand announced layoffs of 1,485 French employees without apprising the French government of these actions. The layoffs occurred at a time when the government was trying to establish a wage policy with employers and unions. Moreover, these moves contradicted the French belief that business, not labor, should shoulder the burden of market adjustments. More recently, the takeover of Chrysler-UK by Peugeot-Citroen in August 1978 created anxieties among the trade unions affected. The new owners made it clear that no ironclad guarantees of continued employment of the work force could be made, but, in addition, Peugeot appeared to be more interested in launching its new cars than in committing itself to the preservation of the U.K. facilities and jobs. These instances illustrate that sometimes multinational corporations act in ways that are considered inappropriate, clumsy, and alien by elements of the host state, including government officials.

Problems associated with controlling the activities of American multinational enterprises are heightened by the influence of the U.S. government (or any other parent state) over corporate policies. American antitrust policies may prevent a merger between the foreign subsidiary of an American firm and a host country enterprise, even when the merger is expressly desired by the host government. Provisions concerning trade with the enemy, which are applicable to the foreign subsidiaries as well as the headquarters of American firms, have prohibited trade with some Communist states. In 1968, for example, a Belgian subsidiary of an American multinational was prevented by the U.S. Treasury Department from exporting farm equipment to Cuba even though the contract had been signed by the Belgian national firm prior to its takeover by an American multinational. There are many such instances. Host state resentment of these extraterritorial extensions of parent state policies are supplemented by fears that foreign subsidiaries may seek support from the government of the parent country in their disputes with the host state. The concerns of Latin America in this regard are well known.[32] In Asia, many countries have similar fears about Japanese foreign investments, and the French government has come to the aid of French firms in trouble with the governments of former French

---

[32]Many Latin American countries have incorporated variants of the Calvo doctrine in their investment laws. This doctrine suggests that foreign enterprises cannot legally turn to their parent governments for protection since they are subject to the laws and legal procedures of the host state.

colonies in Africa. In addition, there is concern that multinational firms will engage in political meddling to establish a favorable investment climate. United Fruit in Guatemala, IT&T in Chile, and the corporate bribery cases in the late 1970s represent attempts by foreign firms to influence not only government policies but also the very structure of government in host countries.

Host governments are, of course, also interested in the impact of multinational corporations on their balance-of-payments position. Critics of these enterprises claim that they generally contribute to a deficit, in that they take more international currency out of the country than they bring in. Negative items (repatriated earnings, charges for royalties, interest, licenses, and various management services, and expenses incurred by importing necessary equipment and component products) far outweigh positive items (the inflow of new capital, savings resulting from import substitution, and earnings gained through exports) in the balance-of-payments accounts. Analyses of the impact of multinational corporations need to be conducted on a case-by-case basis, but in the aggregate critics can point to official U.S. government statistics showing that American multinational enterprises make a substantial positive contribution to the parent country's balance of payments. For example, the Department of Commerce statistics for 1980 indicate that income from American direct investment abroad was $19.8 billion, whereas the outflow of capital funds was only $1.5 billion.[33] This net positive contribution to the United States must, of course, be balanced by a negative effect on the payments position of some host states.[34]

One difficulty faced by host states in their dealings with multinational corporations involves the problem of obtaining accurate information about the firms' activities. Information disclosure about financial transactions, transfer pricing, payments for licenses and royalties, and profit earned is necessary for the development of policies by host countries, but often, because of corporate concern about secrecy and consolidated accounts, such information is not readily available. Consequently, there is the suspicion that multinationals are able to hide behind financial complexities and manipulations to avoid their fair share of taxes.

Depending upon their nature and pervasiveness, multinational manufacturing enterprises may also be accused of undermining the culture and national identity of host states. Jean-Jacques Servan-Schreiber's best-seller, *The American Challenge*, was a plea for Europeans to counteract this challenge

[33]U.S. Department of Commerce, *Survey of Current Business*, August 1981, pp. 23 and 26. Of course, the effects of the import and export activities of multinational corporations must also be considered for a more accurate perspective of their impact on balance-of-payments outcomes.

[34]For an interesting assessment of the negative balance of payments effects of multinational corporations in Latin America, see Ronald Muller, "Poverty Is the Product," *Foreign Policy*, No. 13 (Winter 1973-74), 71–103. A more general critique of the impact of these firms can be found in Richard J. Barnet and Ronald E. Muller, *Global Reach* (New York: Simon & Schuster, 1974).

so that European economic, political, technological, and cultural independence could be preserved. To the extent that multinational firms threaten cultural identity, some host states will become quite concerned. Because of the many linkages between manufacturing subsidiaries and the host state society, the foreign agent-of-change nature of the enterprise may be considered quite threatening. The same effect is somewhat less likely for extractive industries since they rarely are as closely integrated into the host country environment.

Another factor that frightens host state governments, and particularly labor officials, is the mobility and flexibility of the corporation, as opposed to the immobility of the state and its work force. In certain instances, multinational enterprises may be able to leave states in which the investment climate has become less satisfactory, for whatever reason. As a result, states compete with one another by offering more attractive incentives to foreign industry, and companies can play one state against another in pursuit of the more ideal opportunity. An interesting example of this, involving the work force, occurred in Europe when a European multinational firm told its employees in the Netherlands that they would have to operate on three shifts since that was the only way in which the unprofitable facility could be kept open. Furthermore, the Dutch workers were told that the workers in the German subsidiary, which was also liable to being closed down, were willing to accede to management's request. The same story, but in reverse, was related to the German employees in an attempt by management to use its internationalism to coerce its employees. There are no statistics regarding the ease with which multinational enterprises can and do shut down operations in one state in favor of operations in others, but the concern about this alleged mobility is certainly real. Moreover, this mobility illustrates how multinational corporations can take advantage of and indeed manipulate the sensitivity accompanying economic interdependency among states.

Multinational enterprises are often thought to be able to use their internationalism to avoid onerous government policies. Thus, worker safety precautions, pollution control regulations, and restrictions on drugs can be circumvented by an international enterprise by locating in countries where such concerns have not become part of governmental policy.

Many of the aforementioned causes for concern at the governmental level are shared by various economic, social, and political groups within the host state. Labor has been mentioned briefly, and its interest in these issues is obvious. In addition, segments of domestic business experience conflicts of interest with multinational enterprises. Multinational firms are fierce and often successful competitors with local firms for domestic and international markets. Their large size, huge managerial and financial resources, worldwide reputation, and product recognition often mean that multinational firms can literally overwhelm local corporations. Aside from marketing competition, domestic industries frequently face severe competition from multinational firms for skilled workers, research and development scientists, effective managers, and investment capital. The larger and more successful international enterprise can frequently offer higher wages to employees and provide more attractive research facilities for scientists, and it generally sets the pattern that domestic firms must follow. In the financial arena, domestic business interests must compete with the international firms for local capital. Local capital is often used to finance the acquisition and establishment of subsidiaries of multinational firms. Where investment capital is scarce, foreign firms may be using local sources of capital to the exclusion and disadvantage of local enterprises. As Servan-Schreiber plaintively cries, "we pay them to buy us."[35]

Bifurcation of the national economy and the society is one result of this ability of foreign firms to attract scarce factors of production in the host state, a result that is especially likely in the developing countries. The better paid and more skilled employees of the multinational corporations are linked to the global economic system through their employers, but there is an increasingly wide gap between their life-styles and orientations and those of their compatriots who are essentially untouched by the international economy. Consequently, the state develops in an uneven fashion, for a small international-oriented elite co-exists with a more backward and more parochial majority of the population.

Multinational corporations are also criticized for the introduction and aggressive marketing of products that are not necessary for the primary tasks involved in modernization and development. Such efforts draw money from social, health, and educational necessities only to contribute it to the coffers of wealthy corporations. For example, there is the feeling that it is wasteful, indeed immoral, for destitute people to be urged to purchase such things as soft drinks instead of purchasing education, nutritious food, housing, and other fundamentals of life for their young.

These complaints apply to service industries as well as to manufacturing subsidiaries. Furthermore, they are voiced by elements of advanced industrial states as well as by the developing ones, whereas the fears associated with extractive firms seem more applicable to host states that are developing countries. Regardless, within this set of grievances there is ample substance and opportunity for the development of conflict between multinational corporations and host states over the objectives, policies, and even the existence of these firms. Tensions can be expected to rise as host states increasingly insist upon their right to exert more control over foreign investment to increase their benefits and reduce their costs. Indeed, as will be discussed later in this chapter, host states have developed and implemented a wide variety of policies that address the issues raised in these pages.

[35] Jean-Jacques Servan-Schreiber, *The American Challenge* (New York: Atheneum, 1968), p. 14.

Overall, there seem to be three major sources of conflict provoked by the existence and actions of multinational corporations in host states. First, the international corporation is a foreign entity that behaves in a fashion that is unusual, different, or wrong, from the point of view of the host state. Second, the corporation is often perceived as an enterprise that is associated closely with a foreign country—the parent state—that is able to exert its influence on the host state through the mechanism of the corporation. Third, the multinational enterprise is an international entity able to take advantage of economic interdependencies among states without itself being subject to the rules and regulations of a comparable international agency. Consequently, conflict continues between the host states, which seek to determine and control the nature of their relations with multinationals, and the corporations, which desire stability, predictability, and freedom to pursue their business in a relatively unfettered manner.

Host States' Benefits

Although host states hold substantial fears of multinational corporations, most countries of the world not only accept these foreign enterprises but also seek actively to attract them through an extensive array of incentives. Thus, for most states, the benefits of these corporations are worth obtaining, particularly if the negative effects of their operation can be controlled.[36]

One of the more important benefits of multinational corporations for host countries is the mobilization and productive use of investment capital. The developing countries as well as certain regional and industrial sectors of the advanced industrial states often lack the capital to develop industries that tap natural resources, provide useful products, and generate employment and income. In such cases, the mobilization of investment capital, whether it involves a substantial amount of reinvested earnings of foreign subsidiaries or the actual transfer of funds from the parent country to the host country, accelerates industrialization that cannot take place without large infusions of capital. Singapore, Taiwan, and South Korea are often cited as countries that have used foreign investment and trade policies to achieve industrialization, increased export activity, and a remarkable rise in per capita income.[37]

A number of states have taken advantage of the flexibility of multinational corporations to entice them into establishing facilities in depressed areas of a country. A study released in 1973 indicated that one-third of the

---

[36]For an excellent and ground-breaking discussion of why host countries welcome multinational corporations, see Jack N. Behrman, *National Interests and the Multinational Enterprise* (Englewood Cliffs, N.J.: Prentice-Hall, 1970), Chap. 2. Much of the discussion that follows is based upon this chapter.

[37]This topic is addressed at greater length in Chapter 7.

U.S. investment in the United Kingdom was located in officially designated development areas and had created about 150,000 jobs.[38] Multinational firms are frequently more responsive to these incentives than are indigenous corporations. For example, Behrman reports that from 1959 to 1966 Belgian incentives to locate companies in depressed regions attracted three foreign-owned firms for every Belgian firm.[39] Most of the states of the United States have established specific offices to woo potential foreign investors.

Furthermore, most countries are attracted by the employment that foreign investors generate. In the United Kingdom, for instance, American subsidiaries directly employ 730,000 persons.[40] Herbert May estimated that the total employment of American subsidiaries in Latin America in 1966 was 1,230,000, compared with 830,000 persons in 1957.[41] In 1977, according to a Commerce Department study, American-owned multinational corporations employed approximately 7.3 million persons in their foreign operations with compensation amounting to $78.1 billion.[42] Moreover, none of these figures includes the secondary employment by those firms that supply these foreign-owned subsidiaries or service their employees. A study by the Mexican government revealed that, between 1965 and 1970, foreign investment generated nearly four times as much employment as did Mexican companies, although this result is probably somewhat overstated given the acquisition of Mexican firms by foreign multinationals.[43] A special advertising supplement in *Business Week* reported on a study that estimated that in 1978 approximately 625,000 Americans were employed directly and indirectly by the 1,200 Japanese firms operating in the United States.[44]

Host states are concerned about the effect of multinational corporations on balance-of-payments accounts, and, as we have seen, charges of decapitalization are frequently leveled as the result of the disparity between capital inflows to the host states and the outflow of funds for dividends, royalties, and various other services. Raymond Vernon suggested in a study for the United Nations that this argument is inappropriate because it fails to account for the changes that foreign investment can produce in domestic output, changes that in turn often have significant positive effects on a country's balance of payments.[45]

---

[38]Economists Advisory Group, *United States Industry in Britain* (London: The Financial Times, 1973), p. 4.

[39]Behrman, *National Interests*, p. 20.

[40]Economists Advisory Group, *United States Industry in Britain*, p. 5.

[41]Herbert K. May, *The Contributions of U.S. Private Investment to Latin America's Growth* (New York: The Council for Latin America, 1970), p. 19.

[42]U.S. Department of Commerce, *U.S. Direct Investment Abroad, 1977*, p. 6.

[43]As reported in *Business Latin America*, August 6, 1975, p. 256.

[44]As reported in *Business Week*, July 21, 1980, p. 25.

[45]Raymond Vernon, *Restrictive Business Practices* (New York: United Nations, 1972), p. 20.

In addition, the manufacturing subsidiaries of multinational enterprises may provide significant benefits to the host country in terms of import substitution and export promotion. The former refers to products that the host state once imported, therefore causing a drain on its balance of payments, but now produces domestically as a result of the foreign investment. Most available data seem to indicate that the subsidiaries of multinational corporations are more effective in exporting their products, especially manufactured products, than are domestic firms. In the United Kingdom, American subsidiaries in 1970–1971 exported one-fourth of their total output, a much larger share than that of British-owned firms. In fact, American subsidiaries accounted for one-fifth of the United Kingdom's manufacturing exports during that two-year period.[46] Similar figures are available for Latin America that indicate that American subsidiaries accounted for 35 percent of all Latin American exports in 1966. With respect to manufactured products alone, in 1966 American affiliates exported 41 percent of all the Latin American exports of manufactured goods.[47] More recently, U.S. Commerce Department data of 1977 reveal that 38 percent of the sales of majority-owned nonbank foreign affiliates of U.S. firms are sold outside of the host country where production occurs.[48]

Although no generally accepted conclusion can be reached with regard to the ultimate effect of multinational corporations on a host country's balance-of-payments position, the studies by Vernon, May, and John Dunning all conclude that such enterprises probably contribute to a surplus rather than a deficit in the host country. It must be understood, however, that the impact varies according to the country and the specific type of investment.

States also actively court foreign investment because of the benefits received from the transfer of technology and managerial skills. Products and processes developed elsewhere in the multinational network of the corporation are rapidly dispersed throughout the firm, thereby benefiting those countries (both host and parent) that are the recipients of these innovations. Technological developments in multinational corporations have had a great impact on agricultural equipment and office machines in Great Britain, photography and movie production in France, and television throughout Europe, for example.[49] Although quantification of the benefits of technological transfer is nearly impossible, John Dunning reports that in 1970–1971 American subsidiaries used both labor and capital more productively than British counterparts in thirty-five of thirty-nine industries he examined. This advantage was greatest in the capital-intensive and tech-

[46]Economists Advisory Group, *United States Industry in Britain*, pp. 4–5. It is interesting to note that more than 50 percent of all the exports of American subsidiaries are to other affiliates of the same multinational corporation.

[47]May, *Contributions*, p. 1.

[48]U.S. Department of Commerce, *U.S. Direct Investment Abroad, 1977*, p. 318.

[49]Behrman, *National Interests*, p. 17.

nologically leading industries.[50] A Mexican government study revealed that in 1970 worker productivity was on the average twice as high in foreign-owned subsidiaries than in Mexican-owned facilities. Moreover, between 1962 and 1970, production in foreign-owned firms increased at a rate 60 percent higher than did that of locally owned firms.[51] The flow of technology, both scientific and managerial, directly affects customers and users, and this, in conjunction with managerial innovations, stimulates domestic enterprises to improve and modernize their products and procedures to remain competitive. Thus, a frequent side benefit of foreign investment may be a general upgrading of the industrial efforts of the host country.

Host states also appreciate the fact that multinational corporations generate significant amounts of taxable income, which the state can use for its own objectives. In 1977 taxes paid to host states by nonbank foreign subsidiaries of U.S. firms amounted to $54 billion. Of this amount, 75 percent was paid to the developing countries.[52] Host countries have received massive income return from the major oil companies, and through the efforts of the Organization of Petroleum Exporting Countries (OPEC) the host state share is becoming larger all the time. The estimated total revenues for the OPEC countries in 1979 alone was $212.7 billion.[53]

Although many journalistic, academic, and political commentaries emphasize the negative effects of multinational firms on host states, the actions of most host state governments indicate clearly that important segments within host states perceive significant benefits from the operations of these firms. From this perspective, the most important challenge facing host states is how to increase the benefits and reduce the costs of foreign investments. If multinational firms were purely exploitative in their activities, they would be denied access to most countries.

Parent States' Concerns

Until the early 1970s, it was generally assumed that multinational corporations could only be an asset to their parent countries. However, beginning in 1971 American labor, led by the AFL-CIO, mounted serious legislative challenges to the American-based multinationals, challenges that brought to the fore a series of accusations regarding the harm caused by these firms in the parent country. Essentially, labor charged that American international firms profited from their internationalism to the detriment of the American economy and work force. The United States as a whole is not benefiting from this internationalization of production and marketing; only the corporations are.

[50]Economists Advisory Group, *United States Industry in Britain*, p. 6.

[51]*Business Latin America*, August 6, 1975, p. 256.

[52]U.S. Department of Commerce, *U.S. Direct Investment Abroad, 1977*, p. 134.

[53]"The Petro-Crash of the '80s," *Business Week*, November 19, 1979, p. 176.

Of paramount importance to labor, American jobs are being exported by multinational enterprises. This occurs in a number of ways, according to labor leaders. Foreign markets once served by exports from the United States are now supplied by the foreign subsidiaries of American corporations, with a consequent loss of jobs for Americans. Furthermore, some American multinationals, especially in the electrical and electronic appliance fields, have shut down operations in the United States and have opened up new but similar facilities in low-wage areas of the world. The products of these foreign plants are then imported for sale in the U.S. market. This is another case in which jobs seem to have been exported to take advantage of low wages and docile labor in other countries.

Third, labor contends that multinational corporations telescope the technological transfer process so that technology, often developed with the help of federal government funds, becomes available rapidly to other countries by way of local subsidiaries or licensing agreements. Consequently, export markets are lost and so too are important numbers of American jobs as the competitive edge of technology is lost.

The question of the employment effects of multinationals is difficult to evaluate definitively, and the more useful studies clearly specify the sets of assumptions that lead to different conclusions. For example, the Tariff Commission study estimates the impact on employment varying from 1.3 million jobs lost through 1970 to a net increase of 500,000 jobs. Robert Hawkins projected the impact to range from 660,000 U.S. jobs lost to a net gain of 240,000. Frieman and Frank found a net annual loss of 120,000–200,000 jobs but a majority of the workers found new jobs in seven weeks.[54] Robert Stobaugh and his colleagues studied nine industries and concluded that multinationals created jobs but that many of the jobs created were in the white-collar and managerial areas whereas the jobs lost came from the blue-collar ranks.[55] Of course, these estimates of aggregate impacts on U.S. employment tend to mask the fact that dislocations do occur, people do lose jobs, and families do suffer.

Although American labor has been the labor group most concerned about the job export question, several European labor movements, including those in Germany, Sweden, and the United Kingdom, have expressed similar concerns. The revaluations of the German mark and the Japanese yen in the 1970s, along with rapidly rising wage rates in these and other industrialized states, resulted in a shift of production of certain goods from those countries to low-wage countries. This may be acceptable as long as appreciable unemployment does not exist in the parent country, but if

[54]These studies are reported in C. Fred Bergsten, Thomas Horst, and Theodore H. Moran, *American Multinationals and American Interests* (Washington, D.C.: The Brookings Institution, 1978), pp. 102–104.

[55]Robert B. Stobaugh, *U.S. Multinational Enterprises and the U.S. Economy* (Cambridge, Mass.: Harvard University Press, 1972).

unemployment increases, as it has in the early 1980s in Europe, domestic labor will probably react as the AFL-CIO has done. Already, the British labor movement has expressed serious misgivings about the job export matter, and in Sweden one regulation requires a review of the effects of outward investment plans on domestic employment. The potential seriousness of the problem is illustrated by a comparison of wage rates in developed and developing countries. In 1981, the average hourly compensation for Belgian manufacturing workers was $11.29. In South Korea, the average hourly compensation was only $1.17.[56] The potential for production shifts and job exports is obvious.

American multinational corporations are also accused by the AFL-CIO of adversely affecting the American balance of payments. Markets once served by exports are now serviced by foreign subsidiaries, causing a decline in earnings from exports. Moreover, importing electrical appliances, electronic consumer goods, textiles, cars, and other products from the foreign subsidiaries of American multinationals causes an actual outflow of American funds. In addition, the tax deferral provisions of the U.S. tax code enable corporations to retain earnings abroad and avoid U.S. taxation until the profits are actually repatriated. Consequently, profits that could return to the United States and contribute to a balance-of-payments surplus are instead reinvested in other countries. Finally, the actual outflow of dollars in the form of private investment capital is a drain on the balance of payments.

Another result of the tax deferral provisions is that host countries are able to obtain tax revenue from the reinvested profits of the American multinationals; until the profits are repatriated, the United States does not. The reinvested earnings of American multinationals increased from $3 billion in 1970 to over $17 billion in 1980.[57] Also of concern is the tax credit provision that allows American firms to deduct directly from their U.S. tax bill monies paid in taxes to host countries. Vernon estimates that, in 1966, the foreign subsidiaries of American firms paid $10 billion in taxes to host countries, whereas the U.S. government received from the earnings of these subsidiaries less than $1 billion in tax revenues.[58] It should be pointed out that most of the major capital-exporting countries have tax provisions similar to the deferral and tax credit arrangements.

American multinationals have also been attacked for what is alleged to be the "ruthless" way in which their money managers brought about a series of monetary crises during the period 1971–1973 by shifting large

[56]Conversation with personnel in the U.S. Department of Labor, Bureau of Labor Statistics, January 6, 1982.

[57]U.S. Department of Commerce, *Survey of Current Business,* August 1981, p. 25.

[58]Raymond Vernon, "Does Society Also Profit?" *Foreign Policy,* No. 13 (Winter 1973–74), 110. As a result of labor pressure, the Nixon administration in 1973 and 1974 sought to reduce the tax advantage accruing to firms that are multinational.

amounts of currency from a weak dollar to stronger currencies. There was in this action little consideration of what was good for the United States. National loyalty was subordinated to what was best for the corporation. American critics of multinational firms charge that their preoccupation with more efficient and profitable operations generally makes them prone to disregard national concerns about employment, balance of payments, monetary crises, and other matters. Their internationalism allows these firms to operate above and beyond the boundaries of specific states, including their parent country. Indeed, such firms are flexible enough even to dissolve themselves legally in countries such as the United States, Canada, and the United Kingdom to establish legal residence in tax havens such as the Netherlands Antilles.

The effect of American multinational corporations on U.S. foreign policy and foreign relations is another matter of great concern. It has been charged that, because of the vast amount and wide scope of American investment abroad, the United States is obliged to protect its multinationals around the globe. The American economy has become so dependent upon foreign investment in the aggregate and upon the critical raw materials obtained by its extractive firms in the developing countries, it is alleged, that U.S. foreign policy is designed to ensure that host countries continue to be receptive to American investment. This relationship between U.S. foreign policy and U.S. foreign investment is enhanced by the links between executives of big business and the important political appointees in Washington. Both issues are discussed in subsequent chapters.[59]

Although New Left critics typically focus upon these concerns, there is another aspect of the relationship between corporations and foreign policy that needs to be understood. The independent, insensitive, or perhaps even stupid actions of multinational corporations and their subsidiaries can seriously damage relations between the United States and host states. In such cases, the actions of the corporation are taken out of the private context in which they are often undertaken and are transferred into the public domain by elements of the host state that fail to perceive, understand, or accept the distinction between official policies and those of private international firms. When official relations are harmed by private actions, it is the task of U.S. foreign policy to try to improve the relationship. Moreover, in some cases American multinational corporations appeal directly to the U.S. government for help in their conflicts with host countries. For example, they may call for the application of U.S. political power through diplomacy, aid reductions, or other mechanisms by which the American government can attempt to influence other states. In both sit-

[59]The question of American dependence on foreign sources of raw materials is discussed in depth in Chapter 7. The relationship between American business executives and U.S. foreign policy is examined in Chapter 8.

uations, the American government may be pulled into a situation not of its own doing but as a result of actions by a multinational firm. Again, the multinational corporation acts as an entity unto itself; it imposes few restraints upon itself in the form of feelings of national loyalty to any state. Yet it frequently demands protection by the American government when it confronts trouble abroad.

There is also the danger that the parent government may attempt to use its multinational corporations as instruments of its foreign policy, thus causing conflict with the host country. For example, the U.S. government may enforce provisions of the Trading with the Enemy Act, and parent states generally may pursue other, less formal actions through the multinational firm. This has already been discussed as a negative aspect of foreign investment for host states. The mere existence of American, French, or Japanese multinationals may tempt parent state government officials to meddle in the internal affairs of host countries by means of these firms.

For the most part, parent country concerns about multinational corporations are caused by the fear that these firms operate largely beyond the control of the parent state. Public officials in parent states fear that, contrary to the broader interests of their nation, their government will be pushed or pulled into difficult situations by their own multinationals. Furthermore, to the extent that international businesses link the economies of the parent state and host states, these firms increase the interdependency of the parent state with other states, thereby reducing parent state autonomy. This is particularly true of natural resource companies where the firm may become the "captive" of the host country, with the parent state also being a prisoner of the need for a stable source of supply. Consequently, a parent state may be less able to manage either its domestic economy or its international trade and monetary policy. As a result of these concerns, particularly the feelings of helplessness, various groups in parent states are urging their governments to adopt more stringent regulations concerning the operations of their own multinationals. In many respects, these concerns of parent states are similar to those of host states; both feel that the internationalism of multinational corporations gives these firms an alien character and a flexibility that threaten national sovereignty.

Parent States' Benefits

Since the beneficial consequences of foreign investment for parent countries have been questioned seriously by the American labor movement and by other critics, supporters of these enterprises have had to develop a convincing rationale, with accompanying evidence, to counteract the charges. Several of the major arguments offered in support of multinational corporations, specifically those headquartered in America, will be examined here. These enterprises are said to contribute generally to an American balance-of-payments surplus; their international involvement keeps American enterprises competitive in both domestic and foreign markets; and their international nature fosters rather than retards employment in the United States.

A cautious and comprehensive Tariff Commission report based on 1966 and 1970 data found that American multinational corporations do, indeed, contribute to an American balance-of-payments surplus.[60] Their performance far surpasses that of the nonmultinational sectors of the economy. The outflow of funds involved in American direct foreign investment was outweighed by the returns from export activity and the income from repatriated profits, royalties, interest payments, and other fees.[61]

Evidence gathered by the Department of Commerce suggests that multinational enterprises are particularly active exporters, especially to their own affiliates in other countries. For example, in 1977, 27.4 percent of all U.S. non-agricultural exports involved the flow of goods from the American facilities of American-based multinationals to their foreign subsidiaries.[62] Further analysis requires assessing the impact of multinational corporations on an industry-by-industry basis. Petroleum and smelting corporations contributed to a deficit, as opposed to the sizable surplus generated by manufacturing industries.

A corollary argument proposes that, if American firms were not multinational in scope, the overseas markets that are now filled by foreign subsidiaries with significant exports from the United States would be captured by foreign companies. Thus, it is not a question of serving a particular foreign market by either a foreign subsidiary or by increased exports from the United States. In most cases the latter alternative is not available. That is, non-American-based multinationals would move into the market and take away the export option, since local facilities are often less costly in terms of production, transportation, and service costs and are more responsive to local conditions and sales opportunities. A report by Arthur Anderson & Company indicates that in 1965, 69 percent of the largest industrial companies in the world were American, whereas by 1974 only 48 percent of them were. Excluding petroleum companies, the U.S. share of the top firms dropped from 66 percent to 44 percent over the same period. Net income for the nonpetroleum U.S. firms grew by 103 percent from 1965 to 1974; for the non-U.S. firms it grew by 263 percent.[63] Thus, supporters of the multinational corporation claim that an either/or proposition does not exist in this case. Rather, the multinational enterprise must

[60]Senate Committee on Finance, *Implications of Multinational Firms*, pp. 173.

[61]It has been estimated that profits repatriated from U.S. direct foreign investment in 1981 amount to $41 billion, up from $3.6 billion in 1960.

[62]U.S. Department of Commerce, *U.S. Direct Foreign Investment Abroad, 1977,* p. 340.

[63]Arthur Anderson & Company, "U.S. Companies in International Markets—The Competition Factor in Tax Policy," before the Committee on Finance of the U.S. Senate, April 20, 1976.

use foreign installations to service foreign markets; otherwise, the foreign market is lost entirely to American companies and their workers.

Employment is a third factor of great importance in this dialogue. American multinational corporations and their supporters point to the export figures and conclude that American employment would decrease if American firms were not international in scope. Furthermore, not only do multinational enterprises export more than their strictly domestic counterparts, but their domestic investment and employment increase at a more rapid rate than do those of the purely domestic firms. The keystone of the argument is that international operations stimulate the domestic component of a business. International facilities are a substitute neither for domestic production for domestic markets nor for domestic production for foreign markets. Consequently, the international activity represents a net gain for the parent state that is over and above that produced by a strictly domestic firm.

Quite naturally, supporters of the multinational corporation reject the charge that the activities of these firms tend to draw the United States into conflicts with host countries. Although advocates admit to a few instances of such conflict, they believe it is more often the case that the efforts of a firm to increase the benefits to parent and host states are hindered by the policies and behavior of the U.S. government. Such policies—for example, the Vietnam war, the favoritism shown the Israelis over the Arabs, the reaction to the Soviet invasion of Afghanistan, governmental concentration on human rights violations in certain South American countries under the Carter administration, and the often assertive and unilateral actions regarding monetary and trade matters—have all tended to make life more difficult for the multinational corporations, not the reverse.

Moreover, American-based multinationals, along with their counterparts in France, Germany, the United Kingdom, and Japan, emphasize that their internationalism helps to find, mine, and then process raw materials critical to the health and welfare of the parent state economy and society. American multinational oil companies were criticized strongly in 1974 and afterward for their inability to control the source of supply of foreign crude oil and thus prices, largely as a result of the nationalizations of such sources by some OPEC countries. Similarly, manufacturing industries develop important foreign markets for the products of American or other parent state factories. Thus, the conclusion of this argument is that parent states should aid and foster their multinational enterprises because of the many positive effects of their activity. It is interesting to note, regarding this issue, that one of the conscious strategies adopted by a number of advanced industrial states, and now a few developing countries, to meet the challenges of foreign investment is the development of their own multinationals. Thus, multinationals must have some benefit to parent states.

MULTINATIONAL CORPORATIONS
AND CONFLICT IN INTERNATIONAL POLITICS

Thusfar, we have focused on the impact of multinational corporations on host states and parent states.[64] Also important, but the subject of far less attention by both academicians and policymakers, are the effects that multinational firms may have on relations among these types of states. It is important to examine the ways in which multinational corporations, by conscious policies or by unintended effects of their actions, may contribute to the worsening of relations among these other international actors.

Relationships between parent state and host state are particularly susceptible to strain as a result of the actions of multinational enterprises. Since both states seek to utilize the international firm for their own objectives, basic questions of sovereignty and jurisdiction arise, and the corporation may be caught in the middle. Antitrust provisions and the Trading with the Enemy Act have already been mentioned as sore points in the relationship between the United States as a parent government and other countries as host states. Questions of jurisdiction have on several occasions been raised in Canada and in other states regarding legal demands on American multinationals by the U.S. government or its courts. For example, in 1950 the provinces of Ontario and Quebec tried to prevent American subsidiaries from providing documents in compliance with U.S. court rulings by passing laws prohibiting such actions. More recently, the Canadian government prohibited Canadian subsidiaries of U.S. firms from providing data to the U.S. government for use in possible judicial action involving the issue of a uranium cartel. At times, diplomatic negotiations are necessary to unravel the complications resulting from jurisdictional disputes. In all such cases, the existence of the transnational corporation brought into question the fundamental issue of which political entity had jurisdiction. Such problems are inherent in the multinational nature of the enterprise and will inevitably continue to plague relations between parent and host states.

[64]In earlier chapters we have discussed how countries have responded to the growth of trade and the increasing importance of the international monetary system by developing GATT and the IMF as vehicles to "manage" the international nature of these transactions. Regarding the multinational corporations, there is no comparable overarching organization to deal with the internationalization of production and marketing. Instead, there have been a number of largely uncoordinated efforts by many different organizations to control and regulate the international firm. The control efforts of some of these regional and international organizations are discussed in a subsequent section of this chapter. However, the perspective of these organizations has for the most part been to protect its members (states) in dealings with multinational corporations. Thus, the international organizations have acted largely as an extension of its member states and not so much as international political-economic actors in their own right. Even with the IMF and GATT, there has been little analysis by academics or policymakers of the impact of multinationals on the workings of the international monetary and trade systems and their respective international organizations.

The potential for conflict between host states and parent states is exacerbated by the fact that host states and parent states may have very different objectives for the same multinational enterprise and thus may clash in their attempts to achieve these objectives. Balance-of-payments policies constitute an excellent case in point. A parent state trying to correct a deficit might enact regulations designed to hasten and enlarge the repatriation of profits and management fees from the subsidiary, to hinder and restrict the outflow of new capital for investment, thereby provoking the use of local sources of funds within host states, and to expand exports from the parent company and to inhibit imports from the subsidiary. Of course, a host state troubled by a balance-of-payments deficit may institute regulations designed to produce results that are exactly the opposite of those desired by the parent state.

Similarly, parent and host states may also have different objectives about trade, domestic employment problems, currency stability and valuation, location of research and development efforts, and foreign policy matters. It is possible to develop a conflict matrix, such as that in Table 4-4, to specify these and other differing objectives of host and parent states regarding the actions and effects of multinational corporations. A conflict matrix could also be constructed to illustrate the various policy actions that might be undertaken by parent or host states in pursuit of their essentially conflicting objectives. The purpose of such an exercise and of this discussion is to emphasize that the behavior and existence of multinational corporations may be the source of and vehicle for worsening relations between parent and host states, as each attempts to harness such corporations to advance its own interests.

Parent states and host states may also clash as a result of specific actions taken by either host or parent states in the attempt to influence the behavior of multinational corporations. The efforts of Cuba, Peru, Bolivia, and Chile to nationalize American business enterprises within their jurisdiction at one time or another in recent years has produced important conflicts in official

TABLE 4-4   Parent State-Host State Conflicts in Objectives: Multinational Corporations' Effect on Balance of Payments

Issue	Host State Desires	Parent State Desires
Investment capital	Obtained from parent state	Obtained from host state and other foreign sources
Profits	Reinvest	Repatriate
Licenses, royalties, management fees	No payment for services rendered	Full payment for services rendered
Exports	From subsidiary to other subsidiaries and to parent country headquarters	From parent country plants to subsidiaries in host states

governmental relations between these countries and the United States. Canadian government efforts to "Canadianize" the oil industry have caused problems with the U.S. government in support of U.S. foreign investment in that country. Similar problems have occurred involving French firms operating in Africa, and it is highly probable that difficulties will emerge with Japanese enterprises in Asia.

In addition to the fact that multinational corporations may be the object or the source of conflict between parent and host states, they also may be the vehicle by which host and parent countries try to influence each other. There is a widespread fear, with some justifying examples, that multinational corporations may serve as a conduit for foreign policy actions by parent states. The U.S. government sought to hinder the development of a French nuclear force by prohibiting IBM from selling needed equipment. The IT&T-CIA case regarding the Allende government in Chile is a widely remembered example that heightens fear and suspicion that multinationals are vehicles for United States foreign policy efforts.

The reverse is true also. Host states have attempted to influence parent states through multinational firms. In response to President Nixon's 10 percent import surcharge in August 1971, many American firms with subsidiaries in Latin America decried the measure and sought its rapid repeal since Latin America was already running a trade deficit with the United States. Whether out of enlightened self-interest or as a result of direct requests from host state officials, these firms were seeking to influence U.S. policy on behalf of the Latin American host states. The Arab oil embargo of 1973 and 1974 was accompanied by Arab efforts to have multinational petroleum companies influence U.S. and Western policy toward the Middle East. Even prior to the embargo and the Arab-Israeli war, stockholders of Standard Oil of California were sent a letter urging "understanding on our [America's] part of the aspirations of the Arab people, and more positive support of their efforts toward peace in the Middle East." This statement is a good example of a multinational's efforts to influence parent state policy on the behalf of host states. With natural resource shortages and rapidly rising prices of such material, efforts by host countries to influence policies of parent nations through the vehicle of the multinational corporation will probably increase in frequency, intensity, and success. The "special" relationship between Saudi Arabia and the United States is based in part on the active involvement of U.S. corporations in that nation.

The potential impact of multinational corporations on relations between a parent state and a host state is widely appreciated. Less obvious is the likelihood of increased competition among parent states on behalf of their own multinational firms. The expansion and success of American-based multinational corporations in the 1960s has led a number of European states to rationalize and consolidate their own companies with the objective of forming sizable multinationals of their own to compete with the foreign firms. Since these combined firms are often created as a result of government initiative and sometimes with government funds, it is reasonable to expect that the parent governments will sometimes seek to ensure that their firms are successful in their efforts by actively supporting them, to the detriment of international enterprises of a different nationality. Some of the giant European multinationals, such as British Petroleum, Renault, and ENI, are owned partially by their respective governments, and state ownership is becoming a more widespread feature of Western Europe's economic activity. Nineteen of Europe's fifty largest industrial companies are partially owned by the state. The concept of Japan Inc, if often exaggerated, suggests the very close relationship between the Japanese government and its multinational enterprises.

A further stimulus of conflict among parent states stemming from competition among multinational corporations is the current concern about raw material and energy shortages. For example, the lack of sufficient domestic supplies of petroleum, in conjunction with the successful efforts of oil-producing states to control petroleum prices and supplies, has prompted the Japanese government to help its firms explore for oil in other areas. An oil hungry and dependent Europe is also seeking to establish new sources of supply for itself and its own firms, to the disadvantage of Japanese and American firms. Consequently, competition among multinational corporations of different nationalities for what are thought to be vital, scarce resources may well lead to conflict among the parent governments of these firms. The international airline industry, which is characterized by government support of private, quasi-governmental, or totally government-owned firms, may well be the forerunner of conflicts in this regard.

Conflict among host states is likely to occur as they compete to attract the benefits of foreign investment. Already, many host states compete with one another by offering various kinds of inducements to foreign investors. During a 1971 visit to the United Kingdom, Henry Ford made it clear to Prime Minister Heath and the British people that unsatisfactory labor relations in Great Britain might cause Ford of England to restrict new investment or even transfer some existing investment from Britain to other countries. The next day, a group of Dutch business managers and government officials invited Ford to consider further investment in the Netherlands. Although this situation might not happen often, competition for foreign investment does exist among advanced industrial states and among the developing nations.

There are several possible effects of this competitive courtship of multinational corporations. If the competition is severe enough, one result may be an increase in the various states' incentive packages and/or a reduction in the investment risks and costs for the corporations. If states actively pursue foreign investment, they may undercut one another in offering inducements, thereby generally increasing the level of the returns or benefits accruing to multinational corporations and reducing the gains of the host states.

Moreover, the uneven pattern of foreign investment within a region may help to sour relations among potential host states. For example, within a particular region the combination of natural and human endowments, geographical advantages, governmental policies, and other factors may mean that one or two states receive much of the foreign investment and other states very little at all. To the extent that multinational corporations are thought to bring more advantages than disadvantages, the less fortunate states in a region may seek to gain a greater share of the foreign investment through political efforts directed against the more successful host countries.

As a result of competition for investment and concern about the unequal distribution of such investment, some states in a particular region may seek to form a regional group to distribute foreign investment more equitably and purposefully, to harmonize the laws and incentives regarding these enterprises, and generally to reduce the possibility of intraregional conflict over these firms. Among other reasons, the desire to present a united front to foreign investors was a major stimulus for the formation of the Andean Common Market, which comprises Venezuela, Colombia, Ecuador, Peru, Bolivia, and at one time but no longer Chile. The ASEAN countries of Singapore, Malaysia, Thailand, Indonesia, and the Philippines have also joined together to present a combined and more rational approach to regional economic development and the role of multinational firms in the planned development. Thus, in an almost dialectical fashion, competition among host states as a result of multinational enterprises may lead to the development of regional strategies designed to prevent this conflict. This may be thought by some to be a positive result of the activities of multinational corporations.

On the other hand, regional or international efforts to contain interstate conflict may be perceived by some host states as interfering with their ability to try to attract foreign investment or at least to determine their own policies on these issues. Colombia and Venezuela were reluctant initially to join the Andean pact because both countries had relatively satisfactory experiences with a sizable foreign investment sector. Chile withdrew from the pact, and in 1980 the military government of Bolivia intimated a similar possiblity. In another example, Belgium was disturbed when the European Common Market Commission disallowed investment incentives for a certain region of Belgium, an action that the government felt was necessary for the promotion of industry and creation of employment. In essence, the commission felt that the incentives provided an unfair advantage to the Belgians relative to other states in the Common Market. Host state conflict with international or regional organizations emerges when a state feels that it will be able to obtain greater benefits from foreign investment by not subscribing to an international or regional agreement that establishes a common policy toward multinational corporations.

Conflict at the international or regional level may emerge when international organizations, in the form of producer cartels, align host states against a coalition of multinational firms and their parent states. Conflict of this sort threatened to develop between the major petroleum consuming countries and OPEC. In the winter of 1974, the United States attempted to organize major petroleum-consuming countries as a counterweight to OPEC; leadership would have supposedly been assumed by those states that had a number of multinational petroleum companies. The lack of success in this endeavor does not undermine the basic point that conflicts between organized groups of host states and an alignment of parent states are likely to be particularly severe when the dispute involves scarce natural resources or food products.

According to the views advanced by Stephen Hymer, from a more global perspective, it has been suggested that multinational corporations widen the gap between developing countries, as the recipients for foreign investment, and those few advanced industrial states in which the head-quarters of the multinational enterprises are located.[65] Thus, a stratified international political and economic system is created, with significant power accruing to the few headquarters states. There also exists a second tier of regionally important states, similar to middle-management levels of the corporation, that have influence only to the extent to which they serve the interests of the center states. Finally, there exists a large number of passive and very dependent states that are the hewers of wood and haulers of water for the rich states and their multinational enterprises. Hymer and other radical critics predict that this international stratification of states, caused partially and furthered by multinational corporations, will provoke the seeds of its own destruction, for the peripheral states will attempt to overturn the system that dominates them. This will not be achieved readily or without substantial conflict.

POSITIVE IMPACT OF MULTINATIONAL CORPORATIONS ON INTERNATIONAL POLITICS

Advocates of multinational corporations claim that these enterprises have had and will continue to have a beneficial impact on relations among states. In several different ways, multinational enterprises are thought to contribute to regional or functional integration and to other cooperative efforts. First, the threat posed by the existence of multinational corporations may prompt states to adopt common policies to counteract, adapt to, or get the most benefit from them. Concerns about the ability of multinational enterprises to exploit their common market led the Andean group to adopt a set of stringent barriers and regulations to control closely multinational business activities. Similarly, OPEC has presented a more united front to

---

[65]Stephen Hymer, "The Multinational Corporation and the Law of Uneven Development," in *Economics and World Order: From the 1970's to the 1990's*, ed. Jogdish N. Bhagwati (New York: Macmillan, 1972), pp. 113–40.

the giant multinational oil companies and the oil-consuming states. In these cases and others, the multinational enterprise has had a catalytic effect on the formation of coordinated efforts among states that were previously too much in conflict to cooperate.

Second, multinational corporations, as a result of their own integrated nature and their impact on other social units, may help to provide an environment that is conducive to the promotion of integration among states, which is thought by some world leaders to be a desired goal. The ability of these enterprises to surmount national boundaries in the production and marketing of a product contributes to the establishment of a common regional culture and life-style. Integrated production means that workers in a number of different states are linked closely to one another in terms of their work and, of course, their employer. In Europe particularly, regional unions are springing up to represent regionwide interests. Management personnel in Europe are beginning to develop a European perspective and to perceive themselves as having interests and opportunities that range beyond those of their own country.[66] Also, within Europe many products, brand names, and advertising efforts are common to several different states. In sum, the multinational corporation may help both to break down the barriers of separateness and to crystalize some of the common interests and culture that foster regional interest groups and regional orientations. Evidence seems to suggest that, within the EEC, multinational corporations have been useful in promoting integration rather than retarding it.

Some supporters of the multinational corporation claim that it is a force for peace among states since it represents an extremely successful form of internationalism, one that links states more closely. In spite of the political impediments of different national systems and national characteristics, the multinational corporation has succeeded in overcoming these barriers and in making states more interdependent and thus less likely to engage in violent conflict. The former president of the Bank of America and now the president of the World Bank expressed this thesis clearly:

> the idea that this kind of business enterprise can be a strong force toward world peace is not so far fetched. Beyond the human values involved, the multinational firm has a direct, measurable, and potent interest in helping prevent wars and other serious upheavals that cut off its resources, interrupt its communications, and kill its employees and customers.[67]

The previous section indicated many ways in which multinational corporations may adversely affect the patterns of relations between states and international or regional organizations, either as a matter of policy or

[66]See Bernard Mennis and Karl P. Sauvant, "Multinational Corporations, Managers, and the Development of Regional Identification in Western Europe," *The Annals*, 403 (September 1972), 22–33.

[67]Reprinted from "The Internationalized Corporation: An Executive's View," by A. W. Clausen in vol. 403 of *The Annals* of the American Adademy of Political and Social Science, p. 21. © 1972 by The Academy of Political and Social Science.

merely because of competition for their benefits. In this section, we have offered arguments to show the beneficial impact of the multinational corporation on interstate relations. Although serious conceptual and methodological problems as well as fundamental value positions make it difficult to determine precisely the net impact of these enterprises on international politics, it is important to be aware of the positive as well as the negative implications of their existence for relations among states.

MULTINATIONAL CORPORATIONS AND CHANGES IN THE INTERNATIONAL POLITICAL SYSTEM

Up to this point we have examined multinational corporations largely in terms of their relations with states. However, a different perspective is imperative, for not only do these firms have important consequences for states, they also have stimulated the development of international cooperation among other nongovernmental actors. Within this relatively neglected area, some far-ranging and basic changes may be occurring. To oversimplify a bit, it appears that an international economic and political system may be emerging in which multinational corporations are the major institutions as well as the prime stimuli for the development of other structures. However, all this is occurring without a central political authority.

Because of the importance of the international economic system, various international groups organized around common interests are beginning to participate in the international system, as their domestic counterparts do in individual states. The reason for this activity is simply that international economic transactions have direct consequences for the interests of these groups, and as a result the groups seek to exert control over these transactions. Nations have not been particularly responsive to or effective in protecting these organized interests from the impact of the international economic system. Domestic groups are relatively powerless to protect their interests in the context of a highly interdependent world. Finally, the various intergovernmental institutions have not yet developed the ability or the will to represent effectively the concerns of these domestic groups. Thus, there is a need to develop new forms of direct international action among like interests within the global economy.

The lack of a systematic investigation of this phenomenon requires us to illustrate these developments by means of specific examples. The Council of the Americas is a business-oriented group that is somewhat analogous to a lobbying organization in that, among other things, it seeks to promote actions by Latin American governments that favor multinational corporations. The Council also seeks to aid and educate American corporations regarding the problems and prospects of doing business in Latin America. In addition to the Council and a number of other similar organizations, there are various international trade associations of some importance. More broadly, the International Chamber of Commerce has made a significant effort to develop a set of guidelines for multinational corporations, parent governments, and host governments on a variety of issues. The international chamber has been especially eager to assume a leadership and watchdog role on the issue of eliminating improper payments by corporations. It too seeks to represent business interests in the councils of various international organizations.

As a response to the many business-oriented organizations in this emerging international system, other groups are seeking to develop a countervailing force to the multinational corporation. The efforts of international labor union organizations in this regard are most revealing, for the patterns of response that these union organizations are developing may prove to be a model for the actions of other groups. The various national labor movements often feel helpless in the face of the international mobility, flexibility and strength of the multinational corporations. For a variety of reasons, the strategies and tactics used by unions on domestic employers are frequently ineffective when used on multinational employers.[68]

To overcome this disadvantageous position, unions have designed a number of activities to exert some control over the corporations. At the national level, unions from two or more states have cooperated to aid one another in their conflicts with the same multinational employer. At times, this has entailed meetings to exchange information and plan a common strategy for eventual confrontations with management. In other instances, coordinated action has actually been taken against the employer in several different countries. At the regional level, groups of unions have formalized their efforts to coordinate actions taken toward corporations. Through the leadership of the European Metalworkers' Federation, representatives of unions from several states have met with the management of such multinational employers as Philips, AKZO, and others to discuss various issues. Moreover, when a union in one country has struck a multinational employer, counterpart unions in other countries have sometimes refused to work overtime to take up the slack caused by the disruption in production, or they have applied similar types of pressure to the common employer.

Similar activities have occurred at the international level. A number of the international trade secretariats (international union organizations organized according to type of industry), such as the International Metalworkers' Federation and the International Chemical and General Workers' Federation, have formed company councils composed of many of the national unions associated with the same multinational employer. Such com-

---

[68]For a discussion of trade union weaknesses and their responses, see David H. Blake, "Trade Unions and the Challenge of the Multinational Corporation," *The Annals*, 403 (September 1972) 34–35; and David H. Blake, "The Internationalization of Industrial Relations," *Journal of International Business Studies*, 3 (Fall 1972), 17–32.

pany councils have been formed for General Motors, Ford, Volkswagen, Philips, General Electric, Shell, Nestlé and many others. Information exchange, consultation and planning, and joint solidarity actions have been planned and coodinated by these international trade secretariats.

Although these activities do not represent the prevailing pattern of union responses to multinational corporations and the international economic system, they do represent both formal and informal efforts to confront multinational corporations on a regional and international level. To a limited but increasing extent, industrial relations are being internationalized.

This type of development, which is stimulated by multinational corporations, is leading to the emergence of a more truly international economic and political system. Processes and procedures limited formerly to nations are being introduced at the regional and international level because of the international nature of these firms. Although this trend is just developing evidence suggests that it may well be one of the most important long-run effects of the multinational corporations. These enterprises have provoked an operational internationalism that has not yet been achieved by formal political mechanisms. However, in the following section we will discuss the ways in which international organizations have been attempting to increase their monitoring and control of the activities of multinational enterprises.

POLICIES FOR CONTROL

It is natural that some attempts (particularly by host states) would be made to control the extensive impacts of multinational corporations on domestic interest groups, parent and host states, and regional and international organizations and systems. These efforts vary greatly in nature and in degree of success. Some states have not bothered to institute any controls at all, other than those already existing for domestic enterprises. At the other extreme is outright nationalization, whereby the host state obtains total ownership and control of the corporation and the foreign investment is eliminated completely. Between these two extremes is a wide variety of control mechanisms designed to preserve foreign investment while increasing the benefits received by the host state and reducing the associated disruptions and costs.

Overall, the substance of these control policies is quite varied and incorporates most of the concerns expressed by host states. Regarding balance-of-payments questions, some host states insist upon a specific degree of export activity by the multinational enterprise. In addition, they may impose barriers on the import of goods and limits on the repatriation of profits, royalties, licenses, and management fees to the foreign headquarters. Local content regulations require the products of the foreign enterprise to have increasing amounts of domestically produced components or raw materials as opposed to imported parts, and naturally this will reduce a state's balance-of-payments deficit. Brazil, during the space of little more than fifteen years, for example, brought about change in the sourcing procedure of its large car industry to the point where about 99 percent of the component parts are produced in Brazil.

In terms of exerting local control over foreign enterprises, host states often establish requirements regarding the number and position of both foreign and local employees and managers. Some states require a majority of host country citizens on the enterprise's board of directors. Other states go much farther, insisting that the foreign enterprise share ownership— in varying proportions—with national enterprises, local citizens, or government agencies. These demands have been widespread and have affected the global operations of many multinational corporations. Even such companies as IBM, which historically had been able to maintain its 100 percent ownership policy because of its high-technology character, encountered problems of mandated local ownership requirements in India, Indonesia, Nigeria, Malaysia, and Brazil.[69]

Some of these measures, and others as well, enhance the domestic benefits of the foreign investment. Increasing tax rates or the pretax governmental share of profits is a common way by which host countries seek to enlarge their benefits. Mexico and several other states have sought actively to have foreign investors conduct research and development in the host state, thereby increasing the opportunities for local scientists and enhancing the indigenous research and development capability of the host country.

Of course, there are many other measures that host states have adopted to exert some kind of control over the multinational corporation. Some of these efforts to increase the benefits and reduce the costs for the host state take the form of barriers to or requirements for entry. Multinational corporations seeking to invest must meet the specific demands of the host state, often through long, complex negotiations. Some of these provisions may apply to all foreign concerns; others may be ad hoc and specific to the particular investment.

Host state control is also increased through the establishment of new requirements, which must be met by existing foreign enterprises. The firms must then decide whether compliance or withdrawal is the best course to follow. Singapore, for example, instituted an unorthodox policy in the summer of 1979, designed to get multinational corporations to enhance particular state objectives regarding creation of capital-intensive investment. The Singapore government pushed up wage levels countrywide, ranging from 14 percent to 20 percent, to induce multinational corporations

---

[69]"Erosion Extends Around the World," *Datamation*, April 1978, p. 182.

to employ fewer people and set up more capital-intensive operations because of the rising cost of labor.[70] Having made the initial investment and incurred the costs associated with starting a new venture, it is difficult for a corporation not to respond in a fashion that allows it to continue making a profit and at the same time comply with the demands of the state. However, if the operation is marginal at best, or if the process can be easily closed down and opened up in another country, the bargaining power of the state is reduced. As with requirements for entry, these new measures may be applied generally or may be designed for a specific firm.

Just as it is impossible to examine all the types of incentives offered by host states, so it is impossible to discuss the many types of controls placed on foreign investment by host states. As we suggested earlier, the complexity and severity of these restrictions vary widely. States such as Belgium, the Netherlands, Great Britain, and a fairly large number of developing countries are quite receptive to foreign investment and impose few regulations. However, this attitude can change easily, as illustrated by the efforts of the Spanish government to increase its control and benefits from foreign investment. Brazil, too, is a country that has moved from a posture of enthusiastic openness to foreign investment to a more restrictive policy.

Other states have a much more stringent set of controls. For a long time, Japan made it exceptionally difficult for many multinational corporations to establish investment in that country, particularly in those industrial sectors deemed to be most important for Japan's economic plans and success. This policy has been liberalized considerably since 1971, as a consequence of the pressure of the U.S. government and its multinationals. Mexico, too, has traditionally controlled foreign investment in pursuit of its own national objectives. Although Mexican laws regarding foreign investment have been applied rather flexibly, some provisions specify not only a majority share of Mexican ownership but also a high degree of Mexican, as opposed to foreign, management. Coupled with these requirements are regulations overseeing the nature of technology transfers between Mexican enterprises and the subsidiaries of foreign firms and foreign business concerns. The registration of all technological contracts allows the Mexican government to determine whether the arrangement is in the best interests of Mexico. Despite these restrictions, which are applied selectively, foreign investment thrives in Mexico.

Other states have taken an even more restrictive posture on foreign investment, exhibiting a basic reluctance to welcome multinational corporations, but this stand is tempered sometimes with an awareness of the necessity of having some foreign investment in certain specified industries. The terms for admission and operation are much stricter than in Mexico,

---

[70]*The Economist,* December 30, 1978, p. 51.

for instance. Salvador Allende's Chile exhibited this tendency, as did Indonesia in 1965 and Ceylon in 1962 and 1963. Interestingly, the Soviet Union and some of the Eastern European countries are seeking to attract foreign investors, but under clearly specified limitations. Some multinational corporations are willing to operate under these more difficult conditions, but such restrictions, particularly if coupled with governmental instability, tend to scare off many potential investors. Thus, there is the interesting anomaly of President Allende's nationalizing most investments from the United States and other countries and at the same time attempting to attract foreign investment in Europe, without much success. On the other hand, multinational corporations of many nationalities find the huge Soviet market and the stable Soviet investment climate to be potentially interesting in spite of the extensive restrictions on business activities. The adaptability of multinational corporations to restrictive foreign investment climates in the face of great market potential is borne out by the rush of firms to develop relations with the People's Republic of China. Even in the face of unfamiliarity, recent antagonism, and confusing governmental policies, business corporations are enthusiastic about the business possibilities with China, as, for example, the Procter & Gamble executive's commenting on the market potential of selling one billion toothbrushes to the Chinese.

The success of host state efforts to control the activities and impact of multinational corporations while still obtaining desired benefits varies with such factors as the nature of the controls, the stability of the investment climate, the size of the market, the dependence on the raw material, and of course the specific nature of the foreign investment. To put it in different terms, the multinational enterprise weighs the costs of doing business under restrictions with the possible benefits to be received. Nations perform the same type of calculus, but from a different perspective. Speaking generally, the restricted Soviet environment is potentially attractive because of the very large market, in terms of population and stage of industrial development, and the existence of important raw materials. A much smaller and poorer market, even with less onerous and cumbersome restrictions, may be far less attractive to many manufacturing firms. However, if this smaller and poorer country has scarce and critical raw materials, the extractive multinational may put up with governmental controls to gain access to the raw material. In sum, a set of restrictions that controls, without driving out, foreign investment in one country or in a specific industry may be ineffective and disastrous in another country or in a different industry in the same country.

In a general way, it is possible to identify the sources of strength that multinational corporations and host states bring to their negotiations. These are listed in Table 4-5. In the abstract it is not possible to determine whether a specific host country or multinational corporation has the greater power in their conflicts, but some general points can be made.

TABLE 4-5 Sources of Strength in Host Country Negotiations with Multinational Corporations

Host Country	Multinational Corporation
Legislative power	Controls benefits desired by host state (capital, employment, technology, management skill, industrialization, and all the other benefits)
Police and military power	International advantages not duplicated easily (integrated production, established international distribution networks)
Power of the bureaucracy to delay and withhold	Potential parent state pressure
Controls factors that multinationals want (natural resources, labor, market)	Negative host country actions will scare away other investment and international credit
Competition among multinationals for access to factors	Competition among host states for multinationals' investment
Ability to obtain advantages of multinationals from several different sources ("unbundling")	Refusal to expand investment
Nationalized foreign investment	Ultimate power to close down investment

Both sides have an ultimate source of power. The host country is well within the bounds of international law to nationalize properties owned by foreign corporations. Conversely, companies can decide to shut down their investment and leave the country.[71] This type of situation occurred in 1978 between the government of India and IBM. The former said that IBM could continue to operate only if it was willing to share ownership. The company was unwilling to comply and thus withdrew partially from the Indian market.

However, in most conflicts between multinational corporations and host states, reliance upon the ultimate weapons are rare and frequently counterproductive. In the India–IBM case, both parties lost the benefits of the investment. Consequently, most bargaining between host states and multinational corporations involves strategies designed to increase or maintain the benefits and reduce the costs without causing the situation to deteriorate to where both parties lose.

Parent states have also attempted to control the impact of multinational corporations. Since World War II, most current capital-exporting countries have at one time or another imposed controls on outward-bound

---

[71] In some countries, particularly in Europe, the ability of a company to close its operations is becoming severely restricted. Numerous firms have found that it is extraordinarily expensive to go out of business in Europe because of the high price extracted by labor unions and host governments. Firestone recently had to find buyers for facilities in Denmark before it could withdraw from the country.

capital investment. These measures were designed to preserve scarce currency. Other types of controls have been established in response to concerns about antitrust, national security, protection of domestic industry and employment, and punishment leveled at specific countries, such as Rhodesia prior to the formation of Zimbabwe or the Soviet Union after its armed intervention in Afghanistan.

Sometimes the control efforts of the parent state have been designed to ensure that its multinationals behave in an appropriate fashion in host countries. Japan has become quite concerned about the poor Japanese image and hostile relations stimulated by the expanding and insensitive presence of Japanese firms in Asia. Japan has established a set of guidelines in response. Both Sweden and the United States have provisions in their investment-guarantee programs that try to foster good behavior. But, although Sweden has an extensive list of "social conditions," the impact of such efforts is quite limited.

On certain specific items, the U.S. government has attempted to control the behavior of its own multinational firms. Stringent regulations have been imposed on participation by U.S. firms in the Arab boycott of Israel. Companies that comply in any fashion with the boycott, including providing information about trade with Israel to the boycott office, are in violation of the antiboycott legislation. Similarly, in 1977 Congress passed the Foreign Corrupt Practices Act, which leveled severe penalties on firms that engaged in bribery of foreign government officials to obtain business. Both laws are exceedingly complex, ambiguous, and changing, but nonetheless, managers of multinational corporations must be aware of the potentially serious penalties that they and their firms face if they violate these laws.

Of a different sort has been the wide promulgation and acceptance of the Sullivan principles for multinational corporations operating in South Africa. Leon Sullivan, an activist on behalf of black economic development in the United States and a member of the board of General Motors, proposed a voluntary nongovernmental code that established principles of behavior regarding the behavior of U.S. firms with investments in South Africa. These principles seek desegregation at the workplace and demand fair employment practices, equal pay, training programs for nonwhites, increased nonwhite representation in management and efforts to improve the employees' lives outside work. In addition, on-site inspections and reporting of compliance with the principles are basic to the agreements. Many of the major multinationals have abided by the provisions of the principles.

Thus far, we have discussed control efforts undertaken by nations acting alone. An alternate control strategy is concerted action by a group of states regarding the conditions under which multinationals are allowed to operate. Because of the commonly agreed-upon rules and regulations for foreign investment adopted by a specific group of states, their coordinated efforts tend to overcome to some degree the advantages of mobility and flexibility enjoyed by the corporations. These groupings may be organized along geographic and regional lines, as is the case with the Andean Common Market and the European Economic Community, or they may involve cooperation because of a common natural resource, as in the case of OPEC.[72]

The Andean Common Market is an interesting example of a regional effort to control the actions and effects of multinational corporations and still obtain the desired benefits. With respect to control, the five member states have agreed upon a relatively stringent set of rules regarding foreign investment. With respect to benefits, they have joined together as a common market, so that investors abiding by their rules can produce and sell in a market of five states with a combined population of approximately 70 million people. Therefore, from the perspective of the investor, the costs of operating in a more controlled environment need to be measured against the benefits of doing business in a much larger market with a significant reduction of intraregion tariffs.

The Andean experiment is comprehensive in its approach, and, thus, a brief look at some of its provisions regarding foreign investment may be instructive. First, foreign investment is prohibited in a number of industries, including banking, insurance, broadcasting, publishing, and internal transportation. Second, new investment and most existing investment must divest itself of majority ownership (the fade-out formula) within fifteen years in Colombia, Peru, and Venezuela and within twenty years in Bolivia and Ecuador, so that national investor participation will be at least 51 percent. Third, annual earnings repatriated by the foreign firm cannot exceed 20 percent (previously 14 percent) of the investment. Fourth, a foreign subsidiary may not pay its parent company or other affiliate for the use of intangible technological know-how; in addition, clauses or practices that tend to restrict competition or production or otherwise increase the cost of the technology to the host state are prohibited. The Andean code contains other provisions, but these four suggest the extent to which the Andean countries are attempting to control the actions and impact of the multinationals. These five states desire foreign investment, but on their own terms.

At the international level, there has been a growing number of attempts to deal with the international and national challenges presented by multinational corporations. The United Nations and its family of organizations have been especially active. Upon the recommendation of an international panel of experts, the United Nations established a Centre on Transnational Corporations that collects information about multinational corporations and prepares studies on various aspects of their operations. In addition, technical assistance programs are organized to improve the negotiating and regulatory capabilities of host countries. A list of consultants is maintained to aid host countries in these negotiations.

---

[72]OPEC is discussed in detail in Chapter 7.

The United Nations is also developing a series of codes of conduct on various issues associated with foreign investment. The centre is working on a broad code of conduct for multinationals. In addition, UNCTAD has been working on the development of a code on technology transfer, the International Labor Organization has produced a code on labor-related matters, and the United Nations has also developed a code on restrictive business practices.

While other international and regional organizations are developing codes, the most celebrated effort was undertaken by the Organization for Economic Cooperation and Development (OECD). Its Guidelines on International Investment and Multinational Enterprise sought to "improve the foreign investment climate, encourage the positive contribution which multinational enterprises can make to economic and social progress, and minimize and resolve difficulties which may arise from their various operations."[73] After substantial input from labor and business advisory committees, the "guidelines" were agreed to by OECD member countries in 1976 and slightly revised in 1979. This rather comprehensive code is voluntary, but subsequently it has been referred to in court cases. The OECD itself has attempted to monitor the extent of compliance with the code. In other words, these voluntary guidelines have now become an important part of the environment within which multinational enterprises must operate, in some cases actually incorporated into state law. The OECD has also drafted a code on the protection of privacy and the transborder flow of information that seeks to restrict the unfettered and insensitive collection and use of information by multinational corporations and other agencies. Other efforts have been and will be mounted, for the international nature of the activities and impact of the multinational corporation have provoked efforts by governmental organizations and also nongovernmental ones to develop a comparable international presence.

In assessing the effectiveness of attempts to control the behavior and impact of multinational enterprises, a few general patterns can be observed. The efforts to control multinational corporations focus primarily on their relationship with host states and domestic interests within the host states. Parent states have imposed controls to advance their own economic interests and in a few cases to regulate the foreign behavior of these firms. The issue of the impact of foreign investment on the relations among states has received scarcely any systematic attention, and there has been little action to remedy any of the resulting problems.

With respect to the efforts to control multinationals and their actions in host states, much evidence indicates that these firms are willing to operate under regulated conditions as long as it is profitable for them to do so. In other words, many states can effectively harness the activities of these enterprises toward national objectives with the corporations readily adapting

[73]*The OECD Observer,* July 1976, p. 9.

to the new environment. However, not all states are in this fortunate position, and the adaptability of industries and specific firms varies quite widely. Again, the decision to adapt or not depends largely upon management's assessment of the benefits to be gained from continuing operations versus the costs to be incurred.

Developing states and small countries without the benefit of deposits of scarce natural resources are not in a position to exert significantly greater control over foreign investment without threatening to drive away the investments. Basically, the larger and richer state has the best chance to impose controls since this type of state has the most to offer the multinational corporation: expanding markets, labor supply, natural resources. As with trade and monetary matters, it appears that many developing countries are less able than are the more advanced states to obtain the greatest amount of benefit from foreign investment. This peripheral relationship may be improved by joint action such as the Andean Common Market, but the obstacles to such efforts are great.[74]

Of course, if one rejects the objective of industrialization and growth, there is no need for a state to accept investment by multinational corporations. Furthermore, if one views the relationship between host states and these firms in strict zero-sum terms (meaning that corporate benefits are offset by host-state costs), then the implied policy is to nationalize all existing investment and prohibit the entrance of new operations. However, if the relationship is viewed in positive-sum terms, then the challenge for host states is how best to maximize the benefits and reduce the costs associated with foreign investment.

THE MULTINATIONAL CORPORATION
AND THE FUTURE

In the late 1960s and the 1970s, the issue of the multinational corporation was a critical one for host states and for the United States as the largest parent country. Trade unionists, academicians, journalists, politicians, bureaucrats, and ideologues focused their attention on the multinational corporation as a highly visible and tangible-manifestation of global interdependency. Many kinds of social, political, and economic dislocations were blamed on the international firm. However, since those years, the debates about the multinational corporation have become somewhat less strident as the problems of interdependency became more immediate and complex. Economic recession and inflation, energy dependency, balance-of-payments disequilibrium, domestic unemployment, and threats to survival of major companies and industries as a result of foreign competition

---

[74]Chapter 7 examines in depth various strategies available to developing countries.

have reduced somewhat the fixation on the multinational firm. In addition, the challenge to détente and the escalating distrust between and among the major powers have caused a resurgence in military and security matters. Thus, the multinational corporation is a less salient issue in global economic and political relations.

Nations seem to have more confidence in their ability to structure and shape corporate impacts to achieve national goals. This is not to say that there are not major problems and issues to be resolved; rather, there seems to be the recognition by many that multinationals and states will continue to exist together, and efforts are underway to develop the patterns of relationships that will foster this accommodation.

Some feel that slowly but steadily multinationals will change in a way that is more acceptable to the concerns of host states in reestablishing control. Peter Drucker foresees the development of a transnational confederation that takes advantage of its technological, marketing, and managerial skills to link together production-manufacturing centers in various countries.[75] These production-manufacturing centers would be located in developing countries, would be owned by local interests or agencies, and would be woven into a transnational system of production, management, technology, and marketing. The locally owned "subsidiary" would provide labor and perhaps raw materials to manufacture the component parts of the product. The "headquarters" or center firm, erstwhile the multinational headquarters, would contribute technology, management skill, and well-developed marketing skills and international networks. In the transnational confederation, each component part provides the element of the process in which it has a comparative advantage. However, none of the component parts is competitively self-sufficient; instead, each depends upon the complete network for its success.

The confederation arrangement would remove the issue of equity ownership by foreigners, but the complexity of the system does reduce the ability of the host state to influence the whole process, although it can affect the activity taking place within its borders. Central direction is still important in the transnational confederation, but the permanent character of foreign ownership is eliminated.

Whether the multinational corporation evolves into a transnational confederation or not, it is likely that the international firm as we know it today will continue to adapt to the pressures and concerns of state efforts to reduce the costs of foreign investment and general international interdependency. The multinational is still the most tangible and visible element of global interdependency. While states and managers have become more adept at working within this environment, the fundamental issues raised earlier will continue to challenge policymakers and corporate executives.

[75]Peter F. Drucker, *Managing in Turbulent Times* (New York: Harper & Row, 1980), p. 103–110. Note how similar this is to the Japanese trading company discussed on p. 94.

CHAPTER FIVE
AID RELATIONS BETWEEN RICH AND POOR STATES

During the 1950s and 1960s, foreign aid[1] was perceived as perhaps the most critical aspect of economic relations between rich and poor states. While it still constitutes an important and unique dimension of relations between advanced industrial states and less developed countries, other economic channels (such as trade, direct foreign investment, and commercial bank lending) have assumed greater importance over the course of the 1970s and 1980s. Foreign aid, for example, provides only about 10 percent of the total financial flows to less developed countries each year, as compared with over 70 percent provided by export receipts. Foreign aid, nevertheless, remains a critical factor in the development prospects and political-economic viability of a large number of states in the Third World. This is so, in part, because aid can be targeted to specific development priorities by a government more readily than export earnings, foreign investment, or private bank loans from abroad.

The volume of economic aid flowing to less developed countries and to multilateral aid agencies in 1980 is presented in Table 5-1. The United

---

[1]This discussion, consistent with the focus of this volume, will be confined to economic assistance and will exclude military aid. By economic assistance, we mean flows to less developed countries and multilateral institutions provided by governments for the ostensible purpose of development; such flows are concessional in character (lower interest rates, longer repayment periods, grace periods, and so forth) relative to commercial terms.

TABLE 5-1   Foreign Economic Assistance: 1980 (billions of U.S. dollars)

Source	Value[1]	% of Donor's GNP
Total DAC states[2]	$26.6	0.37%
France	4.0	0.62
Germany	3.5	0.43
Japan	3.3	0.32
United Kingdom	1.8	0.34
United States	7.1	0.27
OPEC	7.0	1.46
Communist states	1.8	0.12
Soviet Union	1.6	0.14
Total	$35.2	

[1]Net official development assistance to less developed countries and multilateral agencies. This excludes, for example, private direct investment and portfolio investment, as well as public and private export credits and guarantees.
[2]Total aid for all states represented in the Development Assistance Committee (DAC) of the Organization for Economic Cooperation and Development (OECD). In addition to the states specified in the table, these include Australia, Austria, Belgium, Canada, Denmark, Italy, the Netherlands, Norway, Portugal, Sweden, and Switzerland.

Sources: Data for DAC states: International Bank for Reconstruction and Development, *World Development Report* 1981 (Washington, D.C.: IBRD, 1981), 164. Data for OPEC and Communist states: "Aid in 1980," *The OECD Observer,* No. 111 (July 1981), 22.

States remains the largest national aid donor. America's major economic partners, however, have increased aid to less developed countries at a much faster rate than the United States over the past fifteen years (see Figure 5-1). The United States in 1961 contributed 59 percent of total Western aid. By 1980, the American share had fallen to 27 percent. Indeed, by the customary measure of aid as a percentage of the donor's GNP, the United States presently ranks thirteenth among the seventeen major Western aid donors—ahead of only Austria, Finland, Switzerland, and Italy.

Total aid to less developed countries tripled between 1970 and 1980, but several factors mitigate against over optimistic assessments of recent aid growth and future prospects. Less developed countries' financial needs have escalated dramatically since 1973 in the face of price increases for their oil, food, and industrial goods imports. Removing the effects of inflation, economic assistance grew at the modest rate of only 5 percent annually in real terms after 1973.[2] Aid trends for Western states that look so impressive in Figure 5-1 (apart from the United States) are unlikely to be sustained in the 1980s. Reduced economic growth, inflation, and budget austerity moves are bound to curtail growth in aid disbursements. The OPEC states' emergence as significant new sources of economic assistance in the 1970s was welcomed by less developed countries. But their aid has been focused narrowly on Islamic states. Syria, Jordan, and Egypt (from 1976–1978) have been the major beneficiaries. Economic assistance from Communist states has also

[2]Organization for Economic Cooperation and Development, *Development Cooperation, 1980 Review* (Paris: OECD, 1980), p. 99.

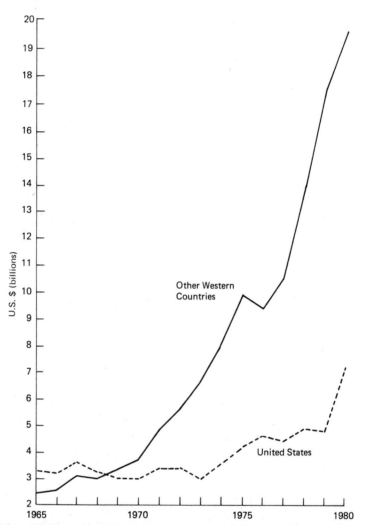

FIGURE 5-1 U.S. Economic Aid as Compared with Other Western States, 1965–1980 **Sources:** Overseas Development Council, *The United States in World Development, Agenda 1980* (New York: Praeger, 1980), p. 230. Updated for 1979 and 1980 with data from International Bank for Reconstruction and Development, *World Development Report 1981* (Washington, D.C.: IBRD, 1981), 165.

been very modest. China virtually discontinued its aid program in the late 1970s. The level of Soviet and Eastern European economic assistance has declined in real terms over the past decade, and about three-fourths of it has gone to Cuba, North Korea, and Vietnam.[3] Most less developed countries with growing financial needs, therefore, cannot afford to rely primarily on increased economic assistance from the major donors in the years ahead— the foundation for significant aid expansion appears to be lacking at present.

[3] Ibid., p. 135.

THE FRAGILE POLITICAL BASE
FOR AID IN THE DONOR
STATES

It is very difficult to generalize about Western aid efforts in the aggregate—
so many diverse tendencies are present simultaneously. Scandinavian states
with few historical ties to the Third World have emerged as strong supporters of development assistance since the 1960s. These countries, along with
some of the smaller European states such as the Netherlands, have assumed
heavy aid burdens for their size. They are also among the most responsive
advanced industrial states to less developed country demands for a wide
variety of international economic reforms. Japan and Germany were in a
defensive international position economically and politically after World War
II. They moved into the economic assistance field boldly only in the 1970s.
Britain committed itself to expand economic assistance in the late 1970s, but
its stagnating economy threatened to undermine that commitment as the
1980s commenced. The United States, as we have seen, has been unable or
unwilling to sustain its earlier postwar posture as the initiator, advocate, and
purveyor of massive amounts of bilateral and multilateral aid to less developed countries. Its aid commitment has immense implications for the global
aid picture because of America's economic importance and the leadership
it has traditionally exercised on international economic assistance issues.

Several factors help to account for the fragile political base upon which
Western aid rests, particularly in the United States. Primary among these
is the gradual evolution in East-West relations from Cold War competition
to limited détente. Through the early 1960s, the Cold War provided the
basic rationale for American economic assistance programs, a national security rationale that was especially effective in mobilizing domestic political
support for large aid appropriations. The emergence of a limited superpower détente during the 1960s and 1970s removed a major incentive for
the United States and the Soviet Union to continue competing with each
other in offering aid to states throughout the Third World. Economic
assistance continued, of course, but it has labored under diminished domestic political support with the erosion of its Cold War underpinning.[4]

Additionally, the experience of the Vietnam war gave rise to serious
doubts about the ultimate consequences of vigorous aid efforts among those
congressional liberals who had previously been major supporters of American economic aid. Senator Fulbright, chairman of the Senate Foreign Relations Committee and other long-time advocates of aid came to view it as

[4]The Cold War reintensified after 1980 with, among other things, the Soviet invasion
of Afghanistan and the election of President Reagan. This might well have provided the basis
for an increase in bilateral U.S. economic assistance, had it not been for America's preoccupation at the same time with domestic economic stagnation and inflation. Growth in economic
assistance to less developed countries, even on Cold War grounds, is not likely in an atmosphere
of national emphasis on tax relief and sharp curtailment of federal expenditures for domestic
programs.

a program that deeply involved the United States in the internal affairs of its aid recipients—even to the point of compelling the United States to make extensive military commitments of questionable value to legitimate American interests. In short, congressional liberals who were among the strongest advocates of an internationalist posture for the United States in its relations with less developed countries, began to argue for a lower profile, one that recognized limits to the desirability and capacity of America to shape the political fabric of states throughout the Third World through aid or other means. This defection of support for aid from liberals marked the end of any vigorous pro-aid constituency within Congress—conservatives have long opposed economic assistance as a "giveaway" program to noncapitalist regimes.

America's social, economic, and political challenges have also undercut domestic political support for U.S. foreign economic assistance. During the 1960s, Americans became sensitized to tremendous social challenges confronting them at home—such as civil rights, medical care, urban decay, and deterioration in public transportation. Programs were initiated to confront these challenges that involved major new commitments of public capital. Even in a period of great affluence, foreign economic assistance fared poorly as it faced greater political competition from "domestic aid" programs for shares of the national budget.

During the 1970s and 1980s, confidence in continued domestic prosperity gave way to reduced rates of economic growth, higher levels of unemployment, and rapidly escalating prices. As the opportunity costs for foreign economic assistance increased in this economic atmosphere, so, too, did political opposition to the program. For example, food exports to less developed countries are one thing when the United States enjoys large, unmarketable grain surpluses; they constitute quite another matter when grain reserves are low and rapidly rising food prices in the United States are helping to drive the country's rate of inflation to record peacetime levels. Thus, proposals for increased food aid to less developed countries in 1973 (and conceivably in the 1980s as well) confronted tough opposition in the United States on the grounds that such aid would aggravate inflation in the American economy.

Additional domestic political opposition to foreign economic assistance comes from American industries and labor fearing loss of domestic production and jobs to less developed countries industrializing with the help of aid. Steelworkers and basic steel manufacturers in advanced industrial states, for example, have lived since the late 1970s with plant closings and massive layoffs because of global overcapacity in steelmaking. They vigorously oppose economic assistance to less developed countries for expanding steel industries—even if poor states view this a vital step toward their overall industrialization goals. Increased economic assistance efforts by the United States and other donors are likely to become casualties of both neomercantilist and anti-inflationary foreign economic policies of such states in an era of stagflation.

To account for the erosion of support for economic assistance, we must also note the emergence of "donor fatigue," particularly on the part of the United States. Most major aid donors deny that they expect gratitude or allegiance from less developed countries as a condition for economic assistance. Nevertheless, they resent the fact that long-time aid recipients so seldom evidence either in sufficient measure. Relative to the early years of economic assistance efforts, there is considerably less conviction in Western states that aid programs bring with them clearly identifiable influence over a recipient country's foreign policy orientation and its domestic political-economic processes. Over the years, all major aid donors have witnessed votes against their position on crucial issues before the United Nations, as well as public displays of hostility (such as attacks on embassies or other facilities) within the less developed countries to which much of their economic aid has flowed. This holds true for Communist aid donors as well as Western states. The Soviet Union has seen anti-Soviet rallies held in stadia constructed with Soviet aid. During the Cuban missile crisis in 1962, Guinea refused to permit Soviet aircraft bound for Cuba to land for refueling at the Conakry airport, which had been constructed with Soviet aid. After years of experience with aid programs, the accumulation of incidents such as these gives rise inevitably to skepticism about the political returns from economic assistance. This is true even if donors insist that no political obligations are connected with development assistance.

In addition to frustration with the foreign policy results of economic aid, the United States and other Western countries have lost confidence in their capacity to determine the development path of poor states through aid programs. Relative to the early postwar years, for example, aid donors are much less confident of their ability to produce predictable political, social, and economic results in poor states through transfers of technology,[5] population control programs, duplication of Western public education and health systems, and capital flows designed to increase the GNP of aid recipients. There is, in addition, much more reluctance on the part of aid donors than there was fifteen years ago to argue that economic assistance is linked in any clearly direct manner to the forging of Western democratic political systems in recipient states. In short, those officials in donor states who see economic assistance as a means of guiding the development efforts of poor states toward preconceived social, economic and political ends are more sensitive to their limitations than in the past. They are also less prone to exaggerate claims about results to be expected from aid programs. These uncertainties about economic assistance make it more difficult in rich states to secure additional resources for economic aid programs.

[5]For a discussion of the politics of transfer of technology, see Chapter 6.

A similar erosion of confidence in the development results of aid is evidenced in appraisals of aid by Soviet analysts. They have expressed doubts about the results of Soviet aid to the state sector in non-Communist less developed countries, as well as about the consequences of Soviet aid recipients' precipitously nationalizing the private sectors of their economies.[6] Soviet leaders have also expressed more general doubts about the nature of socialism espoused by many leaders of Third World states and about the profound differences between these forms of socialism and the "scientific socialism" of Moscow.

REASONS FOR MAINTAINING AID PROGRAMS

The decline in donor states' support of economic assistance efforts is explained largely by these changes in the international political environment, by the erosion of domestic political support for aid appropriations, and by the emergence of "donor fatigue." In spite of these developments, Western states continue to have sufficient interests in less developed countries to maintain economic assistance programs—albeit at reduced levels in relation to their economic capabilities. Economic aid will continue to be a valuable instrument in the diplomacy of advanced industrial states. For example, large requests for aid were an integral part of the Nixon administration's military withdrawal from Indochina and its efforts to settle the Middle East conflict. Two weeks after Secretary of State Kissinger's marathon negotiation of an Israeli-Syrian troop disengagement, and one week before President Nixon's visit to the Middle East in 1974, the administration requested $100 million in economic aid to rebuild Syrian towns along the disengagement line, $350 million in economic aid to Israel, $207 million for Jordan, and $250 million for Egypt. Followng the U.S.-inspired Camp David Agreement on the Middle East in 1977, Israel and Egypt became by far the largest recipients of American economic assistance. Similarly, France has over the years sustained a large economic aid program designed to maintain political and extensive cultural (education) ties between itself and its former colonies. Economic aid will be maintained as a permanent instrument employed by rich states in pursuit of their disparate political goals in less developed countries, whatever the alterations in the philosophical underpinning of their aid efforts or the trend in overall aid flows.

Rich states will also continue economic assistance programs in an effort to promote their national and private economic interests in the Third World. The scarcity in global supplies of certain mineral resources emerged as a clear constraint to the prosperity of all advanced industrial states following

[6]See Robert S. Walters, *Soviet and American Aid* (Pittsburgh, Pa.: University of Pittsburgh Press, 1970), pp. 65–67.

oil shortages in 1973. More than ever before, rich states can be expected to use economic aid, along with other incentives, to secure access to vital raw materials in less developed countries. Japan, for example, made massive aid commitments to oil-producing states in the Persian Gulf and to Indonesia in the aftermath of the Arab embargo on oil shipments during 1973 and 1974.

Rich states also use aid to finance their exports to less developed countries. The provision of financing by Western states for high levels of imports by less developed nations in the 1970s helped to soften the severity of economic stagnation in the West. Western prosperity will continue to be linked importantly with provision of adequate financial assistance (through private and public channels) for less developed states to continue their purchases in Europe, the United States, and Japan. As long as neomercantilism continues to be an important part of advanced industrial states' overall trade policies, rich states are likely to continue economic assistance to poor states as a means of preserving export-related jobs at home and improving their balance of trade. The United States sends 38 percent of its exports to less developed countries.[7] Aid as a supplement to private lending will remain a vital element in stimulating American exports—especially to the less developed oil-importing countries.

The connection between economic assistance and the creation of a hospitable climate for direct private foreign investment is still another reason for the continuation of aid programs by Western states. The United States and other Western aid donors have spoken frequently of economic assistance in the forms of resource surveys, feasibility studies, and infrastructure projects in less developed countries (ports, communication facilities, roads, rail transportation, electric power networks, and so forth) as crucial in creating the necessary preconditions for poor states to finance their future development through private resource flows. In these and other ways (such as investment guarantees for firms operating in poor states, and the threat of denying future foreign aid to less developed countries that nationalize private foreign investment without adequate compensation), economic aid programs are an integral part of securing investment opportunities for firms in donor states. In an age of burgeoning private foreign investment, most Western states will continue to have a vested interest in supporting aid programs on this ground alone.

Finally, advanced industrial states will continue to engage in economic aid efforts because they contribute a unique type of resource transfer to less developed countries. Export earnings and private foreign investment combined may dwarf aid flows to less developed countries, but export earnings and private investment flow, in the first instance, to firms and individuals in poor states. Economic assistance, on the other hand, supplies

---

[7]Overseas Development Council, *The United States and World Development, Agenda 1980* (New York: Praeger, 1980), p. 11.

new investment capital directly to governments in poor states for their use in priority development activities. Thus, systematic improvements in agriculture, education, health, and a variety of other activities crucial for economic development are much more likely to be produced through aid than through revenues generated by trade or private investment in many instances.

The importance of aid in a poor state's overall development is greater than one would expect from looking at the volume of aid flows, shown either as a proportion of total foreign exchange receipts or as a proportion of total investment by less developed countries. It is politically unfeasible for advanced industrial states today to deny their interest in the development of the Third World. Because of aid's unique characteristics, rich states that claim to have an interest in poor states' development must continue aid disbursements, notwithstanding their doubts about the political and economic results.

MULTILATERAL AID

Over the past fifteen years, aid disbursed to less developed countries through multilateral institutions has grown more rapidly than have bilateral aid programs. Multilateral aid presently amounts to over one-fourth of total Western economic assistance.[8] The International Bank for Reconstruction and Development (IBRD), the largest source of multilateral aid, now disburses economic assistance each year on a par with U.S. aid levels. There are contradictory explanations as to the reasons for and the significance of this trend from bilateral to multilateral aid. One view is that multilateral aid is a means by which both donors and recipients can eliminate some of the more nettlesome problems they each associate with bilateral economic assistance. Another view (the radical perspective) is that multilateral aid is merely a more subtle and effective means than bilateral aid of enabling Western states to exercise their domination and exploitation of less developed countries.

According to the first view, multilateral aid substantially removes politics from economic assistance; consequently, it is preferred by both donors and recipients to bilateral aid. Multilateral aid is a way in which to continue economic assistance with less direct involvement on the part of a donor state in the internal affairs of recipients. Thus, liberal U.S. Congress members can support multilateral aid as a means of maintaining an internationalist orientation and simultaneously reduce a specifically American presence in less developed countries; a former colonial power such as the Netherlands can give multilateral aid and thereby avoid charges that its aid efforts are merely an attempt to reimpose its dominance over former colonies. From the donors' perspective, multilateral aid permits a rich state to

---

[8]OECD, *Development Cooperation, 1980 Review*, p. 141.

demonstrate its commitment to the development of poor states in a way that minimizes political attacks from aid critics at home and abroad.

Improved management of certain aid-related problems also provides incentives for increased multilateral cooperation by donors. Bilateral aid flows, for example, have typically been tied to purchases from the donor state. This places constraints on the aid recipient's choice of trade partners and usually results in higher prices for imports flowing to "captive" aid purchasers. Economic assistance must be untied to maximize its effectiveness for promoting development, but few states are willing to do this on a large scale unless all other donors do so. Multilateral aid encourages joint action toward this end.

Recipients, too, can see some major advantages to multilateral aid. Development assistance can be separated more clearly from the narrow political and security interests of various donors if aid is disbursed through an international organization. Even if multilateral aid disbursements are conditioned upon specified policy changes by a recipient, it is easier for a less developed state to accept these conditions from an international institution of which it is a member than to accept them from another state. Membership in the international agencies that disburse aid also gives less developed countries a voice in establishing the criteria for aid allocations. However small their voices, compared with those of rich states in these institutions, it is greater than the voice they have in shaping the bilateral aid policies of donor states. Hence, multilateral aid is attractive to both donors and recipients because it places an international organization between the parties to buffer what is usually a bittersweet relationship.

From the radical perspective, however, Western aid—multilateral as well as bilateral—has never been designed to facilitate the development of poor states. Indeed, in this view aid is merely another instrument that ensures the subordination of states in the periphery to Western states that control the capitalist global economy. This exploitation is crucial for the indefinite continuation of the rich states' prosperity. International economic institutions are purportedly essential to the efforts of rich states to subordinate and exploit less developed countries. The radical perspective with regard to aid is entirely consistent with their view of the function international organizations perform in trade and monetary relations, which we discussed in Chapters 2 and 3. Rich states remain fully in control of the aid policies of international institutions by virtue of their budgetary contributions and voting power, whereas the participation of poor states merely creates the illusion of a genuinely multilateral aid enterprise.

The International Monetary Fund and the International Bank for Reconstruciton and Development are the focus of radical critiques of multilateral aid. The IBRD was established as a sister institution to the IMF. They share the same buildings in Washington, D.C., and, like the IMF, voting in the IBRD is weighted in rough proportion to the amount of capital each country pledges to the institution. In contrast to medium and short-term IMF loans for financing balance-of-payments deficits, however, loans from the IBRD are repayable over much longer periods of time and are linked to internationally approved development programs of recipients. Over the years the IBRD has established the world's most extensive capabilities for monitoring and evaluating development plans and economic assistance. In 1980, over $5 billion in aid was disbursed under its auspices.

As the major source of multilateral short-term credit for less developed countries, the IMF and IBRD impose stringent conditions on their borrowers; conditions, stress the radical analysts, that open the door for their penetration by the trade and investment of rich states. They would view as consistent with this analysis the Reagan administration's call for more stringent international lending criteria and greater reliance by less developed countries on private enterprise, direct foreign investment, and the "magic of the marketplace." Less developed countries not willing to conform to IMF and IBRD suggestions find themselves denied not only loans from these institutions but also credit through private channels or bilateral aid programs. These and other multilateral aid agencies, thus, are merely a subtler and more effective means of attaching poor states to the international imperialist system than is the cruder device of explicit political control.

We are likely to see more emphasis on multilateral aid in the 1980s whether one views economic assistance through multilateral channels as highly preferable to bilateral aid or as merely another instrument for subjugating less developed countries to Western control. The IBRD will undoubtedly remain the centerpiece of multilateral aid efforts, but the institution will have to withstand increased pressure from several directions. Less developed countries are anxious to subject IBRD activities and policies to oversight by the United Nations where they exercise a majority. U.S. government officials, at the same time, have become increasingly vocal in their criticism of a few IBRD loans to governments unfriendly to the West— particularly Cuba and Vietnam. In 1980, the United States threw IBRD programs into disarray by backing away from previous commitments to help replenish capital needed by the IBRD to continue its aid to the poorest states among the less developed countries. New efforts were required to reduce the IBRD's reliance on American donations. While multilateral aid will continue to grow, it is likely to become more highly politicized and contentious as well.

THE AID DIALOGUE
AT THE INTERNATIONAL LEVEL

Global inflation, increased prices for oil dictated by OPEC, and economic stagnation of the advanced industrial states raise the aid needs of most less developed countries and inhibit the willingness of rich states to expand their aid programs. Less developed countries, cognizant of these facts, have attempted to rivet international attention on minimal aid levels "appropriate" for rich states and to push for comprehensive forms of debt relief for the least developed states among them.

Since the U.N.-declared First Development Decade in the 1960s, less developed countries have sought commitments from all developed states to extend economic assistance in amounts equal to at least seven-tenths of 1 percent of their GNP. They are pressing in the 1980s for an increase in this aid target to 1 percent of donors' GNP. The United States has never accepted these or any aid targets as legitimate, in the sense that donor states have any obligation to meet them. Indeed, American aid would have to more than double to comply with the 0.7 percent target. Among the Western states, only the Scandinavian countries (other than Finland) and the Netherlands equal or exceed the aid target.[9] The less developed countries persist in attempting to hold rich states accountable to these international "standards" of aid giving. Even if compliance is rare, a political burden has been placed on every donor country to explain why its aid levels are below the target in virtually all international forums. Without exaggerating their importance, the presence of these targets has placed many rich states on the defensive over the years and has certainly encouraged most advanced industrial states of the West to expand their aid commitments, notwithstanding U.S. intransigence on the issue.

Generalized debt relief for the poorest states emerged as another major dimension of the international aid dialogue as the debt of less developed countries soared during the 1970s. It should be noted that both debt and debt service (repayments of principal and interest) are highly concentrated in the larger, more rapidly industrializing Third World states such as Brazil, Mexico, Argentina, Algeria, Indonesia and South Korea. Generalized debt relief is neither appropriate for, nor desired by, these types of states. They certainly carry high levels of foreign public and private debt, but their rapid economic growth also permits servicing it. They rely heavily on commercial loans through private channels, such as Eurocurrency borrowing (see Chapter 3). Their association with pleas for debt relief would threaten continued access to private lending upon which they rely to finance development.

On the other hand, the poorest of the less developed countries rely extensively on aid rather than on private sources of external financing. With low per capita incomes and much less dynamic growth prospects, these countries (such as Gabon, Guinea, Mauritania, Zambia, Zaire, Bolivia, Peru, Uruguay, and Egypt) face severe challenges in servicing their foreign debt. In various international forums, demands were raised for rich states to assist the poorest countries with debt problems by canceling poor states'

[9]Table 5-1 shows where various major donors stand in relation to these targets. Aid from Communist states would have to increase sixfold, and from Western states it would have to double. OPEC countries exceed the target as a group. OPEC aid donors well in excess of the target are Saudi Arabia, Kuwait, Iraq, the United Arab Emirates, and Qatar.

past foreign aid repayment obligations, consolidating and rescheduling their payments over several decades to private sources of external financing, and creating a new international mechanism to establish principles and guidelines for debtors and creditors to negotiate external debt relief.

The advanced industrial states have opposed generalized debt relief, and they blocked less developed countries' efforts to establish an International Debt Commission under UNCTAD's auspices in 1979. However, certain Western countries (Belgium, Canada, the Netherlands, Sweden, Switzerland, the United Kingdom, and West Germany) have extended debt relief to the poorest less developed countries by converting past aid loans to grants on a selective basis and agreeing to disburse future aid on softer terms. Western powers prefer to deal with less developed countries' debt problems on a case-by-case basis. They have supported expanding resources and easing the conditions attached to loans to less developed countries from the established international lending agencies such as the IMF and IBRD.

As we have seen in our discussion of less developed countries' interests in international monetary relations, debt problems will remain a contentious issue between rich and poor states during the 1980s. A wide gulf separates these groups of states in their basic approaches to managing poor states' mounting debt challenges. Debt management will constitute a central aid focus in coming years.

CONCLUSION

The development gap between rich and poor states is a glaring reminder of tremendous inequalities present in the world (see Table 5-2). As long as it persists, demands for new forms and increased levels of economic assistance will confront the advanced industrial countries, no matter how generous they may feel they have been in the past. The development gap will be a source of increasing international political tensions in the future, just as inequalities among elements of domestic society have been in national politics throughout the world. The focus of the aid dialogue will change from time to time as the various needs of poor states take on greater or less urgency—such as debt service burdens or food supplies. But economic assistance in various forms will remain a critical need for all but one or two dozen of the 120 less developed countries for years to come.

At the same time, it is now more widely recognized than in the past than economic assistance programs can bear only a small share of the burden in producing development for most states. That requires extensive political, economic, and social alterations in the domestic systems of poor states as well as greater progress in improving the gamut of international trade, investment, monetary, and technology transfer relations between rich and poor countries. Economic assistance is likely to take a back seat, except intermittently, to these other pressing challenges to development and international economic peacekeeping in future years.

TABLE 5-2 The Development Gap Between Rich and Poor States, 1979

	35 Low-Income LDCs[a]	141 LDCs[b]	31 Advanced Industrial States	United States
Average per capita GNP	$ 176	$ 597	$6,468	$9,700
Population, millions	1,132	3,244	1,074	220
Average life expectancy, years	49	56	72	73
Infant mortality rate, per 1,000 live births	132	96	18	14
Average literacy rate	35%	52%	99%	99%
Average per capita education expenditures	$ 4	$ 18	$ 286	$ 454

[a]Less developed countries with per capita GNP of less than $300.
[b]Includes the thirty-five low-income LDCs.
For a translation of these statistics into alterations in the standard of living an American would have to make were he or she to live in a less developed country with a per capita income equivalent to that experienced by most people in the world, see Robert Heilbroner, *The Great Ascent* (New York: Harper Torchbooks, 1963), pp. 23–27.

Source: Adapted from Overseas Development Council, *The United States and World Development, Agenda 1980* (New York: Praeger, 1980), Tables A-1, A-2, and A-4.

CHAPTER SIX
TECHNOLOGY TRANSFER AND INTERNATIONAL RELATIONS

Developments in science and technology have become, in recent years, increasingly important elements in world politics with widespread international ramifications. Technological advances have become almost synonymous with economic growth and constitute major factors in assessing shifts in the balance of economic and political power. This is probably why the issue of "technology transfer" has generated so much heated debate among researchers and policymakers alike. The subject matter of "technology transfer" has become

> a prism for a constellation of related issues, among which are the role of science and technology in industrialization, the gap between rich and poor nations and its implications for both, the transnational corporations as both the culprit and savior, and the "new international economic order."[1]

Several different dimensions of the technology transfer issue will be examined in this chapter. The major focus is the technological gap between rich and poor nations, and it will be discussed from the perspective of both types of countries. This issue has important international implications made

[1]Taghi Saghafi-nejad and Robert Belfield, "Transnational Corporations, Technology Transfer and Development: A Bibliography," Worldwide Institutions Research Group, The Wharton School, University of Pennsylvania, Philadelphia, 1976, Introduction, p. 1.

more complex by the concerns of domestic interest groups. Similarly, among advanced industrial states, technological capability is often thought to have some bearing on the perception of a state's strength and power. Thus, technology as a point of contention among advanced industrial states will also be considered. But first, it is useful to discuss what is meant by technology and the transfer of technology.

There are many different definitions of technology that stress different elements of the phenomenon. Some economists define technology as "the knowledge and the techniques with which inputs into the production process are transformed into output."[2] An industrialist says that technology is "the specific know-how required to define a product that fulfills a need, and then to design and manufacture it."[3] The definition most useful in the context of this book is that technology is knowledge and the ability to apply that knowledge. Technology is not products; products are the end result of technology.

The term "technology transfer" itself does not necessarily have a transnational connotation. For example, a distinction has been made between "vertical transfer," as in the stages of the product cycle (e.g., from applied research to product development), and "horizontal transfer," that is, transfer between places or institutions at a given stage of the product cycle.[4] For our purposes, international technology transfer "occurs whenever production in one country benefits from technical knowledge previously available only abroad."[5] The concept of the international transfer of technology as used in this book is the flow of purposeful knowledge across national boundaries "in whatever context for whatever reason to whatever country."[6]

International technology transfer may occur through a variety of processes, including licenses and patents, supplies of machines and equipment, exchanges between scientific bodies of various nations, purchase of technical publications, consulting and engineering services by foreigners, on-site training of indigenous personnel by foreign experts, and students studying abroad. In one form or another, technology has been transferred across national boundaries for centuries.

[2]Franklyn Holzman and Richard Portes, "The Limits of Pressure," *Foreign Policy*, no. 32 (Fall 1978), 81.

[3]Statement by Dr. Maurice Mountain to the U.S. House of Representatives, "Key Issues on U.S.-U.S.S.R. Scientific Exchanges and Technology Transfers," hearings before the Subcommittee on Domestic and International Scientific Planning Analysis and Cooperation of the Committee on Science and Technology, 95th Cong., 2nd sess., October 4–5, 1978, p. 187.

[4]E. Mansfield, "International Technology Transfer: Forms, Resource Requirements and Policies," *American Economic Review* (May 1975), as reported in Philip Hanson, "Technology Transfer to the Soviet Union," *Survey: A Journal of East-West Studies*, 23, no. 2, (Spring 1977), 73.

[5]Philip Hanson, "Technology Transfer to the Soviet Union," p. 73.

[6]Henry R. Nau, *Technology Transfer and U.S. Foreign Policy*, (New York: Praeger, 1976), p. 3.

The development and flow of technology is, however, not distributed evenly among the countries of the world. The major source of new technology has been the advanced industrial states of North America, Western Europe, and Japan. In 1963 and 1964, these states accounted for 98 percent of the world's expenditures on research and development (a total of $29 billion). The United States alone accounted for 70 percent of the total expenditures.[7] Ten years later, total global expenditures on research and development (R&D) increased to $63.5 billion, with advanced industrial states accounting for 97.2 percent of that amount. While the share of the developing countries hardly increased in that period, the U.S. share fell drastically from 70 percent to 50.7 percent, with Western Europe and Japan increasing proportionally. Even though the developing countries' share is projected to have increased to 4 percent of total worldwide R&D expenditures by 1980, the share of these states in developing new technology is still very small.

Since developing countries generate little indigenous technology, their source of supply for new technology has historically been from the advanced industrial states through the mechanism of technology transfer. Consequently, the developing countries, individually and through vehicles like the United Nations, have included technology in the North-South dialogue and discussions of the new international economic order. Technology has become linked inextricably with trade, monetary issues, and direct foreign investment, and at the same time it has become a critical issue in its own right.

TECHNOLOGY GAPS
AND NORTH-SOUTH ISSUES

It is difficult to measure the exact magnitude of the technology gap between rich and poor states, for there are so many approximate or surrogate measures. Nonetheless, the gap is dramatic. A U.N. study that used 1975 per capita gross domestic product of the economically active population as a surrogate measure of technology estimated that "it would take 80 years (for the developing countries) to reach the 1975 levels (of the developed countries) with an annual GDP growth of 3 percent, 60 years with an annual growth of 4 percent, and 50 years with one of 5 percent."[8] In the meantime, of course, the advanced industrial states would not be standing still in technological developments and improvements. The gap can be illustrated further by the fact that in 1973 87.4 percent of the world's R&D scientists lived in the advanced industrial states compared with only 12.5 percent in

[7]Jan Annerstedt, "On the Global Distribution of R&D Resources," Occasional Paper 79/1, Vienna Institute for Development, 1979, Figure 1, p. 4.

[8]UNCTAD Secretariat, report of the Secretariat, *Towards the Technological Transformation of Developing Countries* (New York: United Nations, 1979), p. 34.

the developing countries.[9] Moreover, R&D expenditures per capita of the economically active population were $3.00 for developing countries and $182.10 in the developed countries according to 1973 figures.[10] The data show clearly that most poor countries presently lack the capital and human resources necessary for industrialization and economic growth in the future.

The international political controversies surrounding the technology gap are centered in the almost universal desire of states to exercise control over science and technology—as opposed to acquiring it from external sources, no matter how accessible the technology or generous the terms. Nations want to harness technology to economic, social, and national security policies as defined by the state itself and not as determined by a foreign source. Many developing countries seek greater self-reliance in technology in all sectors of their economies, although many do not possess the capital or human resources to develop a strong technological base. Technology gaps are thought to have a negative effect on a state's economic, political, military, and cultural status. This often results in perceptions that a country's independence and future are dependent upon access to foreign technology and upon the states or corporations that control that technology.

The developing countries seek new technology at low cost, and the advanced industrial states demand a significant return for transferred technology that was developed in their countries. Between these parties, and tied inextricably to the points of contention, are the multinational corporations. The concerns and aspirations of each of these parties are important to an understanding of the technology issue.

CONCERNS OF DEVELOPING COUNTRIES

Probably the overriding concern of the developing countries has been what they consider to be their excessive dependence on the advanced industrialized states for their development (particularly in such areas as industrial technology) and what appears to be an inevitable perpetuation of that dependence. The developing countries feel entangled with the advanced industrial states by a variety of asymmetrical relationships that are largely the result of the dominant role that the industrialized states exercised during the colonial era. Trade patterns that developed between the advanced industrial states (i.e., the North) and the developing countries (i.e., the South) during colonial times form a key historic element of this asymmetric dependence.

For instance, the commodities produced in the South and sold in the international market largely reflected the demands and tastes of the markets in the North. Similarly, the consumer goods of interest to developing coun-

[9]Annerstedt, "On the global Distribution of R&D Resources," p. 4.
[10]Ibid., p. 6.

tries reflected the production patterns and tastes of the North. Because the Northern states possessed more elaborate technical know-how, patents, finance, and management techniques, the underdeveloped Southern states looked to the North for their supplies of capital-intensive consumer items, which were too complex to manufacture in the South. To industrialize, the developing countries had to import expensive technology, often in the form of products, from the already industrialized states, and that required them to expand their export base, selling more commodities primarily to the commodity hungry North. Efforts by the developing countries to establish their own manufacturing industries threatened some of the exports from the industrialized states. The North's advocacy of freer international trade to facilitate the most efficient and profitable distribution of factors of production served to undermine the efforts of the developing countries to build a manufacturing base with its attendant technological advantages. The Southern states thereby felt relegated to becoming "hewers of wood" and had to be dependent on the North for whatever transfer of technology would be forthcoming, at the latter's own inclination and pace.

Other external factors that further heightened the asymmetry between the North and South included the establishment of the General Agreement on Tariffs and Trade (GATT), brought into being mainly by the Northern states who then supervised and controlled international trade. Whether or not this power was ever used by the North in directing trade flows is immaterial. The fact is that trade patterns have continued to reflect the dominance of the North as depicted in Table 6-1.

This table shows that over 69 percent of total world export trade occurs between countries in the North and that substantially greater trade flows exist among the advanced industrialized states (North-North) and from the developing countries to the industrialized states (South-North) than vice versa (North-South) and that much less exists between the developing countries themselves (South-South). Admittedly, these figures do not reflect only technology-related exchanges, but this asymmetrical trade pattern is symbolic of the nominal transmission of technical knowledge from the developed to the developing countries and the subordinate role of developing countries in technological advancements.

TABLE 6-1   Direction of World Exports by Value, 1980 (in percentages)*

Exports from	To North	To South	To Centrally Planned Block
World	69.1%	27.8%	3%
North	67.6%	27%	3.2%
South	66.1%	26.5%	3%

*Some unallocated figures have not been included.

Source: Calculated from "International Monetary Fund, *Direction of Trade Statistics, 1981 Yearbook*, Washington, D.C., 1981, pp. 2-23.

The asymmetry of technical knowledge in favor of the advanced industrial states is seen most vividly in the negligible ownership of patents by developing countries compared with the developed countries. Studies by UNCTAD have revealed that only 6 percent (200,000) of the world's 3.5 million patents in existence in 1972 were held by the developing countries and that less than one-sixth of that total (30,000) were held by nationals of those countries.[11] The remaining 170,000 patents were held by foreigners, mostly multinational corporations.[12] Apparently, Western dominance of Third World patents has, if anything, been increasing. In Chile, for example, nationals held 34 percent of all patents in 1937, but only 5 percent thirty years later.[13]

Another concern of the developing countries relates to the "appropriateness" of the technology transferred by the advanced industrial states. The developing countries maintain that much of the technology transferred is typically capital intensive and labor saving, whereas the chief problem in most developing countries is unemployment. The different circumstances under which such technology is developed and the unwillingness of the developed countries and the multinational corporations to adapt it to the local setting make it inappropriate for the developing countries given their need to provide employment. Conversely, machinery and equipment transferred to the developing countries have been labeled "inappropriate" because they were machines of older vintage. Not only was the technology out of date but also the developing countries or consumers in these countries were being charged high prices for the old technology.

Even where the technology transferred from the developed countries is welcomed by the developing countries, there is generally a dissatisfaction with its price. The developing countries maintain that the cost of transferred technology is unnecessarily inflated. For example, it is charged that members of the pharmaceutical industry are among the highest-cost sellers of technology and dramatically overprice their products. A recent OECD report stated (on the evidence of U.S. Senate reports) that some ingredients were overpriced by 1,000 percent or even 5,000 percent.[14] The developing countries consider technology already developed to be part of human heritage and that all countries have a right of access to such technology to improve their standards of living. Moreover, they are of the view that they have paid enough to the developed countries through the exploitation of

[11]UNCTAD Secretariat, "Transfer of Technology—Technological Dependence: Its Nature, Consequences and Policy Implications," TD/190 (New York: United Nations, 1975), p. 11.

[12]Issam El-Ziam, "Problems of Technology Transfer—A Point of View from the Third World," Occasional Paper No. 78/6, Vienna Institute for Development, 1978, p. 2.

[13]Ibid

[14]A. C. Cilinigiroglu, "Transfer of Technology for Pharmaceutical Chemicals," October 1974, as reported in Dimitri Germidis, ed., *Transfer of Technology by Multinational Corporations*, Vol. II (Paris: Development Center of OECD, 1977), p. 26.

their natural resources that facilitated the development of the advanced industrial states at their expense. The developing countries are therefore incensed by the fact that payments for technology, in their attempt to industrialize, strain their balance-of-payments position. An UNCTAD study estimated that the Third World would pay over $10 billion for the right to use patents, licenses, process know-how, technical services, and trademarks by the end of the 1970s.[15] The chief technology exporters—the United States, France, and Britain—netted $5.4 billion worldwide in 1974 from payments for technology,[16] and in 1980 receipts by U.S. firms from royalties and fees totaled nearly $5.7 billion, many times more than the amount paid out in royalties and fees by U.S. firms.[17]

One contributor to the unnecessarily inflated price of technology, as seen by the developing countries, is the fact that technology is often sold in packages. For example, tie-in clauses in certain contracts compel a licensee to purchase unpatented goods from the licensor; in other cases, technology may be supplied only through turnkey operations where the supplier undertakes full responsibility for construction of a plant and managing it until local personnel are ready to do so. Particularly where the recipient of the technology is a subsidiary of the supplier, as often is the case, the recipient country acquires little, if any, "new" technical know-how. What the developing countries find repugnant is that some elements of the package may be overpriced, unnecessary, or available locally. One study revealed that 83 percent of Bolivia's contracts and 86 percent of Ethiopia's involved such clauses.[18] There has consequently been a drive for disaggregation or "unbundling" of package contracts by the developing countries. In the Andean pact countries, for instance, royalty payments from subsidiaries to parent companies are prohibited. Moreover, a requirement is imposed for disaggregation: the import of every item of technology must be cost justified separately on the basis of comparison with other available technology.[19]

As part of their strategy to facilitate technological development and minimize the cost of imported technology, the developing countries have been trying to get the multinational corporations operating in their jurisdiction to establish research and development centers in the local setting. They have been unsuccessful in their endeavor. One OECD-sponsored

[15]UNCTAD Secretariat, report of Secretariat, *Major Issues Arising from the Transfer of Technology to Developing Countries,* (New York: United Nations, 1973), p. 2.

[16]El-Ziam, "Problems of Technology Transfer," p. 31.

[17]U.S. Department of Commerce, *Survey of Current Business* (Washington, D.C.: GPO, August 1981), p. 30.

[18]El-Ziam, "Problems of Technological Transfer," p. 31.

[19]Chamber of Commerce of the United States, report of the Task Force on Technology Transfer, "Technology Transfer and the Developing Countries: Guidelines and Principles for Consideration in Development of National Policies Governing Transfer of Technology Between Industrial and Developing Countries" (Washington: Chamber of Commerce, April 1977), p. 7.

study of sixty-five subsidiaries of more than twenty multinational corporations in twelve countries of varying levels of development, economic structure, size, and geographical locations revealed that R&D activities in centers attached to subsidiaries were practically nonexistent[20] but were concentrated mostly in the parent company's home country. There are good reasons for this, including the economies of scale involved in centralizing R&D, the availability of highly trained scientific and engineering personnel, close interactions between members of the scientific community, and more effective management of the R&D function.[21] But the technology gap is widened, not narrowed, as a result of such policies.

One of the results of this phenomenon, which is of great concern to the developing countries, is what is known as "reverse transfer of technology" or "brain drain." Not only are the developed countries and their multinational corporations unwilling to establish R&D and other facilities that could employ and train local skilled labor, but, paradoxically, the developing countries in need of foreign assistance are an important source of highly qualified personnel for the developed countries. UNCTAD studies estimate that, for the fifteen-year period from 1960 to 1975/1976, skilled migration from the developing countries (consisting of engineers, scientists, physicians and surgeons, and technical and kindred workers) to the three major developed countries of immigration—the United States, Canada, and the United Kingdom—amounted to over 300,000 persons.[22] That estimate does not take into account skilled migration to other developed countries. At the same time there has been a gradual shift in the skill-level composition of persons emigrating from the developing to the developed countries. Officials in the latter have attempted to make their immigration policies responsive to their domestic labor markets by applying more selective criteria for immigration applicants.[23] For example, in the United States, high on the list of priorities are those people with education and skills needed in the U.S. labor market; very low on the list are unskilled workers. Consequently, scientists, engineers, doctors, and the more highly skilled are more likely to gain permission to immigrate to the United States than are other less skilled categories; this contributes to the brain drain from those countries desperately in need of building their indigenous technological capabilities. In terms of absolute flows, nearly 61,000 physicians and surgeons, over 100,000 engineers and scientists, and another 123,000 technical and kindred workers migrated from the developing regions to

[20]Dimitri Germidis, *Transfer of Technology by Multinational Corporations: A Synthesis and Country Case Study*, Vol. I, (Paris: Development Center of the OECD, 1977), p. 52.

[21]William A. Dymza, "Regional Strategies of U.S. Multinational Firms That Affect Transfers of Technology to Developing Countries," in *Transfer of Technology by Multinational Corporations*, Vol. II, ed. Dimitri Germidis (Paris: Development Center of OECD, 1977), p. 99.

[22]UNCTAD Secretariat, report of Secretariat, *Technology: Development Aspects of the Reverse Transfer Technology* (New York: United Nations, 1979), para. 6.

[23]Ibid., para. 9.

the United States, Canada, and the United Kingdom between 1961 and 1975/1976.[24] In the latter part of the 1970s, the migration of people from the developing countries represented 70–80 percent of the total migration of skilled persons to the United States. From 1961 to 1965, the developing countries provided only 37 percent of the total skilled migrants.[25] The brain drain is working to the disadvantage of the developing countries.

These considerations provide substantial justification for developing countries' concern about whether the "trickling down" of technology from the advanced states is occurring effectively. Some developing countries have been agitating for the development of indigenous R&D capacities that would simultaneously facilitate growth and preserve their self-reliance. One outcome of the present system is an uneven distribution of the fruits of technology transfer and a substantial widening of domestic income gaps. The consequences of this situation have been stated succinctly by Frances Stewart, an Oxford economist:

> 5–15 percent of the labor force is equipped with modern technology. The rest suffers from complete neglect. The minority, equipped with advanced-country methods, have high productivity and high incomes; the majority, lacking all modern equipment and deprived of most investment resources, suffer from very low productivity. The wide disparities in incomes between the sector using advanced technology transferred from the advanced countries and the rest of the population is largely responsible for the unsatisfactory income distribution in many developing countries, and for the employment problem.[26]

Because of a dependency upon technology transfer via multinational corporations, many developing countries feel unable to control either the direction or pace of technological and industrial development. While some remedies of control are possible, the economic realities of their position mean that in many cases countries are largely passive recipients of the technological efforts of others. Autonomy and self-direction are difficult to achieve.

In addition, the tendency for some multinational corporations, in pursuit of more favorable production costs, to allocate low-skill-level operations to subsidiaries in developing countries may have long- and short-term effects on the international division of labor. The developing countries may be frozen into production activity characterized by low wage costs and

[24]Ibid., para. 12.

[25]Ibid., para. 10, based on unpublished data supplied by the U.S. National Science Foundation.

[26]Frances Stewart, "Technological Dependence in the Third World," paper prepared for OECD Seminar on Science and Technology and Development in a Changing World, DSTI/SPR/75.33, Paris, April 21–25, 1975, as quoted in Ward Morehouse, "Science and Technology and the Global Equity Crisis: New Directions for United States Policy," Occasional Paper No. 16, The Stanley Foundation, Muscatine, Iowa, 1978, p. 18.

low technology levels, whereas the more high-paying functions requiring the development and application of new technology will remain the province of the advanced industrial states. Thus, the developing countries retain their status of economic and technological colonies with few opportunities to develop their own technological strength.

ADVANCED INDUSTRIAL STATE
VIEWS AND THE TECHNOLOGY GAP

The concerns of the developed nations with respect to technology transfer differ significantly from those of the developing countries; hence, the debate. One primary issue upon which there is disagreement is the view that existing technology is part of human heritage and should therefore be free. The advanced industrial states maintain that technology is proprietary knowledge, a human product based on ingenuity and capability that merits commercialization and that should be sold only at the owner's (and developer's) discretion. Its transfer, however achieved, should neither be interfered with nor should it be compelled.

The arguments by the developed countries on this issue may be summarized as follows: First, the developing countries fail to realize that the majority of transferable technology is privately owned by corporations and that the governments of the advanced industrial states cannot mandate transfer of technology even if they wanted to. A report by the Chamber of Commerce of the United States stated that

> The ownership of technology constitutes a property interest entitled to recognition as such. There is no doubt that this statement represents the position of the United States government of both political parties, of economists and lawyers of nearly every persuasion and of both American business and American labor.[27]

Second, as with any other commercial item, technology will be transferred only if the conditions for it are suitable. Moreover, the owners of the technology usually seek profits from its use. A report that contributed to the development of U.S. policy for the General Conference on Science and Technology for Development in Vienna, in August 1979, stated that

> it seems clear that the extent of private technology flows to developing countries will depend on whether conditions in each country (markets, regulations, institutional and business capabilities, and so forth) attract such flows.[28]

[27]Chamber of Commerce of the United States, "Technology Transfer," p. 20.

[28]National Research Council, report of the Council, *U.S. Science and Technology for Development: A Contribution to the 1970 U.N. Conference,* Background on Suggested U.S. Initiatives for the U.N. Conference on Science and Technology for Development, Vienna, 1979 (Washington, D.C.: GPO, 1978), p. 5.

Third, it is only appropriate that the developed countries demand a "fair" return for the technology transferred to the developing countries because technology is expensive. The total expended of all countries in 1973 on research and experimental development amounted to $96.4 billion. Of that, $93.6 billion was spent by the developed countries.[29] Also, funds earned from existing technology are needed for the development of new technology. The advanced industrial states, especially the multinational corporations, maintain that survival and growth of their enterprises are dependent on profits often generated by the development and application of new technology. Consequently, bowing to the demands of the developing countries for free or undervalued technology is considered suicidal.

Instead of allowing economic forces to regulate technology flows, the aggressive political activism of the developing countries in their quest for technology is objectionable to many of the advanced industrial states and the multinational corporations. This posture of the developing countries is thought to be counterproductive to the long-term growth interests of the developing countries. The chairman of OECD's Development Assistance Committee has stated that the developing countries "do themselves a disservice by not recognizing more clearly that a further unleashing of the international market mechanism at this juncture is the most promising means for moving toward their goal of a new international economic order."[30] In effect, many in the advanced industrial states feel that developing countries should seek expansion of technology and its application rather than pursue policies that will restrict technology and its transfer to countries needing its benefits.

The interests and concerns of the advanced industrial states coincide largely with those of the multinational corporations that serve as the major conduit for the transfer of technology. They are particularly disturbed by the restrictive practices of the developing countries, ranging from national legislation to the call for international codes of conduct, many of which are considered to inhibit economic activity and efficiency. A growing number of developing countries have adopted laws and created regulatory agencies to control the flow of technology and the payments for such technology. For example, the Andean pact members have made technology transfer payments an important part of their overall regulation of foreign capital.[31] In Brazil, payments for technology are screened by a National Institute on Industrial Property before foreign exchange is released by the central bank.[32] Argentina has a similar law. Mexico, among other countries, recently denied or severely restricted patent protection for pharmaceuticals, fertilizers, pes-

[29]Annerstedt, "On the Global Distribution of R&D Resources," p. 6.

[30]Report of the OECD Development Assistance Committee, John P. Lewis, chairman, "A Possible Scenario for the Development Strategy," OECD Observer, 101 (November 1979), 6. This view was also propounded by President Reagan at the Cancun Conference in 1981.

[31]Chamber of Commerce of the United States, "Technology Transfer," p. 12.

[32]Ibid., p. 12.

ticides, and the like as well as for a variety of chemical and metallurgical processes, antipollution apparatus, and nuclear technology.[33] At the international level, the code of conduct proposed by the developing countries in UNCTAD is seen as a list of "do's and don'ts" for multinational companies. In response, the Chamber of Commerce of the United States has stated in its guiding principles that

> the United States should react to impairment or threats of impairment of industrial property rights of American citizens as it does to the impairment of rights in tangible property.[34]

The developed countries and the multinational corporations sometimes find confusing the apparent contradiction between the often-expressed demands for easier transfer of technology to developing countries and their demands for the strengthening of local capability to innovate and produce or adapt technologies more appropriate to the local environment and markets. The developing countries are seen to be undecided and unclear about their needs and capabilities and consequently frustrate the potential development of adequate technology flows.

The arguments of the developed countries and multinational corporations about technology appear so contrary to those of the developing countries that the two sides appear to be on a no-win path. But an apparent desire to resolve the conflict is reflected in the numerous research studies and conferences at regional and international levels that have occurred in the past decade.

In addition to the disagreement over how the developing countries should react to technology, some groups in the advanced industrial states have serious misgivings about the export of technology from such states. Some in the United States have even agitated for a curb on the export of technology to both developing and developed countries.

Fortune reported that "quite a few U.S. businessmen are beginning to worry that the U.S. is exporting too much technology for its own good . . . [and] that a lot of foreign products incorporating technology acquired from the U.S. are beating out American products in markets around the world— including the U.S. itself."[35] For example, in the field of semiconductor electronics, U.S. corporations developed seventeen or eighteen innovations, twelve of which came from Bell Laboratories. Yet, the U.S. industry and related employment has suffered because corporations have exported their know-how to foreign manufacturers. Currently, the U.S. trade balance in the category of electronic and communications equipment is deeply in the red. The United States has failed to capture as much of the world market

---

[33]Ibid., p. 15.

[34]Ibid., p. 20.

[35]Herbert E. Meyer, "Those Worrisome Technology Exports," *Fortune,* May 22, 1978, p. 106.

as it should in view of its laboratory prowess.[36] Fujitsu, the Japanese computer manufacturer, has received the know-how it needs to help close the technology gap between it and the U.S. computer industry as a result of its investment of about $23 million in Amdahl Corporation, a U.S. computer company founded by a former IBM computer designer.[37]

Along the same lines as the *Fortune* article cited, an academic observer of the technology issue has noted that

> U.S. firms may contribute to both the deterioration of the U.S. trade balance and to the loss of U.S. technical leadership by establishing foreign manufacturing affiliates and by licensing their technology to foreign manufacturers.[38]

Grave concern is expressed about a new generation of technology transfer arrangements to foreign companies in which the U.S. firm holds no equity and over which it has no managerial control. Examples of such arrangements include a commitment by Cummins Engine Company to share its newest generation of diesel engines with Komatsu, its licensing affiliate in Japan and a leading tractor and construction equipment manufacturer;[39] General Electric's joint venture with SNECMA, the French government-controlled manufacturer of military aircraft engines, in 1971, to design ten 15-ton civilian prototypes;[40] and a $223 million contract between General Telephone & Electronics and SONELEC, Algeria, in 1972, to build a completely integrated electronics plant.[41]

Robert Gilpin in *U.S. Power and the Multinational Corporation* argues that the eagerness of U.S. multinationals to invest overseas has seriously damaged the competititve position of the United States.[42] Not only has foreign investment replaced investment at home, but the technological advantage enjoyed and needed by American companies has been reduced sharply through the transfer of technology in its various forms. Thus, U.S. economic and political leadership, as well as domestic economic strength and health, have been seriously compromised. Gilpin calls for a policy that stimulates research and development efforts in the United States but that then seeks to retain the global advantages gained for the benefit of American workers and industry. This neomercantilist view sees a competitive global system, with the United States losing out to other countries because of misguided domestic and international economic policies.

[36]Ibid., p. 108.

[37]Ibid., p. 107.

[38]Jack Baranson, "Technology Exports Can Hurt Us," *Foreign Policy*, No. 25 (Winter 1976–77), 180.

[39]Ibid., p. 181.

[40]Ibid., p. 183.

[41]Ibid., p. 183.

[42]See Robert Gilpin, *U.S. Power and the Multinational Corporation: The Political Economy of Foreign Direct Investment* (New York: Basic Books, 1975).

The most vocal and persistently critical group on the issue of technology transfer is the labor movement. It has spearheaded the verbal assaults on the multinational corporation for excessive transfer of technology. The gist of their protectionist position is that the export of technology, be it in the form of know-how, machinery, or plants, has a long-term damaging effect on the U.S. economy as a whole and on U.S. employment in particular. Earlier chapters discussed American labor's concerns about the effect of American subsidiaries overseas and the "unfair" trade practices of other countries that threatened employment levels in the United States.[43]

The current protectionist stance of U.S. labor is a major shift from labor's position in the 1950s and 1960s, when it advocated freer trade. Then, labor felt that removing impediments to trade facilitated potential growth in U.S. exports, thereby creating more jobs for U.S. workers who enjoyed a substantial technological advantage over workers elsewhere. With the increasing interventions in markets by the developing countries, such as export performance requirements, local content regulations, and technology review boards, U.S. labor has become frustrated and has been pressing both industry and the government to take actions to prevent a loss of U.S. industrial employment.

One reason why labor is disturbed by the export of technology to the developing countries is the latters' tendency to erect high tariff barriers to restrict the inflow of American products based on that technology, once the domestic expertise is developed. A case in point involves light aircraft trade between the United States and Brazil. Until the early 1970s, Brazil was a leading purchaser of light aircraft manufactured in the United States; in 1974, 408 Cessna aircraft were purchased by Brazil. The Brazilian government wanted to create a domestic light aircraft industry and entered into co-production with the Piper Aircraft Corporation to manufacture in Brazil. The Brazilian government later put a 50 percent tax on all imported planes even from Piper. In 1976, Piper Aviacao do Brasil supplied about 75 percent of the domestic Brazilian market, while the United States export market share fell from about 100 percent in 1970 to less than 1 percent in 1976. Moreover, in 1976, the Brazilian Piper subsidiary had begun to export aircraft to Uruguay, Chile, Peru, Colombia, Venezuela, and some African nations. It even sought to sell Brazilian-made planes in the United States.[44] By labor's estimate, the creation of a light aircraft industry in Brazil has damaged employment in the U.S. aircraft industry. Similar developments have occurred in other industries, especially as developing countries established local content regulations for subsidaries of foreign multinationals.

[43]See the discussions on this point in Chapters 2 and 4.

[44]See the National Research Council, *Technology, Trade and the U.S. Economy* (Washington, D.C.: National Academy of Sciences, 1978), pp. 74–75; and Harold W. Berkman and Ivan R. Vernon, *Contemporary Perspectives in International Business* (Chicago: Rand McNally, 1979), p. 138.

INTERNATIONAL ATTEMPTS
TO RESOLVE THE CONFLICTS

As in so many cases described in this book, both the North and the South have legitimate concerns about the other party's point of view. As a result, the conflicts are not easily resolved. Particular problems between a multi-national corporation and a developing country are often settled through negotiations, although in some cases no agreement can be reached. However, there are also major efforts to address, if not resolve, the North-South technology issue in a variety of international settings. UNCTAD has been a pivotal forum for attempts to reach an understanding.

In 1974 the developing nations proposed an International Code of Conduct on Transfer of Technology that sought initially to curtail drastically the concept of ownership of technology. The issue is so sensitive and so linked with other international economic issues that drafts are still being debated. The developing countries feel that mandating technology transfer will provide increased and cheaper access to technology. The advanced industrial states are convinced that practices that undermine the ownership and control of technology by its developers will reduce the transfer of technology, for there will be little incentive to engage in such transfers.

One of the major points of contention is whether the code should be voluntary or mandatory and whether it applies to parent-affiliate relationships. An additional issue is how disputes over technology transfer should be settled. Should there be arbitration, by whom, and whose laws should apply? Some developing countries feel that the country receiving the technology should have the right to choose which set of laws is applicable. On the other hand, the advanced industrial states seek to uphold "commercially sound" principles as a basis for the code, for to do otherwise would retard the transfer of technology. Some parts of the code have been accepted by both parties; others have not. The final outcome is still to be determined.

The Andean Common Market and ASEAN countries have also established their own rules and regulations regarding technology. The Organization of American States has sought to develop an understanding about the different perspectives of advanced and developing countries. The OECD has addressed the issue of technology transfer directly in several ways, including having a section on that issue in its Guidelines for Multinational Enterprises, which was discussed in Chapter 4.

In spite of these and other efforts, the issue of technology transfer is unlikely to be resolved soon. Technology transfer is linked inextricably with the other international political economy issues addressed in this book. In addition, technology is an important part of the demand of the developing countries for a dramatic transfer of resources and wealth from the North to the South. The issues are clear; the different viewpoints are well founded; but the controversy is so linked to different sets of values that its resolution is extraordinarily difficult.

TECHNOLOGY GAPS AMONG
DEVELOPED COUNTRIES

Dissatisfaction with technology gaps has not been limited to the developing countries and the North-South conflict. Advanced industrial states also are concerned about their technological strength, growth potential, and independence. In the mid-1960s, a technology gap emerged as an important political issue among advanced industrial states. Europeans, particularly the French, took note of the seemingly unassailable scientific and technological predominance of the United States relative to other Western states. In the decade 1957–1966, the United States devoted over three times the resources to research and development ($158 billion) as did all the industrialized states of Western Europe combined ($50 billion).[45] From 1951 to 1969, scientists in the United States received twenty-one of thirty-eight Nobel prizes in chemistry and twenty-three of forty Nobel prizes in medicine and physiology.[46] Giant American-based multinational firms such as IBM and Kodak were capable of devoting resources to research and development that were equal in magnitude to the gross sales of their competitors in Europe.[47] Indeed, IBM spent as much on the development of its model 360 computer ($5 billion) as the French government planned to spend on the Force de Frappe, its nuclear deterrent, from 1965 to 1970.[48]

In the 1970s, the Japanese emerged as a technological threat to other advanced industrial states including the United States. As just one example, many view the robotics industry as being critical to the future economic power of an industrial country. Japan has installed 50,000 robots in its industry, a figure that is six to seven times greater than all those in operation elsewhere in the world.[49] Japanese success in this endeavor is the result of a conscious policy of stimulation and cooperation by the Japanese government and its industry. Tax write-offs, special loans for smaller- and medium-sized companies, and government subsidies for robot leasing programs have all served to stimulate this future-oriented high-technology industry while at the same time increasing Japanese competitiveness in world markets.[50]

[45]Organization for Economic Cooperation and Development, *Gaps in Technology*, analytical report (Paris: OECD, 1970), p. 115. During the mid-1960s American expenditures on research and development were fifteen times those of West Germany and ten times those of Britain. Raymond Vernon, *Sovereignty at Bay* (New York: Basic Books, 1971), p. 90.

[46]Vernon, *Sovereignty at Bay*, p. 90.

[47]Kenneth Waltz, "The Myth of National Interdependence," in *The International Corporation*, ed C. Kindleberger (Cambridge, Mass.: M.I.T. Press, 1970), p. 217; and John Dunning, "Technology, United States Investment and European Economic Growth," in *The International Corporation*, p. 165.

[48]Waltz, "The Myth of National Interdependence," p. 217.

[49]Paul Aron, "Robotics in Japan," Paul Aron Report No. 22, July 3, 1980.

[50]See Julian Gresser, "Japanese Government Policies for the Robotics and Machine Tools Industries—The Productivity Problem from Another Perspective," U.S. House, Subcommittee on Trade, Ways and Means Committee, Hearings, Quality of Production and Improvement in the Workplace, 96th Cong., 2nd sess., October 14, 1980.

The international political controversies surrounding these technology gaps are centered in the universal desire of states to exercise control over science and technology, and thus its industrial future as opposed to acquiring it from external sources, however accessible the technology or generous the terms. All states want to harness science and technology to national economic, social, and security policies. This is widely perceived to require national control over research and development, which in turn can be assured only with a broadly based, indigenous science and technology capability. To the extent that a nation lacks this capability, feelings of acute economic vulnerability and outright resentment toward foreign sources of technology are likely to arise. These feelings can lead to severe international tension, particularly in cases where states find it beyond their capacity to produce internally the technology necessary for innovation in economic sectors that are vital to their national autonomy and international economic competitiveness. Just as resource-rich developing countries need the most advanced techniques for processing mineral resources, a country such as France needs the latest computer technology to support its political and economic policies.

Indigenous scientific and technological capability is widely associated with greater power status in world politics. The French, in particular, have made this connection. Robert Gilpin summarizes the French position:

> Today Great Power status accrues only to those nations which are leaders in all phases of basic research and which possess the financial and managerial means to convert new knowledge into advanced technologies. In the case of the two superpowers, eminence in science and technology go hand-in-hand, and it appears unlikely that any nation or group of nations can ever again aspire to a dominant role in international politics without possessing a strong, indigenous scientific and technological capability. International politics has passed from the era of traditional industrial nation states to one dominated by the scientific nation states.[51]

On no occasion was the validity of this general position manifested more clearly to France than in its efforts to develop an independent nuclear force during the 1960s. The vulnerability of even an advanced industrial state that is dependent upon an ally for foreign sources of technology was revealed when the U.S. government initially prohibited the French purchase of certain IBM computers required for its Force de Frappe on the grounds that the nuclear test ban treaty forbade America's assisting a nonnuclear power to obtain nuclear weapons.[52] In the eyes of the French and numerous

[51]Robert Gilpin, *France in the Age of the Scientific State* (Princeton, N.J.: Center of International Studies, Princeton University Press, 1968), p. 25.

[52]Ibid., p. 54. These IBM computers were to be purchased from the French affiliate of IBM. This case is a good example of the political implications of multinational corporations for host state-home state relations. These implications are discussed in Chapter 4 of the present volume.

other states on the wrong side of the technology gap, the achievement of a greater degree of self-sufficiency in science and technology is a prerequisite for the capacity to forge an independent stance in global political and economic relations.

Particularly high stakes seem to be associated with technological dependence upon the United States, or any foreign country, in the field of electronics. Jean-Jacques Servan-Schreiber states the case very dramatically:

> Electronics is not an ordinary industry: it is the base upon which the next stage of industrial development depends. In the nineteenth century the first industrial revolution replaced manual labor by machines. We are now living in the *second industrial revolution,* and every year we are replacing the labor of human brains by a new kind of machinery—computers.
> A country which has to buy most of its electronic equipment abroad will be in a condition of inferiority similar to that of nations in the last century which were incapable of industrializing. Despite their brilliant past, these nations remained outside the stream of civilization. If Europe continues to lag behind in electronics, she could cease to be included among the advanced areas of civilization within a single generation.[53]

Thus, technology gaps have a profound impact on states' economic, political, military, and cultural status. These gaps can produce a visceral reaction in states in which vital national, political, and economic aspirations are perceived to be dependent upon access to foreign technology, for this means that national aspirations are also vulnerable to sabotage by states or corporations beyond national control. As such, technological dependence is an issue that rapidly becomes transformed into one of intense nationalist feelings.

To avoid being merely a technological consumer, many advanced industrial states have adopted policies designed to enhance their technological capability. This is done by positive measures such as state subsidies for research and development, focused educational programs, stimulated purchasing of new technology by companies, and others. However, states have also adopted measures that create disadvantages for technology imports from other countries. "Buy National" provisions that allocate a percentage of local purchases to domestic firms have been introduced in certain industrial sectors in many states including the United States and Japan. One strategy pursued by the Japanese to increase their technological capability after World War II was to keep out imports from other countries so that their firms could become competitive and technologically adept under the protection of the government. European countries are reversing the situation by seeking to limit imports of some products from Japan.

---

[53]Jean-Jacques Servan-Schreiber, *The American Challenge* (New York: Atheneum, 1968), pp. 13–14. Italics in original.

Because of the perceived importance of technology to a country's economic and political strength, technology, like trade, investment, and monetary policy, has become a critical aspect of global economic relations. While the debate among the advanced industrial states may not be as strident as that of the developing countries, their concerns are just as real and have the potential for poisoning relations among allied states jockeying for economic power.

CHAPTER SEVEN
OPEC AND OTHER STRATEGIES FOR STATES IN THE PERIPHERY OF THE GLOBAL POLITICAL ECONOMY

In the view of most observers, less developed countries have failed to maximize their position in global economic and political relations. Why this is true, however, is a matter of dispute. It may be the result of their own social-political-economic choices, or of a conscious policy on the part of advanced industrial states to exploit them over several centuries, or of the rich states' preoccupation with economic relations among themselves and their relative neglect of the impact of these relations on poor states. Whatever the explanation, it is important to examine alternative strategies that less developed countries, acting individually and in concert, can employ to augment their share of the benefits from international economic transactions.[1] Success, of course, implies that Third World countries will simultaneously strengthen their political position in the international arena.

The oil cartel administered through the Organization of Petroleum Exporting Countries (OPEC) is far and away the most successful exercise of leverage among a variety of strategies pursued by states in the periphery of the global political economy. The emergence and impact of OPEC deserves and will receive primary attention in our discussion of alternative strategies

---

[1]Less developed countries' policies toward foreign investment will constitute the focus of this chapter, although other forms of economic transactions, such as trade and aid, will be discussed in passing. Strategies for poor states to secure greater gains from trade were discussed in Chapter 2.

being pursued by Third World states to enhance their international and domestic positions. Yet, it is important to recognize that, for all OPEC's success, it is a technique of applying economic and political leverage that very few less developed states can employ successfully. For this reason a number of other strategies—less dramatic in impact, but applicable to a much broader population of less developed countries—will be outlined. While the strategies are outlined separately, they are related with each other. Less developed countries will sometimes pursue several approaches simultaneously. At other times, states will adopt a particular development and bargaining strategy as a remedy to deficiences revealed in previous experience with a different approach. We will come back to these points at the conclusion of the discussion.

LIBERAL ECONOMIC STRATEGY

If the leadership of a less developed country accepts the basic tenets of liberal economic thought, one way in which to enhance that state's benefits from global economic transactions is simply to attract more of those transactions to it. The strategy here is to forge national policies in a manner designed to exploit the highly sensitive international economic interdependence characterizing the contemporary world.[2] Taking advantage of the sensitivity of multinational corporations to business opportunities all over the globe, a less developed country can occasionally attract foreign capital, increase its exports, and otherwise channel foreign capital and technology in accordance with its national economic priorities by the use of selective economic incentives.[3]

    This strategy has been adopted most successfully by a number of rapidly industrializing less developed countries—such as Brazil, Mexico, Hong Kong, Singapore, Korea, Taiwan, Malaysia, and the Philippines. While there are vast differences among these states, they have all placed great emphasis on outward-oriented growth policies as a means of promoting rapid industrialization. Their policies typically include special tax incentives to local and foreign investors (especially for production of exportable goods); duty-free entry of imports (raw materials, intermediate goods, machinery) necessary for producing goods to be exported; currency devaluations to maintain a competitive position for national production in world markets; income policies designed to keep wages low; and maintenance of an hospitable environment for direct foreign investment.[4] In addition, these countries possess

[2]See Richard Cooper, "Economic Interdependence and Foreign Policy in the Seventies," *World Politics*, 24, no. 2 (January 1972), 159-81.

[3]For a more complete presentation of an "exploitative response" to international economic interdependence, see Cooper, ibid., p. 168.

[4]Organization for Economic Cooperation and Development, *The Impact of the Newly Industrializing Countries* (Paris: OECD, 1979), p. 48.

a disciplined, skilled labor force; an active, indigenous entrepreneurial class; and a stable (often authoritarian) government.[5]

The less developed countries mentioned here have, through these sorts of policies, enjoyed spectacular economic success over the past decade. From 1970 to 1978, their economies grew at an average rate of 7.8 percent per year compared with 4.9 percent for less developed countries as a group and 3.2 percent for advanced industrial states.[6] Their growth in the manufacturing sector averaged 10.3 percent versus 5.9 percent for less developed countries generally and 3.3 percent for advanced industrial states.[7] They are vigorous exporters of a variety of increasingly sophisticated industrial products. Their exports of manufactured goods to Western nations increased 30–50 percent annually during the 1970s.[8] They also account for the bulk of direct foreign investment and private bank loans going to Third World nations in recent years.

These newly industrializing countries obtained their progress primarily through outward-looking growth policies exploiting opportunities afforded by a liberal economic order. Their continued success will depend upon the willingness and capacity of advanced industrial states to make structural adjustments in their domestic economies as the manufacturing and exporting capabilities of the less developed countries expand. The efficacy of these policies as a strategy for growth and industrialization by less developed countries will be undermined if the advanced industrial states stress protection rather than adjustment in their national economies.

The growth and development strategy of these rapidly industrializing states entails certain costs that make it unpopular, or even politically impossible, to sustain in many less developed societies. To maximize a nation's international competitiveness and its attractiveness to foreign investors, a premium is often placed upon ruthlessly imposed political stability and suppression of wages at the expense of domestic economic and social justice. Successful efforts to attract direct foreign investment may result in extensive foreign control over, and denationalization of, the host state's economy. Financing growth and trade deficits through commercial borrowing can lead to staggering debt-service burdens and exposure to intrusion upon domestic political and economic decisions by one's international creditors.

All these criticisms have been leveled against Brazil's economic miracle, for example. The military regime has maintained a tight grip on political life in Brazil. Inequalities in the distribution of income between the richest 5 percent of the population and the rest of the country have increased dur-

---

[5]Ibid.

[6]Calculated from International Bank for Reconstruction and Development, *World Development Report, 1980* (Washington, D.C.: IBRD, 1980), pp. 112-13.

[7]Ibid.

[8]Robert D. Hormats, "The Policy Context," in *Western Economies in Transition*, eds. Irving Leveson and Jimmy W. Wheeler (Boulder, Colo.: Westview Press, 1980), p. 6.

ing the period of rapid economic growth[9]—due largely to a repressive wage structure for laborers. Foreign firms accounted for over 40 percent of Brazil's exports of manufactured goods and a similar proportion of the country's total sales in manufacturing.[10] Foreign firms accounted for an even larger share in overall Brazilian investment.[11] Brazil has accumulated the largest foreign debt of any Third World nation ($55 billion in 1980) through its extensive commercial borrowing.[12] Its debt service equaled 28 percent of Brazil's exports in 1980.[13] As it entered the 1980s, Brazil was approaching limits to its borrowing capacity and was coming under closer scrutiny by the international banking community and the IMF.

Brazil, therefore, exemplifies the best and the worst of the outward-oriented growth strategy followed by a number of rapidly industrializing less developed countries. Its growth in production, industrialization, and exports as well as its access to foreign capital and technology through foreign investment and bank lending make Brazil the envy of the Third World, in some respects. On the other hand, its remarkable economic success has been accompanied by an authoritarian political regime, an erosion of national autonomy, an exacerbation of income inequalities within society, and dependent development.[14] Brazil and the other newly industrializing countries are frequently cited as models of development by liberal analysts, while at the same time radical analysts condemn them.

REGIONAL EFFORTS TO ATTRACT AND REGULATE INVESTMENT

The common investment code of the Andean Common Market is an example of an attempt by six less developed countries[15] to avoid the economic denationalization associated with the Brazilian-type experience while seeking the capital, technology, and services of foreign investors. Through regional integration, these countries hoped to create a unified market that would strengthen their economic and political position in relation to the large states in Latin America (Brazil, Argentina, Mexico) and to advanced industrial states outside the continent.

[9]Werner Baer, "The Brazilian Growth and Development Experience," in *Brazil in the Seventies*, ed. Riordan Roett (Washington, D.C.: American Enterprise Institute, 1976), p. 48.

[10]Peter Evans, *Dependent Development* (Princeton, N.J.: Princeton University Press, 1979), p. 80.

[11]See "Foreign Investment in Brazil: A Survey of the Impact on the Economy," *Business Latin America*, February 18, 1971, p. 52.

[12]*World Business Weekly*, December 8, 1980, p. 29.

[13]IBRD, *World Development Report, 1980*, p. 134.

[14]See Peter Evans, *Dependent Development*, for a thorough discussion of these points.

[15]Peru, Colombia, Ecuador, Bolivia, Venezuela, and Chile (which withdrew in 1975).

Multinational firms are uniquely equipped to take advantage of the opportunities presented by the regional integration efforts—as previous events in Western Europe had indicated. The Andean pact states sought to spur direct foreign investment in manufacturing industries through offering the attractions of a common market. On the other hand, they wanted to prevent loss of control over the course of their national and joint industrialization plans as a consequence of multilateral corporations' policies. A common investment code (Decision 24) of the Andean Common Market was designed to strengthen the bargaining leverage of host states and local firms vis-à-vis multinational corporations operating in the region.[16]

The members of the Andean pact varied greatly in their inclinations and capacities to administer their common investment code. Since the code relies upon national implementation, its effectiveness in controlling multinational corporations fell considerably short of the objectives formulated in 1970.[17] Nevertheless, for most less developed countries, concerted action vis-à-vis foreign investors is likely to offer greater potential than individual action if the aim is both increased investment and more stringent host state regulation. If a single state imposes strict investment controls, multinational corporations sensitive to differences in national regulation of their activities will avoid that state and locate elsewhere in the region.[18] If, on the other hand, a number of states in a region adopt and implement an identical investment code, multinationals that wish to operate in the region will find it much more difficult, perhaps impossible, to avoid the constraints. The connection of such investment controls with movement toward a regional common market is a particularly interesting strategy because the prospect of an integrated regional market, rather than a number of small national markets, may offer the incentive necessary to attract foreign investment even under strict controls.

NATIONALIZATION

The approach of the Andean pact may appear as a halfway measure to economic nationalists in less developed countries. The Andean states are, after all, still interested in attracting foreign investment, albeit under stringent conditions. Nationalization of major foreign operations within the state

[16] The types of controls exercised by the Andean pact states through their common investment code are described in Chapter 4, p. 130.

[17] For an assessment of the investment code's implementation see Lynn K. Mytelka, *Regional Development in a Global Economy* (New Haven, Conn.: Yale University Press, 1979), pp. 62–113.

[18] This is more the case for small states than for larger, more highly developed countries. For example, Mexico has attracted foreign capital quite successfully with investment controls similar in some respects to the Andean investment code. See Chapter 4 for a more detailed discussion of controls imposed on foreign investors by host states.

is sometimes prescribed as a more appropriate strategy for an individual less developed country in its attempts to increase its share of benefits from global economic relations. The strategy of nationalization, usually on a highly selective basis, is likely to appear most attractive to those less developed countries in which government revenues are generated largely from exports of primary products whose extraction and international sales are controlled by foreign capital.

This is true for several reasons. Foreign-owned extractive enterprises engaged in the exploitation and shipment abroad of finite natural resources give the appearance of removing national wealth rather than creating it, as a manufacturing enterprise does. Thus, foreign investment in extractive industry is particularly resented in less developed countries, and it is more prone to nationalization than is foreign investment in the manufacturing sector, for example.[19] In addition, the return on foreign direct investment in extractive industries is typically much higher than is the return on investment in manufacturing industries.[20] Even though the host state's share of earnings from extractive enterprises controlled by foreign capital has increased substantially over the years, host states have a compelling urge to nationalize these enterprises and to acquire *all* the earnings from these particularly lucrative investments. This movement is certain to gain strength as the limits to available mineral resources are appreciated throughout the globe and as the prices of these products begin to reflect this fact.

The nationalization of foreign investments in extractive enterprise is an extraordinarily appealing strategy for those less developed countries fortunate enough to possess major supplies of primary products.[21] Nationalization holds the promise of increased government revenues and foreign exchange earnings in a way that appears to reduce the dependence of a poor state upon rich states and the multinational corporations operating from them. This policy has immense domestic political appeal in those less developed countries in which the general population is highly sensitive to dependence upon, and perceived expoitation by, rich states and foreign firms.

Seductive as this policy may be for less developed countries, it does not necessarily result either in increased revenues or in reduced dependence upon multinational firms. Unless a number of special circumstances

[19]Stephen Kobrin found that, in states expropriating only the most sensitive foreign investments, extractive industries accounted for 59 percent of all takeovers. Manufacturing investments accounted for only 11 percent of all expropriations by these states. See his "Foreign Enterprise and Forced Divestment in the Less Developed Countries," *International Organization*, 34, no. 1 (Winter 1980), 77.

[20]See U.S. Congress, Senate Committee on Finance, *Implications of Multinational Firms for World Trade and Investment and for U.S. Trade and Labor,* 93rd Cong., 1st sess., 1973, p. 445.

[21]We will focus our discussions of nationalization on extractive industry since this is such a salient export sector to many Third World states. It is very difficult to analyze the pros and cons of nationalization with any precision unless one focuses on particular economic sectors or products.

are present, nationalizing local production of primary products for sale abroad is likely to place a less developed country in the unenviable position of being a supplier of last resort. As a result, it faces great uncertainty in the amount of its export earnings and government revenues from year to year. Moreover, it is also likely to remain as dependent upon multinational corporations for marketing the product internationally as it had been dependent upon them previously for production of the primary product.[22]

The production and sales of most mineral resources, such as petroleum, copper, tin, nickel, and aluminum, are typically controlled by an oligopoly of vertically integrated multinational corporations that are at once the major producers *and* the major consumers of the mineral resource. Vertical integration is a compelling goal of large enterprises that seek to avoid risk either as suppliers or as consumers of mineral resources. A firm that begins as a producer of, say, copper creates affiliates that process and/ or fabricate products from the mineral in an effort to assure its sales of copper in a buyer's market. A firm that begins as a producer of finished goods requiring massive amounts of copper inputs creates affiliates to produce copper itself in an effort to assure its supply of the mineral in a seller's market.[23] This behavior results ultimately in the oligopolistic control of international markets in mineral resources, a condition faced by almost any less developed country contemplating nationalization of foreign-owned extractive industry. This situation often reduces the efficacy of nationalization as a strategy to enhance the economic returns and national autonomy of a less developed country possessing valuable mineral resources.

Nationalization is likely to bring a steady increase of economic returns to a less developed country to the extent that (1) the stage of production represented by a foreign firm's operations in the country is the greatest barrier of entry into the vertically integrated production and sales process,[24] (2) the state that nationalizes the foreign firm either continues to cooperate with, and participate within, the oligopoly controlling international distribution of the mineral resource[25] or to develop an international distribution capability of its own—one that is seen by refiners, fabricators, and consumers of the mineral as a dependable source of supply at stable prices.[26]

---

[22] In addition to these problems, one must also take into account the effect that nationalization of extractive industry might have on efforts to attract foreign investment in other economic sectors or efforts to secure international loans. The discussion that follows relies heavily upon the work of Theodore Moran. In particular, see "New Deal or Raw Deal in Raw Materials," *Foreign Policy*, No. 5 (Winter 1971-72), 119–36; "Transnational Strategies of Protection and Defense by Multinational Corporations: Spreading the Risk and Raising the Cost for Nationalization in Natural Resources," *International Organization*, 27, no. 2 (Spring 1973), 273–88; and *Multinational Corporations and the Politics of Dependence: Copper in Chile* (Princeton, N.J.: Princeton University Press, 1974).

[23] Moran, "New Deal or Raw Real in Raw Materials," pp. 122–23.

[24] Ibid., pp. 124–27.

[25] Ibid., pp. 129–31.

[26] Moran, *Multinational Corporations*, p. 242.

Unless these circumstances prevail, the state that nationalizes foreign-controlled extractive operations will find itself a supplier of last resort, because multinational firms will seek "safer" sources of supply, even at higher cost.

If the stage of production represented by the foreign firms' operations within a particular less developed country is not the greatest barrier of entry into the vertically integrated production and sales process, nationalization of the foreign operations will not result in increased revenues or in control over marketable production of the mineral for international consumers. If alternate sources of supply of the mineral can be developed, the multinational firm whose mining operations are nationalized will develop them. Even if these alternate deposits are more expensive to develop, they will be attractive to multinational firms seeking to avoid risk in securing supplies of the mineral. Thus, in response to the threat of nationalization of their mining operations in Chile and other areas, large corporations in the copper industry have recently focused their efforts on extracting copper from lower-grade ore deposits in more "secure" areas of the world, such as Australia, Canada, and the United States.[27] Copper is a mineral resource for which access to unprocessed reserves is the greatest barrier of entry to a vertically integrated production and sales process. Even so, after nationalizing foreign-based copper industries in 1971, Chile faced the loss of its major consumers and thus, reduced economic returns from its international sales of copper. Attempts at nationalization by less developed countries to maximize revenues from international sales of other mineral resources, such as aluminum and tin, are even less likely to succeed over the long run because the greatest barrier of entry to the vertically integrated production and sales of these minerals is possession of highly sophisticated processing technology and immense amounts of capital, not access to ore deposits.[28]

The other major requirement a less developed country must meet to sustain increases in economic returns from the nationalization of extractive industry is to maintain its reputation as a dependable supplier of the mineral to consumers abroad. This means continued participation within the international oligopoly of multinational firms which often control the bulk of international sales of mineral resources. In this way, the production of the nationalized operation continues to enjoy a sustained volume of sales at controlled price levels in international markets. Unless this is accomplished, or unless the less developed country develops an international sales network of its own that is just as dependable in supplying the mineral at steady price levels, the income generated from nationalizing production is likely to be reduced or very uneven from year to year.[29] The development

[27] Ibid., pp. 32–33. For an interesting discussion of the corporate strategy employed by Kennecott in anticipation of and defense against nationalization of its operations in Chile, see Moran, "Transnational Strategies of Protection and Defense by Multinational Corporations."

[28] Moran, "New Deal or Raw Deal in Raw Materials," p. 126.

[29] Ibid., pp. 129–33; and Moran, *Multinational Corporations,* pp. 240–41.

of its own sales and distribution network is often beyond a less developed country's economic capacity or administrative skills; it is, in addition, always a long-term enterprise. The threat of interrupting supplies for political purposes is, in any case, not compatible with maximizing earnings from nationalized production over the long run. Thus, the country that nationalizes foreign-controlled production of its mineral resources finds that it must continue to cooperate with the same firms, or with firms similar to those it nationalizes at home, for the sales of its products abroad.

These facts pose a major dilemma for less developed countries attempting both to maximize revenues from sales abroad and to reduce dependence upon multinational corporations (and their parent states) by nationalization of local operations of extractive industry. The government that chooses this policy will usually have to decide which of these goals to pursue, since they tend to be mutually exclusive. Policies designed to obtain steadily increasing, or even stable, economic returns from international sales of nationalized mineral exploitation require cooperation with, and continued dependence upon, multinational corporations. But this is politically difficult and often unacceptable for a regime whose domestic support rests upon its confrontation with foreign firms over the production and sale of these economic resources. Refusal to cooperate with multinational firms may minimize dependence upon them (and their parent states), but a less developed country will thereby most likely suffer great fluctuations in its receipts from international sales. The regime may feel that a redistribution of income within the country and a sense of national identity and pride accompanying nationalization are more than adequate compensation for the loss of stable or increased export earnings. Our point, however, is simply that nationalization of foreign capital in local extractive industry seldom results in *both* increased revenues and reduced dependence upon foreign firms.

However, if global demand for a particular mineral resource continually exceeds production and if there are no economically feasible synthetic or natural substitutes, certain less developed countries may find success in nationalization without risking continued dependence upon foreign firms for international sales. To the extent that the world begins to approach the limits of global mineral resources, such a situation could conceivably emerge in regard to numerous products in the not too distant future. At present, petroleum is the product enjoying this market situation, but even in this case the oil-producing states have pursued a strategy that differs in several crucial respects from unilateral nationalization of the sort we have been discussing.

This analysis of nationalization as a strategy for less developed countries suggests in most cases that it is not likely to produce all the results that at first glance make it attractive to economic nationalists. We have focused upon nationalization of extractive industry, but our basic argument can, with minor adjustments, be applied to the nationalization of numerous types of production marketed internationally. Of course, a very different situation and calculus exist with regard to the efficacy of nationalization of foreign firms that produce only for consumption within the domestic market of a less developed country.

COMMODITY PRODUCER CARTELS:
THE EXTRAORDINARY CASE OF OIL

If, in general, nationalization of foreign-controlled extractive industry by individual less developed countries has little chance of yielding all the benefits claimed, unified action by a group of less developed countries that together possess the major deposits of the same mineral resource should offer greater hope of success. In this case, the strategy involves concerted action by major producer states confronting an industry or oligopoly as a whole, rather than a single producer state confronting only the firm (or firms) located within its borders. If less developed countries possessing the major sources of a particular mineral resource can maintain a common front vis-à-vis all the major multinationals in that industry, none of these states can be relegated to the position of a supplier of last resort. Collectively, they would still be able to exert considerable weight in international distribution and sales. This is, of course, the strategy that has been employed so successfully by oil-producing states since 1970.

The oil-producing states were in a very weak bargaining position relative to the international oil industry prior to 1970. The seven giant oil majors (Exxon, Texaco, Mobil, Standard of California, Gulf, Shell, and British Petroleum) dominated international oil markets. These firms determined both the level of production and the price for oil in virtually all oil-producing states. Throughout the postwar period until about 1970, there was a substantial surplus of oil relative to global demand. As a result, the posted price of oil, upon which the producing states' royalties and tax revenues were based, remained very low. Indeed, in 1959, oil firms imposed a *reduction* in the posted price of oil from all oil-producing states. This act prompted the creation of OPEC in 1960.[30] Less developed oil-producing states heavily dependent upon oil export receipts vowed to oppose, through OPEC, any future attempts by the international oil firms to reduce their oil revenues. Joint action was imperative because any oil-producing state confronting the international oil industry alone risked reduction of its oil output and revenues. The international firms could freeze "troublemakers" out of world markets since they controlled production and marketing net-

---

[30]OPEC is composed of Iran, Iraq, Kuwait, Saudi Arabia, Venezuela (the original members), Indonesia, Algeria, Libya, Nigeria, Ecuador, Qatar, Abu Dhabi, Dubai, Sharjah, and Gabon.

works throughout the non-Communist world and had access to alternative sources of crude oil supplies in numerous countries. OPEC's activities had little economic or political impact for the first decade of its existence, however, in the face of abundant global oil supplies.

The convergence of several developments enabled the oil-producing states to wrest control of pricing and production of their oil from the international oil firms in the early 1970s.[31] During this period, all the advanced industrial states in the West were enjoying economic prosperity and were operating simultaneously near the peak of their business cycles. This extraordinary level of aggregate economic activity placed immense pressure on existing global oil production. The international oil market that was characterized previously by great surpluses became very tight.

At about the same time, America's voracious consumption of oil began to exceed its capacity to supply its needs from domestic production. The United States lost its virtual self-sufficiency in petroleum production in the late 1960s and was forced to enter world markets for oil purchases in increasing amounts yearly.

The oil-producing states in the Middle East occupied the pivotal position in the world oil market of the early 1970s. Middle Eastern production costs could not be matched anywhere. The region accounted for approximately 40 percent of the world's oil production, and it provided the logical location for future expansion of oil production as 60 percent of proven global oil reserves were located there.

These dramatic developments in the global energy picture at the end of the 1960s had been preceded by a gradual, and exceedingly important, alteration in the structure of the international oil industry. During the 1950s and 1960s, the oil majors that had long dominated international petroleum markets found themselves in vigorous competition with oil independents (such as Occidental, Marathon, Hunt, and Getty) seeking to develop access to their own supplies of crude oil.[32] The independent oil companies were able to secure concessions alongside the oil majors as new oil fields were developed and expanded rapidly over the course of the 1950s and 1960s in states such as Algeria and Libya. In short, the number of important firms in the international oil industry was expanding. The oil majors were less firmly in control of the oligopolistic international oil market that they had dominated successfully for decades.

---

[31] The discussion that follows is treated in greater detail in numerous publications. Two brief recitals of these events are Edith Penrose, "The Development of a Crisis," in *The Oil Crisis*, ed. Raymond Vernon (New York: W. W. Norton, 1976), pp. 39–57; and John M. Blair, *The Control of Oil* (New York: Pantheon, 1976), pp. 211–34.

[32] The oil independents were following the traditional pattern of vertical integration, seen so frequently in the emergence of multinational corporations (see the section on Nationalism). Price competition between the oil majors and the independents led directly to the reduction in oil prices of 1959 that spurred the creation of OPEC.

Against this backdrop of developments Qaddafi, the aggressive new leader of Libya, made a bold move in 1970 to renegotiate the terms governing the oil industry's development of Libya's oil concessions. His success set in motion a chain of events that culminated in OPEC's dramatic assertion of control over oil pricing and production in just three years (after a decade of frustration and impotence).

Qaddafi took advantage of Libya's unique attractiveness as an oil exporter in the tight oil market of 1970. He argued that the price of Libyan oil should be increased and maintained above the price of Persian Gulf oil (including production from Iraq, Iran, Kuwait, Saudi Arabia, and others) because (1) Libyan crude has a very low sulfur content, making it especially attractive to refiners and consumers of heating oil in Western economies facing strict environmental standards, and (2) Libyan oil was far more economical to deliver to markets in Europe and the United States than was Persian Gulf oil, which, after 1967 and the closure of the Suez Canal, had to be shipped all the way around the continent of Africa. Accordingly, Qaddafi demanded an increase in Libyan oil prices and threatened to shut in Libyan oil production to sustain the price increase, if necessary (i.e., he sought greater revenues through a lower volume of output at higher prices, thus conserving Libya's oil reserves). In early 1970, oil companies in Libya were told to raise the posted price of oil they produced there or face confiscation of their Libyan oil operations. The oil firms were extremely vulnerable to pressure from Qaddafi, not only because of Libya's market position, but also because of the deep divisions within the international oil industry between the independents and the majors.

Both the independents and the majors operated concessions in Libya. The independents such as Hunt, Occidental, Continental, and Marathon had little alternative but to accede to Qaddafi's demands. They controlled few or no alternative sources of crude oil outside of Libya and, hence, could not afford to risk the loss of their Libyan concessions. The oil majors (such as Exxon, Mobil, and British Petroleum), on the other hand, had numerous alternatives to their Libyan crude supplies. Giving in to Qaddafi's demands would invite all other oil-producing states in which the majors operated to raise similar demands for revenue increases and for a voice in determining production levels. The oil majors' access to alternative supplies of crude oil and the prospect of having to renegotiate their numerous concessions elsewhere gave them the capability and the incentive to orchestrate oil industry resistance to Qaddafi's demands.

A common front by the oil companies against Libyan demands proved impossible to sustain, however, because of the differing vulnerabilities and interests of the oil majors and independents. Exploiting this division, Qaddafi successfully negotiated a price increase with Occidental Petroleum—a particularly vulnerable independent international oil firm that relied almost totally upon its Libyan concession for crude oil. With this break in the ranks, other oil independents and majors in Libya quickly followed Occidental's precedent in renegotiating the terms of their oil concessions.

As the oil majors feared, Libya's success prompted other oil-producing states in the Middle East to demand price increases for their oil production as well. The oil majors were caught in a cycle of leap-frogging demands between Libya and other oil-producing states on the Persian Gulf. If the Middle Eastern oil-producing states secured price increases, the price premium Libya demanded for the lower transportation costs and lower sulfur content of its oil would be negated. Middle Eastern producer states' success, therefore, would generate a new round of Libyan efforts to renegotiate its oil prices. This, in turn, would prompt Middle Eastern producers to renegotiate, and so on.

To avoid this terrifying prospect, the oil industry as a whole took the unprecedented move of engaging all the oil-producing states in the Persian Gulf and North Africa in comprehensive, multilateral negotiations to establish a mutually acceptable, stable price structure for oil. These efforts culminated in the Teheran and Tripoli Agreements of 1971, which called for an increase in the posted price of oil from $1.80 to $2.50 per barrel with orderly annual price increases of 2½ percent through 1975.

Unfortunately for the international oil industry, events during 1972 and 1973 outran the Teheran and Tripoli Agreements. Global demand for oil pushed actual market prices higher than the posted prices negotiated in 1971. Devaluations of the dollar in 1971 and 1973 meant a loss of real earnings for the oil-producing states, which received payment for oil exports in dollars. The OPEC countries scheduled a meeting with the oil industry for October 1973 to revise price levels to take account of these unanticipated developments in the oil market following the Teheran and Tripoli Agreements. Of course, in October 1973 the world also witnessed the outbreak of war in the Middle East. Arab oil-producing states shortly thereafter imposed a selective embargo of oil shipments to the United States, the Netherlands, and Portugal in retaliation for their support of Israel in the war. The embargo and concomitant production cutbacks tightened global petroleum markets even further and introduced great uncertainty throughout the world about assured access to uninterrupted supplies of oil. Oil-importing states responded by competing frantically for oil deliveries at ever higher prices. At the end of 1973, all OPEC states (Arab and non-Arab) took advantage of this volatile market situation to impose a fourfold increase in the posted price of oil to $11.67 per barrel.

This extraordinary series of events in the early 1970s constituted a revolution in world oil markets. The oil firms that had traditionally maintained unilateral control over oil prices and production levels found themselves unable to do so any longer. Changes in the structure of the international oil industry brought about by the rise of independents, and a very tight oil market altered fundamentally the bargaining strength between the industry and oil-producing states. The Teheran and Tripoli Agreements initiated by the oil industry to assure market stability revealed, instead, a new-found strength for oil-producing states after decades of impotence. Within the next two years, through OPEC the oil-producing states were able to determine unilaterally prices and production levels for their crude oil entering world markets.

In addition to securing control over pricing and production levels, the oil-producing states systematically assumed majority or complete national ownership of the companies' crude oil concessions within their jurisdiction. While they pushed the oil multinationals into a minority equity position, they did so without forcing the firms to disengage from the oil-producing states. The companies surrendered their exclusive equity position, but remained for the time being as operators of their previous concessions and continued to distribute and market much of the OPEC states' oil internationally. In this way, the producing states gained national control over their natural resources while still securing the benefits of the oil corporations' technological expertise, managerial skills, capital, and distribution and sales networks. Sheik Yamani, the Saudi Arabian Minister of Oil and Minerals, referred to the post-1970 arrangements between OPEC states and the oil industry as a "catholic marriage between the producer countries on the one hand and the consumers and the major or independent oil companies on the other hand by linking them to a state where it is almost impossible for any of them to divorce."[33] It was clearly a marriage, however, that the producing states forced upon reluctant partners and in which they hold the upperhand. Oil industry officials have referred to it as a "shotgun wedding."[34]

These arrangements differ significantly from the nationalization efforts outlined previously. The traditional form of nationalization seeks to expel selectively foreign firms from the host state, whereas OPEC states seek to exploit them. Nationalization leads to open conflict with foreign firms upon which the less developed countries often depend for new technology, capital mobilization, and international sales. OPEC states have been able to forge continued cooperation between themselves and the multinational investors at all stages of the production and sales process. The host states remain firmly in control of the terms of the relationship since the oil firms are hostage in the short and medium terms to the OPEC states' crude oil supplies.

Political-Economic-Security Impacts of OPEC Success

Their assumption of control over production and pricing in international petroleum markets introduced massive alterations in the global political economy and, of course, enhanced immensely the political and

---

[33]*The New York Times*, October 8, 1972, Sec. 3, p. 7.
[34]Ibid., Sec. 4, p. 3.

TABLE 7-1 Global Distribution of Oil Reserves, Production, and Consumption—1980 (Percentage of World Total in parenthesis)

Country/Region	Oil Reserves[a] (billions of barrels)		Oil Production[b] (millions of barrels per day)		Oil Consumption[c] (millions of barrels per day)	
OPEC	431	(66)	27.3	(44)	NA[d]	
Middle East	354	(55)	18.8	(30)	1.6	(3)
United States	26	(4)	8.6	(14)	16.4	(26)
West Europe	23	(4)	2.6	(4)	14.0	(23)
Japan	—[e]	(0)	—[e]	(0)	5.0	(8)
Communist states	86	(13)	14.6	(23)	12.7	(21)
Others	83	(13)	9.5	(15)	12.0	(19)
World total	649	(100)	62.6	(100)	61.7	(100)

[a]*Oil and Gas Journal*, December 29, 1980, pp. 78-79.
[b]*BP Statistical Review of the World Oil Industry, 1980*, (London: British Petroleum Corporation, 1981), p. 6.
[c]Ibid, p. 8.
[d]Not available in these data. Included in "Others".
[e]Negligible.

economic salience of OPEC states. The dominance of OPEC states in global oil reserves, production, and trade can be seen from the data presented in Table 7-1. Two-thirds of the world's oil reserves and 44 percent of the world's oil production are accounted for by OPEC. The Middle Eastern and North African OPEC states occupy a particularly important role in the global oil picture and within OPEC—these states possess about 90 percent of OPEC's oil reserves and generate over three-fourths of OPEC's oil production. During the late 1970s Western Europe and Japan relied upon oil imports from OPEC states in the Middle East and Africa for over 75 percent of their oil consumption.[35] The United States met over 25 percent of its oil needs from these OPEC states.[36]

Since 1973, the OPEC states have exploited their dominance over global oil supplies by raising the price of their oil fifteenfold in seven years. These price increases, sustained by production shut-ins when necessary, have produced the largest "peacetime" international transfer of wealth in history. OPEC revenues from oil exports, which amounted to $15 billion in 1972, were running over $300 billion a year by 1980. Between 1974 and 1980, a handful of OPEC states had accumulated well over $300 billion in financial surpluses—international reserves in *excess* of their purchases of goods and services abroad.[37] Of course, these OPEC payments surpluses

[35]American Petroleum Institute, *Petroleum Industry Statistics*, (Washington, D.C.: API, July 1978), Section X, Table 5.

[36]Ibid., Section XIV, Table 3.

[37]*World Business Weekly*, November 3, 1980, p. 29. These oil revenue surpluses are concentrated in the OPEC states with large production capacity and low population—Saudi Arabia, Kuwait, Qatar, Libya, and the United Arab Emirates. Saudi Arabia alone had accumulated financial surpluses of approximately $120 billion (*World Business Weekly*, November 3, 1980, p. 33). It is important to note that during the late 1970s half of the OPEC states operated with payments deficits in spite of increased oil revenues.

must be reflected in huge payments deficits for oil-importing states. America's oil import bills, for example, increased from $4.8 billion in 1972 to $80 billion in 1980. This has been a key factor in America's persistent balance-of-trade deficits throughout the 1970s.

Domestically, these jumps in oil prices have increased inflation dramatically, produced wrenching imbalances among various sectors of the economy, and retarded economic growth. OPEC's financial gains from international oil sales are, therefore, obtained at high domestic and international costs to America and the rest of the world. The staggering global impact of OPEC's financial success is perhaps most apparent when we recognize that the United States is better equipped to absorb and minimize these international and domestic economic shocks than is any other country in the world.

The dramatic, intermittent price increases for OPEC oil confronting all oil-importing states have followed a well-established pattern since 1973. Oil consumers have competed with each other in frenzied pursuit of oil at virtually any price during periods when an unanticipated reduction in oil production occurs in a major oil-exporting country for any length of time. A tight international oil market, maintained by OPEC production shut-ins, amplifies the effect of short-term price escalations accompanying uncertainties in oil deliveries. When OPEC states see frenzied competition among consumers generating short-term price escalation, they capture and perpetuate the "temporary" panic market by formally raising the posted price of oil governing their longer-term oil contracts. For example, the posted price of Saudi Arabian oil increased relatively slightly from $11.65 per barrel in 1974 to $14.34 per barrel on January 1, 1979. During 1979, however, domestic turmoil in Iran, which resulted in the Shah's departure and continued long after Khomeini's assumption of power, reduced Iranian oil production and exports abruptly. In the face of this unanticipated shortage of global oil supplies, prices for oil in the "spot" market (auctions of discrete lots of oil to the highest bidder, unlike longer-term contractual oil sales at posted prices) in 1979 shot up to $40 per barrel. The OPEC states, arguing that spot market prices indicated clearly that the posted price of oil was too low, responded by more than doubling their posted prices of oil. By January 1, 1981 Saudi Arabian oil under long-term contract sold at $32 a barrel (versus $14.34 two years earlier).

The same dynamic occurred in 1973 during the Arab oil embargo, when oil prices were increased fourfold. We can expect OPEC states to increase oil prices dramatically whenever any disturbance involving major oil-producing states induces desperate consumers to push the spot market price for oil far above the established OPEC price level. This pattern creates grave concern because regime instability and international conflicts pose a constant threat to most OPEC states in the Middle East.

The pattern described here is likely to repeat itself in the future, notwithstanding the existence of some periods during which pressures on the global oil market soften. During 1981, for example, oil prices softened as a result of economic recession in most advanced industrial states, increased conservation in the face of oil price increases in 1979, and Saudi Arabia's policy of producing oil in quantities well above its normal production ceiling. Such periods may lead to Western perceptions of a substantially decreased vulnerability to OPEC oil leverage. Yet Western economic recovery and a Saudi Arabian decision to limit production for any number of conceivable economic or political reasons can quickly restore world oil markets to that precarious balance between supply and demand that produces dramatic price increases in the face of disturbances affecting major oil-producing states.

Through price increases, OPEC's massive accumulation of wealth and financial surpluses has placed immense burdens of adjustment on states throughout the global economy. In the process OPEC has gained great potential to exercise additional international influence. Their quotas in the IMF have been doubled, and, as we saw in Chapter 3, IMF capital needs in the 1980s are likely to be met only by accommodating the central political-economic interests of Saudi Arabia and other key OPEC states.

Oil producers with financial surpluses have deposited most of their assets in Western banks. Any wholesale movements of these reserves into and out of the major international currencies can wreak havoc on exchange rates and national economies. This gives them substantial leverage over Western states. Precipitous removal of Saudi Arabia's $45 billion deposited in the United States in 1980 would, for example, have resulted in a collapse of the dollar's value in international markets. On the other hand, such a move would also have resulted in substantial losses for Saudi Arabia, 80 percent of whose international reserves are held in dollar assets around the globe. So, while foreign assets accumulated by OPEC states provide them with potential leverage over Western states, these assets also leave the oil-producing states exposed to potential counterpressure from the West. Iran certainly found this to be the case when it threatened to remove its billions of dollar-assets from American banks as part of its economic and political warfare with the United States in 1979. President Carter responded by freezing all Iranian deposits in American institutions. The seizure of these exposed Iranian finances later provided critical leverage for securing the release of diplomats held hostage in Teheran. Oil wealth deposited abroad is a double-edged sword for OPEC countries.

The dramatic success of OPEC since 1973 is one of those seismic events in world affairs that affects directly virtually all dimensions of international political activity. Among other things, OPEC has intensified the sharpness of the Third World's demands for a new international economic order

(NIEO), it has introduced severe strains among the Western allies over energy policy and diplomacy in the Middle East, and it has thrust the Persian Gulf region into the forefront of America's security concerns.

Most Third World countries took great pleasure in seeing the non-Western oil-producing states of OPEC wrest control over the international oil market from Western states and their oil multinationals. It marked an end to the West's previous domination of virtually every important dimension of international economic exchange. The OPEC states moved quickly and adroitly to cement ties with the Third World states by using their oil power to press the long-standing demands for international economic reform of importance to all less developed countries. (We have already examined the less developed countries' concerns in the areas of trade, aid, investment, and monetary relations.)

Just months after the oil price hikes and the Arab oil embargo of 1973, OPEC states led the call for convening a special session of the United Nations General Assembly to address the problems of raw materials and development. At this session was passed the U.N.'s "Declaration on Establishment of a New International Economic Order" of interest to all Third World states. OPEC states declined Western initiatives during 1974 to negotiate an orderly oil production and pricing scheme for the sake of reducing turmoil in the international economy. Instead, the OPEC states succeeded in creating a negotiating forum including other Third World states as well as the Western states and OPEC. These negotiations were based on an expanded agenda that addressed the gamut of less developed countries' commodity trade, industrialization, and international financing interests in addition to oil production and pricing. The OPEC states linked the threat of further oil price increases in late 1975 to the Western states' willingness to negotiate seriously with the Third World within this larger framework. These negotiations took place in Paris in the form of a specially created Council on International Economic Cooperation (CIEC) that functioned from late 1975 through early 1977. While the substantive accomplishments were modest, it was within the CIEC framework that the Western states agreed to create and contribute to the Common Fund as part of UNCTAD's Integrated Program for Commodities (see Chapter 2).

OPEC states also initiated economic assistance programs for less developed countries amounting to over $5 billion per year by the late 1970s. At these levels, OPEC aid, as a percentage of the donors' GNP, was several orders of magnitude higher than Western aid during the same period. Even though OPEC aid has been concentrated primarily in a half dozen states with large Moslem populations and amounts to only a small fraction of the increased import bills that less developed countries must now pay for oil, the initiation of these aid efforts has helped OPEC to retain good relations with Third World countries.

Through all these activities OPEC has managed to forge a loose economic coalition with Third World states and to provide the cutting edge in their dialogue with Western states over international economic reforms. Yet the concrete financial burden placed upon oil-importing less developed countries by OPEC's price increases will certainly introduce severe strains on this relationship. For example, Brazil's oil imports increased from $4.2 billion in 1979 to $10.5 billion in 1980 due to oil price increases imposed by OPEC. These financial burdens aggravated an already imposing foreign debt challenge facing Brazil. Taken as a whole, less developed countries' oil import bills doubled between 1978 and 1980 when they rose to $50 billion. The current account deficits and debt accumulation by these states, due largely to higher oil prices, were examined in Chapter 3. However, Third World states are unlikely to challenge OPEC openly in spite of these burdens, because Western nations have given little indication that less developed countries can expect additional economic assistance to meet their increasing energy and development needs by joining Western efforts to oppose OPEC.

The pivotal position of the Middle East in international oil markets since 1973 has altered Western states' diplomacy dramatically vis-à-vis the region and opened up deep cleavages among the advanced industrial states. Through implementation of their embargo in 1973 against the United States, the Netherlands, and Portugal along with production cutbacks, the Arab oil-producing states demonstrated their capacity to employ the oil weapon with political success. European and Japanese dependence on oil supplies from the region since that time has led them to virtually embrace the Arab position in the conflict with Israel to assure uninterrupted access to oil. The United States, whose imports from the Middle East and Arab states in North Africa have increased substantially over the course of the 1970s (see Figure 7-1), moved from a clearly pro-Israeli position in the 1960s to that of a mediator between Israel and Arab states between 1973 and 1976. Under the Carter administration, the United States became an active participant in forging an Israeli-Egyptian bilateral peace treaty and a framework for a more comprehensive Arab-Israeli agreement. OPEC's success in 1973 and since has permanently altered politics in the area.

Asymmetries in the degree of dependence upon Middle Eastern oil have rendered deep cleavages between the United States and its Western allies. The United States is a major producer of oil with only about 16 percent of its oil needs met from Middle Eastern and North African supplies. Moreover, immense reserves of coal and oil shale provide America with viable potential alternatives to OPEC oil in the long term. In contrast, Europe and Japan rely upon imports from this region for over three-fourths of their oil needs and do not possess fossil fuel alternatives in abundance as is the case for America. These differences have led European states and

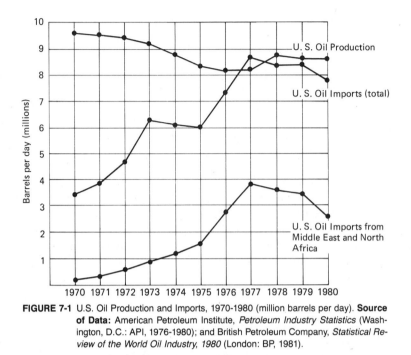

FIGURE 7-1 U.S. Oil Production and Imports, 1970-1980 (million barrels per day). **Source of Data:** American Petroleum Institute, *Petroleum Industry Statistics* (Washington, D.C.: API, 1976-1980); and British Petroleum Company, *Statistical Review of the World Oil Industry, 1980* (London: BP, 1981).

Japan to shy away from bold challenges to OPEC or to important oil-producing states in the Middle East, which the United States has sought on occasion. Such was the case of the unwillingness of Japan and the European states to apply stringent economic sanctions in support of the United States during its confrontation with Iran over the seizure of American diplomatic personnel as hostages between 1979 and 1981.

More generally, it is important to note that, in the Middle Eastern war of 1973 and in the Iranian revolution in 1979, the United States, not Europe or Japan, has been the primary target of OPEC states' threatening to use supply interruptions as a political weapon. It is not surprising that America's allies would attempt to put some distance between themselves and the United States in its Middle Eastern confrontations, given their greater dependence on Middle Eastern oil and the fact that the United States has typically been the target of oil states' wrath, not they. Differences in energy vulnerability and in preferred political/economic/military strategies in the Middle East will continue to create major strains among the Western allies. That is an important legacy of the strength demonstrated by oil-producing states since 1973.

While the United States enjoys considerably more flexibility than do its major allies on energy matters, it remains extremely vulnerable to shocks from oil-producing states in the Middle East. America's reliance upon oil imports and especially imports from the Middle East can be seen in Figure 7-1. At the time of the Arab oil embargo in 1973, the United States imported 36 percent of its oil needs and only 17 percent of its imports came from the Middle East and North Africa. At the peak of its vulnerability in 1977, America met 47 percent of its oil needs through imports. The Middle East and North African states supplied 43 percent of America's imports (19 percent of its total oil consumption). Indeed, the United States in 1980 relied upon the particularly unstable Persian Gulf states for 30 percent of its oil imports.

The oil-rich region lies in the shadow of the Soviet Union—a shadow that was elongated ominously by the Soviet invasion of Afghanistan in 1979 (notwithstanding the fact that Afghanistan is not an oil producer). In addition, religious cleavages, secular-religious conflicts, ethnic-nationalist rebellions, modernist-traditionalist splits, and interstate confrontations threaten the viability of regimes and interruption in oil production from key states throughout the region. The dangers of hostilities surrounding the Arab-Israeli conflict and the Palestinian question remain, of course, ever present. American and Western economic dependence on oil production from a region in such domestic and international political turmoil poses a security challenge to the United States of the highest magnitude.

America entered the 1980s lacking the capacity to stabilize the Persian Gulf area. There is little the United States can do to defuse the multitudinous, complex sources of tension confronting regimes throughout the region. A substantial buildup of American military power in the area will not throttle the central domestic and regional challenges to the authority of regimes in the Middle East. Indeed, most regimes recognize that they will face heightened political opposition by open military alliance with either superpower.

The United States in the 1980s is unlikely to stabilize the region or to enhance its influence by forging extensive military ties with important client states as was the case with Iran prior to the fall of the Shah in 1979. Moreover, the immediate proximity of the Soviet Union compared with the necessity for the United States to project its power 6,000 miles will enable the Soviet Union to retain conventional military superiority in the Persian Gulf.

This is not to suggest that the Persian Gulf area upon which the West relies for so much of its energy needs will necessarily fall within the Soviet orbit. The wariness of both superpowers by all states in the area will probably prevent either the Soviet Union or the United States from dominating the Persian Gulf in an intensely nationalist era, in spite of the Soviet's greater capacity to project conventional military power there than the United States. What should be clear is that the United States will be unable to eliminate its vulnerability to oil supply interruptions and price shocks from this unstable area by relying primarily on military means.[38] It can do so only by a comprehensive energy policy designed to reduce the importance of these oil-producing states in meeting America's energy needs.

American Energy Policy: The Response to OPEC

The United States has attempted through both multilateral and unilateral efforts to deal with the security and economic challenges posed by OPEC's seizure of control over international oil markets. In 1974 Western states, with the exception of France, created the International Energy Agency (IEA) to coordinate their response to OPEC. Its major accomplishment to date has been the erection of a multilateral mechanism to deal with any significant supply interruptions from OPEC, whether directed consciously at Western states (as the Arab oil embargo of 1973) or not (such as the elimination of production through domestic turmoil or war). IEA agreements call for each member state to accumulate an emergency petroleum reserve equivalent to at least 90 days' supply of its national oil consumption.[39] In addition to being able to draw upon these reserve stocks in a future oil emergency, states in the IEA have commitments to share equally any reduction in oil consumption in excess of 7 percent due to an interruption of imports. In a word, a selective embargo of oil of the sort imposed by the Arab states in 1973 would be met by a common IEA strategy for Western states to share equally their available supplies of energy oil reserves, oil imports, and domestic oil production. It is hoped that knowledge of these commitments among Western states will deter or render ineffective any OPEC states' efforts to bring pressure on Western countries through interrupting oil supplies.

While these multilateral arrangements would, presumably, provide some security for Western states in the face of supply interruptions, they do not confront the threat to their economic security posed by massive OPEC oil price increases. To do that, Walter Levy, a prominent oil consultant, suggests that through the IEA the Western states must forge an agreement to refrain jointly from competing for oil in world markets at spot market prices above OPEC price levels. They would also need to agree to share equally the burdens of adjusting to oil shortages that might well

---

[38]Most American analysts in the early 1980s felt the United States should enhance its capability and preparedness to intervene militarily in support of key oil-producing states in the Persian Gulf if it clearly serves American interests. The point is that no credible capacity exists for the United States to stabilize the Persian Gulf and international oil deliveries through primary reliance on a military presence in the area—in fact, exactly the opposite would probably occur.

[39]The U.S. strategic petroleum reserve was to reach 1 billion barrels by 1985—later revised downward to 500 million barrels. Storage accumulated by the end of 1980 amounted to approximately 100 million barrels, the equivalent of about a week's consumption or two weeks of imports. Additions to the reserve increased in 1981.

arise by their refusal to purchase oil at high spot market prices.[40] An agreement of this sort would confront directly the dynamic underlying the pattern of OPEC price increases since 1973, outlined previously.

A reduction in vulnerability to Middle Eastern oil-producing states necessarily requires a combination of moves by oil-importing states that would reduce the level of oil imports and develop energy alternatives to petroleum. While multilateral cooperation is highly desirable along these lines through the IEA, effective results will have to come primarily from implementing comprehensive national energy policies. The basic structure of such an energy program is clear in the case of the United States, even though the means of its implementation and priorities among the various components has inhibited its implementation.

The program requires effective conservation of energy use. Americans use far more energy per capita than do people in any other nation. Conservation through improving gasoline mileage for automobiles, more extensive reliance on mass transportation, construction of more energy-efficient buildings, reduction in overheating and overcooling of buildings, and so forth offer the greatest opportunity for short-term improvement of the energy challenge confronting the United States. In addition, an energy program requires limiting the growth and the level of oil imports from the Middle East. Proposals toward this end include the introduction of quotas or tariffs on oil imports. Strenuous efforts must also be made to stimulate oil production outside the Middle East and OPEC. Great attention has been focused recently on enhancing America's domestic oil production through extracting residual oil from previously worked reserves, expansion of production and new exploration on the continental shelf and in Alaska, and exploitation of petroleum reserves on federally owned lands. Oil production from major new fields being developed in the North Sea, Mexico, China, and the Soviet Union provide further foreign alternatives to OPEC oil. If the United States must continue to rely heavily on oil imports, more widely dispersed sources of crude should reduce the risk of supply interruption. An effective energy policy requires encouraging new exploration and production outside of OPEC states.

In the long term, the United States has the capacity to develop energy alternatives to petroleum: nuclear power, biomass, solar energy, and immense reserves of coal and oil shale in the West offer a potentially abundant energy environment for America. Yet, in addition to being years away, these energy alternatives carry substantial ecological challenges and extremely high costs compared with even rapidly escalating OPEC oil prices. Nuclear power must be accompanied by the development of safe means for permanently discarding waste materials—that has yet to be done. Coal, if used

---

[40]See Walter Levy, "Oil and the Decline of the West," *Foreign Affairs*, 58, no. 5 (Summer, 1980), 999–1015.

in its traditional form, threatens air quality in populated areas. If liquified or gasified, coal costs escalate. Exploitation of coal located in the plains and mountain states on a scale sufficient to meet our future energy needs will require huge capital resources for the development of adequate rail and/ or pipeline transport infrastructures. As with oil shale and biomass production, coal will have to compete directly with desperately needed agricultural production for scarce land and water in the American West. Over the course of the 1970s the price estimates for commercial exploitation of oil shale have remained between one and a half and two times higher than OPEC oil prices. Thus in 1980, when OPEC oil cost $32 per barrel, estimates for commercially viable oil shale production were approximately $60 per barrel.[41]

Every component of an energy program outlined here (conservation, import reduction, development of new oil production, development of energy alternatives to oil) is stimulated by higher energy prices. But through price controls on its domestic oil production, the United States has kept oil prices far below those prevailing in Europe and Japan.[42] By 1981 these price controls were dismantled to bring domestic oil prices up to world market levels. Price decontrols were placed at the heart of a comprehensive energy program for America.

The United States entered the 1980s taking only the first steps toward a meaningful energy program. It is important to recognize that this is a long-term proposition involving complex and far-reaching trade-offs for Americans. Unlike most advanced industrial states, the United States possesses the capability over the long run to virtually eliminate its vulnerability to continued oil dependence upon OPEC—despite the developments of the 1970s in international oil markets. This enhanced energy and economic security vis-à-vis OPEC and states of questionable political stability must be purchased, however, with a substantial reduction in American standards of living as energy alternatives to oil are likely to continue for some time to cost much more than OPEC oil. Great disparities will emerge in the burdens of adjustment borne by different regions of the country, different industries, and different segments of society as new, higher-cost energy replaces lower-priced oil. A bold energy policy will have to be accompanied by massive social-economic programs to ease the most serious strains in the adjustment process.

U.S. interests dictate an effort to reduce dependence on oil imports, particularly those from the Middle East. The various means for doing so in the long run are well understood. What remains is the major political challenge of determining which alternatives will be stressed and the nature of the sacrifice Americans are willing to make to achieve their goal. Everyone

[41]*The New York Times*, August 4, 1980, p. D2.

[42]In 1980, for example, gasoline costs in Belgium and Italy were almost three times higher than those in the United States.

may want greater energy and economic security from OPEC, but at what level of sacrifice of real income? at what level of prices for gasoline and heating oil? at what level of prices for food? at what levels of inflation and unemployment? at what levels of environmental deterioration? These are the sorts of opportunity costs associated with enhanced energy independence. It is important to recognize and confront them as difficult as they are to estimate precisely. The resolution of these sorts of questions will determine the fate of any comprehensive energy program to reduce U.S. vulnerability to OPEC over the next ten to fifteen years.

The Generalizability of OPEC

OPEC's dramatic success and durability despite conflicts among its members (including a war between Iraq and Iran in 1980) has so enhanced the economic and political position of the oil-producing states that less developed countries possessing large shares of raw materials or commodities other than oil have attempted to develop variants of OPEC's producer cartel strategy. Associations now exist among producers in less developed countries of such diverse commodities as bauxite, copper, iron ore, rubber, timber, and bananas. These producer associations can be expected to test their market strength over the years. Some of them may enjoy intermittent success in increasing government revenues from existing and future concessions, securing the location of processing facilities within the jurisdiction of producer states, and assuming minority or majority ownership over raw materials' production. They are not likely, however, to have much success in exercising decisive control over world market prices and production levels in the manner of the OPEC states since 1973. The combination of conditions enabling OPEC states to secure a stranglehold over world oil markets does not appear to be present for Third World producers of other commodities.

Producer cartels for raw materials among less developed countries are likely to succeed as a strategy for seizing market control to the extent that (1) access to the product in its primary stage constitutes the greatest barrier of entry into the vertically integrated production and sales process; (2) the dominant portion of the world's supply of the mineral is concentrated in a very limited number of less developed countries whose political outlook and economic situation are sufficiently congruent to make concerted economic action possible; (3) global demand for the product is rising steadily over the years; (4) natural and synthetic substitutes are not available or are extremely costly to employ; (5) production cutbacks to hold or increase prices do not significantly increase unemployment in the producing states; and (6) financial reserves are large enough to allow limits in output without seriously curtailing imports necessary for development. Oil would appear to be the exception, not the rule, for commodity producers in the Third World.

It should also be noted that, even if all these conditions for successful cartel activity should emerge for another commodity, there is no raw material that approaches crude oil's economic and political potency as a lever on advanced industrial states. In 1975 the combined value of all food and raw material exports from less developed countries amounted to only 35 percent of the value of OPEC's oil exports.[43]

A NEW INTERNATIONAL
ECONOMIC ORDER

OPEC exemplifies a strategy whereby less developed states cooperate and bargain along industry lines to enhance their economic and political position in international relations. There are also numerous multilateral efforts structured along regional and universal lines by less developed countries that extend well beyond confrontation with a particular industry. These efforts have seldom provided the drama of OPEC confrontations with advanced industrial states and the oil multinationals, but they constitute an important dimension of less developed countries' attempts to extract more benefits from their economic relationships with rich states and multinational firms.

Universalist multilateral strategies for systemic economic reform took shape with the creation of the United Nations Conference on Trade and Development (UNCTAD) in 1964. The cleavage between periphery and center states in the global economy was formalized in UNCTAD by a group system[44] in which 120 poor states (originally 77) adhered to united positions in making concrete proposals for reform in the gamut of international economic relations between rich and poor states. During the 1970s common less developed countries' proposals for international economic reforms (first made explicit and given coherence by UNCTAD) evolved to comprise a set of formal demands for a new international economic order. Since 1974 the NIEO has provided the agenda for North-South diplomacy in a wide variety of institutional settings.

In substance, the NIEO consists of the aggregated demands for economic reforms of interest to less developed countries in the various issue areas discussed throughout this volume. The demands would assure increased resource transfers from rich to poor states on improved terms and

[43]Calculated from United Nations, *Monthly Bulletin of Statistics*, 31, no. 6 (June 1977), xxviii.

[44]For a discussion of the group system, see Branislav Gosovic, "UNCTAD: North-South Encounter," *International Conciliation*, No. 568 (May 1969), 14–30.

with little accountability on the part of the less developed countries. Among other things the list would include:[45]

1. Implementation of UNCTAD's Integrated Program for commodities along with the establishment of the Common Fund as its centerpiece.
2. Liberalization and extension of the Generalized System of Preferences for less developed countries' exports of manufactured and semimanufactured goods to advanced industrial states.
3. An increase in the less developed countries' share of the world's industrial output to 25 percent by the year 2000. (In 1979 less developed countries accounted for only 9 percent.)
4. Establishment of a link between the creation of new special drawing rights in the IMF and development assistance.
5. Increased stabilization of the value of international reserves and exchange rates by movement away from the dollar as the linchpin of the international monetary system.
6. Increased access to IMF and commercial loans with lower interest rates, longer repayment periods, and less conditionality.
7. A comprehensive international approach to the management of debt rescheduling or cancellation confronting less developed countries.
8. Conformity of all advanced industrial states with the target of 0.7 percent of GNP in official development assistance to less developed countries.
9. Development of an enhanced research and development capacity within less developed countries.
10. Enhancement of science and technology transfers more appropriate to the particular needs of less developed countries, at reduced cost.
11. International regulation of multinational firms to prevent their most pernicious impacts on the social, cultural, economic, and political development of poor states.

As we have seen before, the less developed countries make these and additional demands with the conviction that the liberal international economic system dominated by Western states has produced a maldistribution of income and influence at the expense of Third World states. The resource transfers demanded in the NIEO would, in their view, eliminate the international sources of their economic and political weakness.

In addition to resource transfers, NIEO demands also focus on the need for universal recognition of new principles that less developed countries would like to see guiding international economic relations. In this sense, the NIEO is as much a demand for alteration in standards of conduct and norms governing economic relations as a demand for resource tranfers.

[45]For an excellent, concise summary of less developed countries' demands for a new international economic order, see Donald J. Puchala, ed., *Issues Before the 35th General Assembly of the United Nations 1980–1981* (New York: United Nations Association of the United States, 1980), pp. 73–104.

Less developed countries have pressed hard to legitimize these new principles through passage of numerous U.N. resolutions.[46] The principles advanced in the NIEO assert the rights that less developed countries claim for themselves and the duties they would impose upon advanced industrial states. Consider the following points taken from the Charter of Economic Rights and Duties of States passed by the General Assembly of the United Nations in December 1974:

1. "Every state has and shall freely exercise full permanent sovereignty, including possession, use and disposal, over its wealth, natural resources and economic activities."

2. "Each state has the right to nationalize, expropriate or transfer ownership of foreign property in which case appropriate compensation should be paid by the state adopting such measures taking into account its relevent laws and regulations and all circumstances that the *state* considers pertinent. In any case where the question of compensation gives rise to controversy, it shall be settled under the *domestic law of the nationalizing state and by its tribunals . . .*" (italics added).

3. "It is the duty of states to contribute to the development of international trade of goods particularly by means of arrangements and by the conclusion of long term multilateral commodity agreements, where appropriate, and taking into account the interests of producers and consumers."

4. "All states have the right to associate in organizations of primary commodity producers [such as OPEC] in order to develop their national economies to achieve stable financing for their development, and in pursuance of their aims assisting in the promotion of sustained growth of the world economy, in particular accelerating the development of developing countries. Correspondingly all states have the *duty to respect the right by refraining from applying economic and political measures that would limit it*" (italics added).

These and similar norms for international economic relations advanced by less developed countries would result in enhancing the sovereignty of Third World states, altering long-standing principles of international law regarding rights of foreign investors, and replacing the market mechanisms with commodity agreements and/or commodity cartels in international commerce for raw materials. The advanced industrial states have not accepted these principles being advanced by less developed countries in the NIEO. The U.N. resolutions asserting them carry no legal or politically binding authority. Through the resolutions the less developed states are attempting to draw public attention to their aspirations and to establish a foundation for altering international economic practices in the future.

[46]See, for example, "The Charter of Economic Rights and Duties of States," *UN Monthly Chronicle*, 12, no. 1 (January 1975), 108–118; "The Declaration on Establishment of a New International Economic Order," ibid., 11, no. 5 (May 1974), 66–69; and "Program of Action on the Establishment of a New International Economic Order," ibid., pp. 69–84.

A third dimension of less developed countries' demands for a new international economic order involves institutional reforms that would enhance their power in international economic decision making. Most Third World states had not obtained independence at the time the major international economic institutions were established after World War II. They were able to exercise little influence over the formulation of international law or the operation of international organizations affecting most directly their conduct of international economic relations. To enhance their position and voting power in multilateral economic decision making, less developed countries have pressed for (1) expanding the membership of existing organs of the U.N. family of institutions (such as tripling the size of the U.N. Economic and Social Council with increased less developed countries' participation), (2) bringing negotiations of economic importance from forums excluding less developed countries into institutions where they are represented (such as moving key deliberations on international monetary relations from the Organization for Economic Cooperation and Development to the International Monetary Fund's Group of Twenty), and (3) creating entirely new international economic institutions to champion particular less developed countries' interests (such as UNCTAD, the United Nations Industrial Development Organization, [UNIDO], and the U.N. Commission on Transnational Corporations). Overall, the developing states are trying to subordinate multilateral decision making on economic matters in the IMF, IBRD, GATT, and elsewhere to the authority and supervision of organs in the United Nations, where less developed countries enjoy an overwhelming voting majority. This was at the core of their dispute with the United States and other advanced industrial states in the North-South negotiations at Cancún, Mexico in 1981.

A new international economic order along the lines advocated by less developed countries would constitute wholesale redistribution of resources and political-economic power in the international system from the advanced industrial states of the West to countries in the Third World. For this reason Western states cannot be expected to move voluntarily toward a comprehensive implementation of the NIEO. In addition to considerations of wealth and power losses, however, the leading Western states profoundly disagree with the basic premises of the NIEO demands. As opposed to the NIEO assumption that underdevelopment is primarily a result of past and present inequities in the international economic system, the United States and others are inclined to view domestic policies of less developed countries as the greatest obstacle to their development. Western states are opposed to a massive restructuring of international economic institutions and the norms of behavior that, in their view, have served most states well. They are very reluctant to replace market mechanisms, despite their imperfections, with an elaborate array of formally negotiated agreements governing resource flows as called for in the NIEO.

The advanced industrial states are likely to respond to the NIEO demands by agreeing to highly specified, selective reforms in international trade, financial, or investment relations that take into greater account the particular economic needs of less developed countries and with which most Western states are in agreement (such as the Generalized System of Preferences). The Western states will remain opposed to sweeping alterations of the basic principles and institutions that have provided the framework for international economic relations since World War II.

While the aggregated demands of 120 less developed countries for reform of the international economic system are unlikely to be met in any comprehensive fashion, the continued emphases in the NIEO have performed an important agenda-setting function for less developed countries. It has provided the means by which Third World states have placed their political-economic priorities alongside Cold War issues and intra-Western economic concerns in contemporary international diplomacy. This is a considerable accomplishment for a group of states that only forty years ago were objects of world politics rather than actors in it.

The NIEO demands also provide legitimacy and a more coherent rationalization for bolder regional and national policies of less developed countries in their foreign economic relations. In short, the greatest impact of the NIEO is likely to be seen in increased multilateral economic cooperation among Third World states and emboldened unilateral bargaining by less developed countries with foreign firms, public and private financial institutions, and advanced industrial states. We should not look only at formal universal agreements consummated between advanced industrial states and less developed countries in evaluating the success or failure of the NIEO as it evolves.

RADICAL STRATEGIES

With the exception of nationalization, this discussion of alternative strategies for states in the periphery seeking to improve their position in the global political economy has focused on a positive-sum view of international economic relations. That is, both poor and rich states are believed to secure benefits from their various economic transactions; the struggle is over attempts to increase the relative share of these benefits going to the poor states. Radical thinkers see the global economy in zero-sum terms, however. Benefits secured by rich states in their economic transactions with states in the periphery are seen as a direct measure of the economic loss suffered by the poor states. In short, the contemporary poverty of states in the periphery is seen by radicals as the product of their continued economic relations on present terms with advanced industrial societies. When prescribing strategies by which less developed countries might reduce losses or increase benefits from international economic relations, radicals emphasize the need to interrupt economic transactions with rich Western states—indeed, to rebel against the existing global system.

Consistent with this logic, a less developed country might choose to withdraw from international economic relations to the maximum extent possible. Such a strategy is an insulatory response to a situation in which a poor state associates economic exploitation and political and cultural penetration with active participation in the contemporary global economy. Tanzania, for example, has adopted a variant of this basic posture in its insistence upon self-sufficiency. It has minimized international economic contacts and has subordinated the values of rapid economic growth and development of heavy industry to the values of national autonomy, self-reliance, and the preservation of traditional social relationships. This strategy may involve the nationalization of foreign assets, but it differs from the typical strategy of nationalization. Nationalization is usually proposed not as a means to withdraw from, or minimize reliance upon, international economic relations but rather, as a means to increase the returns from these relations. In the case of the withdrawal or self-sufficiency strategy, the choice between rapid economic growth and national autonomy has been faced and resolved in favor of the latter. As we have seen, proponents of nationalization often fail to see that these values might be incompatible.

When taken to its logical conclusion, the radical position implies an aggressive strategy of confrontation between states in the periphery and the center states.[47] The United States and other Western powers are seen as owing their commanding economic and political position in the world to their capacity for continued access to and exploitation of states in the periphery. The only way for less developed countries to improve their lot significantly is to act in concert to destroy existing exploitative economic relations and the present American role in the world economy. Radicals imply that this could be done by denying the United States and other Western countries the export markets, investment opportunities, and raw materials of the Third World upon which the center states' prosperity depends. Unlike the other strategies for which one can find some empirical referent, this strategy is exclusively theoretical at the present time. Because of this, we will address only briefly the question of the extent of the center states' dependence upon Third World states and the economic capacity and political efficacy of this proposed action. Since most of the relevant literature pictures the United States as the linchpin of contemporary international economic relations, this examination will be confined to the United States as the target of the Third World.

[47]See for example, André Gunder-Frank, "Sociology of Development and Underdevelopment of Sociology," in *Dependence and Underdevelopment*, J. Cockroft, A. G. Frank, and D. Johnson eds. (Garden City, N.Y.: Doubleday, 1972), pp. 321–98.

There is no question that the United States would be hurt economically if all less developed countries joined together to terminate their imports of U.S. goods and their acceptance of U.S. direct foreign investment. What position do the less developed countries occupy in American trade and investment? In 1979, U.S. trade turnover (exports plus imports) with less developed countries amounted to 6 percent of its GNP.[48] During 1979, American direct foreign investment in less developed countries equaled 4 percent of expenditures for new plant and equipment in the United States,[49] and income from United States direct foreign investment in less developed countries amounted to 5 percent of U.S. corporate profits in 1978.[50] The rates of return on American investments in less developed countries are, indeed, higher than are those for investments in the United States and in other advanced industrialized states. However, the difference is largely accounted for by extraordinary returns on U.S. foreign investments in petroleum. The rates of return on direct foreign investment in manufacturing and other areas of economic activity in the less developed countries differ little from the rates of return on similar investments in America and other Western economies.[51]

These data suggest that U.S. trade and investment in less developed countries are certainly important to American economic prosperity. In the aggregate, however, there is little to suggest that the United States could not cope with an attempt by less developed countries to sever trade and investment relations with America. The American economy remains more self-sufficient than all but a handful of countries in the world—as measured by the ratio of foreign economic activity to domestic activity. The less developed countries as a group occupy a relatively small proportion of America's international economic transactions. Sixty percent of U.S. trade and 75 percent of its direct foreign investment are directed to other advanced industrial states. More to the point, it is hard to conceive of realistic situations in which a large group of less developed countries would unite effectively to confront the United States with a cutoff of trade and investment ties, even assuming the emergence of highly radicalized leadership. The more likely pressure would be toward maintaining or increasing trade and investment relations with alterations in their terms of exchange and composition, not an abrupt interruption of economic relations that less developed countries need more than the United States.

[48]Calculated from *Economic Report of the President, 1980* (Washington, D.C.: GPO, 1980), pp. 203 and 319.

[49]Calculated from U.S. Department of Commerce, *Survey of Current Business*, August 1980, p. 17; and ibid., September 1980, p. 23.

[50]Calculated from ibid., August 1980, p. 25; and *Statistical Abstract of the United States, 1979* (Washington, D.C.: GPO, 1979), p. 567.

[51]See, *Survey of Current Business*, August 1980, p. 22; and *Economic Report of the President, 1980*, p. 301.

The capacity of less developed states to secure global economic reform by threatening to withhold mineral resources appears more impressive than their capacity to do so through the denial of their markets to American exports and capital. For example, Harry Magdoff lists six critical materials necessary for the production of jet engines and points out that imports account for 75 to 100 percent of American consumption of four of these materials (columbium, nickel, chromium, and cobalt).[52] By means of this illustration Magdoff very dramatically makes the point raised by many radicals that the overall American economy is highly dependent on raw material imports that in many cases are supplied by less developed countries. It is a small step to conclude that concerted action by the Third World to deny these resources to the United States would indeed accomplish the goal of forcing the United States to agree to major alterations in the terms upon which it conducts foreign economic relations.

The major problem in implementing a collective denial of mineral resources vital to the American economy is the extremely remote possibility that major suppliers would agree to such a policy. Table 7-2 explains why. It is unlikely that states such as Brazil, Canada, Mexico, and Malaysia would elect to cooperate in this endeavor. To implement a concerted strategy of denying mineral resources to the United States would require the emergence and cooperation of radical regimes in most of the states listed in Table 7-2. But even radical regimes might not wish to take such action. Those states that have individually nationalized foreign-owned extractive enterprises have usually done so to increase their returns from sales of the mineral resources to advanced industrial states rather than to halt deliveries to major consumers and purposefully disrupt the global economy. This is true notwithstanding the Arab oil embargo of the United States in 1973 and 1974. It must also be realized that the United States retains considerable capabilities of its own to which it could resort should a direct confrontation along these lines be attempted by producers of mineral resources. "The United States and Canada today control a larger share of the world's exportable supplies of grain than the Middle East does of oil."[53] It is hard to conceive the form that "victory" would take should a commodity war erupt between the Third World and the United States.

Short of actually denying raw materials to the United States, there are possibilities for securing changes of American policy for long-standing issues of economic importance to less developed countries through the leverage afforded by OPEC states. Radicals would presumably like to see the oil-producing states demand in concert the construction of a new economic order that would be more beneficial to all poor states as the quid

[52] Harry Magdoff, *The Age of Imperialism* (New York: Monthly Review Press, 1969), pp. 51–52.

[53] Lester Brown, "The Next Crisis? Food," *Foreign Policy,* No. 13 (Winter, 1973–74), 21.

TABLE 7-2   Major Suppliers of Mineral Resources of Which 50 Percent or More of American Consumption Is Imported

Mineral or Metal	% of Consumption Imported, 1977	Major Foreign Suppliers (1973–1976)
Columbium	100%	Brazil, Thailand, Nigeria, Malaysia
Mica (sheet)	100	India, Brazil, Madagascar
Strontium	100	Mexico, Spain
Manganese	98	Brazil, Gabon, South Africa
Cobalt	97	Zaire, Belgium and Luxembourg, Norway, Finland
Tantalum	97	Thailand, Canada, Australia, Brazil
Platinum group metals	92	South Africa, Soviet Union, United Kingdom
Bauxite and alumina	91	Jamaica, Australia, Surinam, Guinea
Chromium	89	South Africa, Soviet Union, Turkey, Rhodesia
Tin	86	Malaysia, Thailand, Bolivia, Indonesia
Asbestos	85	Canada, South Africa
Fluorine	80	Mexico, Spain, Italy, South Africa
Nickel	70	Canada, Norway, New Caledonia, Dominican Republic
Potassium	66	Canada, Israel
Gold	60	Canada, Switzerland, Soviet Union
Zinc	58	Canada, Mexico, Australia, Peru
Antimony	52	South Africa, People's Republic of China, Bolivia
Cadmium	51	Canada, Australia, Belgium and Luxembourg

Source: U.S. Department of Interior, *Mining and Mineral Policy*, annual report of the Secretary of Interior Under the Mining and Minerals Act of 1970 (Washington, D.C.: GPO, 1978), p. 60.

pro quo for assurances of adequate supplies of oil at stable prices to the United States and other rich states. In addition, should less developed countries be successful in instituting producer cartels in commodities other than oil, the opportunity would be present for a confrontation between *coalitions* of commodity producer cartels and advanced industrial states. This would add even more leverage to demands for radical reforms in the conduct of global economic and political relations.

Radical thinkers are prone to assert that aggregate data on the Third World's portion of American export trade, foreign investment, and raw material supplies both understate American economic dependence on the poor states and miss the point. They hold that the economies of advanced industrial nations, particularly the United States, "are so intricate that the removal of even a small part, as in a watch, can stop the mechanism."[54] Most evidence suggests, however, that the leverage the less developed countries have is basically that of raising costs and producing some major, but probably manageable, adjustments throughout the American and global economies. Pursuit of concerted action of this sort might result in increasing a few less developed countries' share of the benefits in various types of international economic transactions, but it is likely overall to produce further stratification among rich and poor states. Moreover, except in the broadest terms, radical thinkers fail to identify the mechanisms through which, and the terms upon which, international trade, capital, technology, and services will be conducted should this strategy succeed in revolutionizing the existing global economy.

CONCLUSION

To bring greater coherence to the themes of this chapter, the alternative strategies are summarized in Table 7-3.

The strategies shown in the first two columns of the table rest upon an assumption consistent with liberal economic thought that global economic relations are essentially positive-sum in character—that is that poor as well as rich states benefit from economic cooperation.[55] The main difference we wish to convey between the strategies in the first and second columns is that, in the case of the former less developed countries are for various reasons in a position of greater strength than are most poor states in their relations with rich states or multinational firms. Hence, they will be less wary of contacts with the established global economy than will states pursuing the strategies labeled as attempts to secure reforms within the existing framework of the global economy. The third column, in contrast, contains strategies that rest upon assumptions consistent with radical thought: that national autonomy is a supreme value and that global economic relations between rich and poor states are essentially zero-sum. This typology may exaggerate the disparities between various strategies, but it is useful in providing an overall perspective of diverse modes of economic and political behavior.

[54] Gabriel Kolko, *The Roots of American Foreign Policy* (Boston: Beacon Press, 1969), p. 50.
[55] The reader may wish to refer back to the general discussion of the differences between liberal economic thought and radical thought presented in Chapter 1.

Less developed countries never rely exclusively on a single strategy to improve their position in the global political economy. Often, the simultaneous pursuit of different strategies can lead to mutually reinforcing results. For example, the regional investment code of the Andean states may help to stimulate universal oversight of multinational corporate behavior through UNCTAD, which in turn would strengthen the hand of many less developed countries struggling with foreign investment policy. However, a special difficulty arises for a less developed country when it approaches one economic sector (such as extractive industry) in zero-sum terms, and at the same time wishes to cooperate within other economic sectors (manufacturing or service industries) on the basis of positive-sum assumptions. Thus, Chile's nationalization of copper was inconsistent with its efforts through its membership in the Andean pact to attract foreign capital in other economic sectors.

It would be gratifying if on the basis of this discussion a general policy prescription could be suggested that would dramatically enhance these states' position in the global political economy,[56] but it would be a mistake to do so. Some presently less developed countries such as Brazil and some oil-producing states will indeed become rich and politically important. Other poor states may in the future be catapulted into a position of wealth and political potence should they sit astride mineral resources that are subject to the intense global demand of the sort we see for petroleum today. Dankwart Rustow's observations about political modernization seem compelling as a general assessment of the problem.

> When one starts searching for causes, a country's rapid progress will always turn out to be closely related to very special and very favorable circumstances in its location or heritage [or in international market conditions]. The most admirable achievement seems least susceptible of imitation . . . What is encouraging is the length and diversity of the list . . . There is no reason to search for a single universal recipe, and even less to despair if any of its alleged ingredients are missing. Instead, each country must start with a frank assessment of its particular liabilities and assets; and each will be able to learn most from those countries whose problems most closely resemble its own.[57]

[56]This is not to say that less developed states employing these and other strategies are unlikely as a whole to increase their economic or political position in the global economy. Advanced industrial states and multinational firms can expect to find states in the periphery extracting a greater share of the benefits from international economic transactions than they were able to do prior to the 1970s. The era of low prices for primary products and virtually complete control of international commodity markets by Western firms has passed. However, notwithstanding some alteration of the less developed states' general position in the global political economy, these states are unlikely overall to secure economic and political gains, *relative to advanced industrial states*, that will even approach the magnitude that will be necessary to alter their perception that they must function in a global economy in which they are relegated unjustly to a peripheral position.

[57]*A World of Nations: Problems of Political Modernization* (Washington, D.C.: The Brookings Institution, 1967), pp. 275–76.

In efforts to prescribe policies by which less developed countries might obtain greater benefits from global economic relations, it is important to make explicit the values that are to be maximized (for example, aggregate economic growth or national autonomy), the costs (social and economic) involved in the pursuit of these values, the political and economic conditions at home and abroad that must obtain for the succesful pursuit of a specific policy, and the probability that such conditions are likely to be present or produced. These considerations will generate different assessments of the prospects for different countries, and even for the same country as it operates in different economic sectors. Proponents of both liberal economic thought and radical thought would do well to focus on these basic considerations instead of indulging their penchant to propose policies that are deduced from prior assumptions and that are seen as generally applicable to all states in the periphery and to all varieties of their economic transactions.

TABLE 7-3   Alternative Strategies for States in the Periphery of the Global Economy

State Action	Taking Advantage of the Existing Global Economy	Securing Reforms Within the Existing Framework of the Global Economy	Revolutionizing or Insulating Oneself from, the Global Economy
Individual	Exploit sensitivity of international economic interdependence (Brazil)	National effort to attract foreign economic activity under strict control of host state (Mexico)	Nationalize assets of foreign firms (Chile— copper) Minimize participation within global economy (Tanzania)
Concerted	Exploit majority control of mineral resources vital to global economy (OPEC)	Regional attempts to attract foreign capital under strict control of host states (Andean pact) Universal attempts to redistribute income to poor states (NIEO)	Deny export markets, investment opportunities, and raw materials to the United States and center states on existing terms (radical theorists)

CHAPTER EIGHT
FOREIGN ECONOMIC POLICYMAKING IN THE UNITED STATES

The United States is still the leading economic and political power among the center states and within the global economic system. Of course its hegemony is challenged at home and abroad; frequently it is unable to get its own way; and in some regions of the world, other states exercise more economic influence than does the United States. Yet, in terms of the breadth and intensity of its economic and political links throughout most of the world, it is the preeminent state in the global economic system. Developments within the United States as well as specific American policies are likely to have widespread implications for countries throughout the world. Consequently, an analysis of the politics of the global political economy requires an examination of the policymaking process in the United States. This will be done by juxtaposing radical and liberal perspectives of the American foreign policy process, recognizing that there are important differences within both camps.

THE RADICAL PERSPECTIVE

The Substance of Foreign Policy

Our purpose is to examine the foreign economic policymaking process within the United States. From the perspective of various radical analysts, however, the assumption must first be made about the substance of U.S.

foreign policy. Basically, although with some variation, radical critics feel that the foreign economic and political interests of the United States are synonymous. Therefore, the process by which foreign policy is made is essentially the same, regardless of whether the issue is an economic or a political one. Indeed, for most radicals a distinction between the two is not appropriate.

On this question and on others as well, there is some disagreement among radical analysts.[1] One group, of a Marxist-Leninist orientation, tends to feel that the capitalist system of the United States largely determines its political concerns and that capitalism demands international economic and political involvement to overcome its many domestic shortcomings. According to this view, perhaps represented best by Harry Magdoff, capitalism is a system that inequitably withholds from its workers their fair share of income and wealth. Consequently, the limited purchasing power of the proletariat, coupled with an insatiable appetite for growth by corporations, results in a surplus of manufactured goods and investment capital. The domestic U.S. market cannot absorb enough new production to sustain corporate growth since the proletariat is not earning enough to purchase more goods. Less new investment capital is needed and less is able to be employed profitably in the United States. Therefore, the capitalist American system needs foreign outlets for its excess goods and investment capital. The foreign political and military policy of the United States is designed to secure and maintain these foreign markets for the benefit of the American economy. As Magdoff states, "the underlying purpose [of imperialism] is nothing less than keeping as much as possible of the world open for trade and investment by the giant multinational corporations."[2]

Magdoff and others go beyond this relationship to point out how dependent the United States is upon a host of critical raw materials found elsewhere in the world. Because these natural resources are necessary for the continued functioning of the highly developed American economy, American foreign policy seeks to safeguard the sources of these materials. This leads quite naturally to an expansionist and adventuresome foreign policy that knows few geographical or political limits.[3] Because of natural resource dependency and the need to have foreign markets absorb goods and capital, the foreign political policy of the United States is designed primarily to serve and advance its economic interests.

[1] Pat McGowan and Stephen Walker identify five radical approaches to the formulation of foreign economic policy. The general discussion that follows does not explore the diversity of these views or the richness of each. For a more comprehensive treatment, see Pat McGowan and Stephen G. Walker, "Radical and Conventional Models of U.S. Foreign Economic Policy Making," *World Politics*, 33 (Winter 1981), 347–82.

[2] Harry Magdoff, *The Age of Imperialism* (New York: Monthly Review Press, 1969), p. 14. See Vladimir I. Lenin, *Imperialism* (New York: International Publishers, 1939) for the classical Marxist-Leninist view of imperialism.

[3] This issue has been examined in greater depth in Chapters 6 and 7.

Another group of radical critics, especially Michael Hudson, feels that American economic interests and policy are really servants of an expansionary political policy.[4] He observes a self-assertive U.S. government that seeks to dominate other countries or at least to ensure their compatibility with the American system. The expansion of American investments and trade is a conscious policy fostered by a government that is anxious to enhance the overall power of the United States. This outward thrust of state capitalism is based on a different cause-and-effect relationship than that advanced by Magdoff, but in both cases foreign economic policy and foreign political policy are thought to be so highly correlated as to be synonymous.

Richard Barnet combines the two previous radical positions when he ascribes American expansionism to its society and institutions. Like Hudson, he emphasizes the importance of the national security managers (officials in the State Department, Defense Department, National Security Council, CIA, and so forth) who have decision-making authority in foreign policy matters. However, Barnet, like many other radicals, stresses the business background of these officials and the dominance of business interests and attitudes in the government and in the society more generally. The crux of the relationship as he views it is that "the corporations continue to exercise the dominant *influence* in the society, but the *power* keeps passing to the state."[5] The congruence of foreign economic and political interests in American international relations is once more clearly indicated.

Regardless of differences among them, radical critics rarely make a distinction between the American foreign policymaking process regarding political and security matters and the process for economic issues. Since the interests and objectives of business and government regarding both economic and security matters are basically similar, separate policymaking processes do not exist. In other words, decisions on Cuba, arms limitation agreements with the Soviet Union, trade reform, and revision of the international monetary order spring from the same fountainhead of policymaking.

The Formulation of Foreign Policy

Admitting the differences among radical analysts but recognizing their shared conviction that American foreign economic and political interests are similar, several views of how foreign policy is made in the United States can now be examined. It is important to note that discussions of the foreign policymaking process by radical analysts focus frequently on the procedures by which policy is made on political, security, and military issues. Some radical critics like Magdoff discuss the *substance* of American economic policy, but they fail to explore specifically the process by which foreign economic policy is made. Others have addressed this issue more directly.

---

[4]Michael Hudson, *Super Imperialism: The Economic Strategy of American Empire* (New York: Holt, Rinehart and Winston, 1968).

[5]Richard J. Barnet, *The Roots of War* (Baltimore: Penguin Books, 1972), p. 185.

Consequently, an examination of radical analysts' views of the formulation of foreign economic policy in the United States rests upon a combination of direct statements about the policy process and interpretations of their writings on other subjects like political and security issues.[6]

One group of radical thinkers, the instrumentalist school, perceives a U.S. foreign policymaking process that is primarily a reflection of and a response to the interests of the capitalist class and its big corporations.[7] It is a system in which economic and political interests, as defined and advanced by large business enterprises, dominate the substance of political and economic policy as well as the process by which foreign and domestic policies are made.

These radical analysts argue that business dominance is achieved as the result of the congruence between what is good for the United States and what is good for its large business concerns. Radical critics often rely upon statements by policymakers and corporate executives to prove their point. One of the most often-quoted remarks is that of Assistant Secretary of State Dean Acheson in 1944 before a congressional committee concerned about postwar economic planning. Drawing upon the frightening possibility of a new depression after the war, Acheson said, "We have got to see that what the country produces is used and sold under financial arrangements which make its production possible. . . . You must look to foreign markets."[8] The prospect of limiting production only to what could be consumed in the United States "would completely change our Constitution, our relations to property, human liberty, our very conceptions of law. . . . Therefore, you find you must look to other markets and those markets are abroad."[9] Thus, he continued, "We cannot have full employment and prosperity in the United States without the foreign markets."[10] Businessman Bernard Baruch was more succinct when he emphasized the "essential one-ness of United States economic political and strategic interests.[11]

Business influence over the foreign policymaking process is ensured by the recruitment of foreign policy officials from the highest ranks of the corporate and financial elite. Consequently, many of the national security managers not only represent business interests but in essence are corporate

---

[6]One further caveat is that we are attempting to describe briefly views of a number of analysts as if there were no differences among them. Of course, there are; thus, what follows is a short synthesis of the thoughts of many.

[7]See McGowan and Walker, "Radical and Conventional Models," for a useful summary of this view and that of the structuralist position which follows.

[8]Quoted in William Appleman Williams, "The Large Corporation and American Foreign Policy," in *Corporations and the Cold War*, ed. David Horowitz (New York: Monthly Review Press, 1969), p. 95. Parts of this passage have also been quoted in David Horowitz, *Empire and Revolution* (New York: Random House, 1969), pp. 233–34; and Lloyd C. Gardner, *Architects of Illusion* (Chicago: Quadrangle Books, 1970), p. 203.

[9]Williams, "The Large Corporations and American Foreign Policy," p. 96.

[10]Ibid.

[11]Quoted in Benjamin J. Cohen. *The Question of Imperialism: The Political Economy of Dominance and Dependence* (New York: Basic Books, 1973), p. 125.

officials serving the government for a few years in the foreign policy apparatus. In the process, of course, they also further the interests of their corporations and of business in general. G. William Domhoff and Richard J. Barnet present analyses of foreign policy managers in the White House and the departments of State, Defense, and Treasury that reveal that a significant proportion of these officials held top-level positions in corporations, financial institutions, and related corporate law firms prior to their recruitment into government service. Barnet points out, for example, that between 1940 and July 1967, seventy of the ninety-one secretaries and undersecretaries of defense and state, secretaries of the three branches of the armed forces, chairmen of the Atomic Energy Commission, and directors of the Central Intelligence Agency came from large corporations and leading investment houses.[12] Thus, the link between business and foreign policy is forged by a direct sharing of executives by government and business.

More indirectly, but just as critical, is the unrepresentative social and educational background of many of the most important foreign policy officials and their counterparts in business. The similarity in their backgrounds would tend to provide them with basically the same outlook on many economic and political issues. They are likely to move in similar social and intellectual circles. Many of them share the characteristics of significant family wealth, membership in exclusive clubs, listing in *The Social Register,* attendance at select private preparatory schools, and graduation from Ivy League-type colleges. For example, a study by the Brookings Institution revealed that 32 percent of the political appointees to the departments of State, Treasury, Defense, Army, Navy, and Air Force (all of which are important in the making of foreign policy) attended a select list of eighteen private preparatory schools.[13] Political appointees to cabinet departments, regulatory agencies, and other commissions that are less involved in foreign policy matters were much less likely to have attended these prep schools (only 11 percent of them did so).

All this means that this corporate-based power elite will find it quite easy to move between business and government positions, thereby ensuring a foreign policy posture that is compatible with and supportive of big business interests. In the words of a leader in this type of analysis of the elite, "American foreign policy during the postwar era was initiated, planned, and carried out by the richest, most powerful, and most international-minded owners and managers of major corporations and financial insti-

[12]Richard J. Barnet, "The National Security Managers and the National Interest," *Politics and Society,* (February 1971) p. 1:260.

[13]These figures were derived from Table D.9 in David T. Stanley, Dean E. Mann, and James W. Doig, *Men Who Govern* (Washington, D.C.: The Brookings Institution, 1967), pp. 124–25.

[14]G. William Domhoff, "Who Made American Foreign Policy 1945–1963?" in *Corporations and the Cold War,* p. 25.

tutions."[14] Thus, the unrepresentativeness of foreign policy managers in terms of socioeconomic background and prevous positions in and allegiances to corporate America suggest strongly that big business interests help determine the foreign policymaking process.

According to the instrumentalist view, the influence of big corporations on the foreign policymaking process is enhanced further by the activities of a number of important groups that serve to transmit the business point of view to government officials. These transmission belts include a few of the large foundations based on corporate wealth, special blue-ribbon presidential advisory committees, and a small number of research and discussion committees. The Ford Foundation, the Carnegie Corporation, and to a lesser extent the Rockefeller Foundation have been active supporters of programs at universities and of foreign-policy related groups that represent business concerns in the foreign policymaking process. The special presidential committees are blue-ribbon citizens groups selected largely from corporate elites to analyze and to make recommendations regarding specific foreign policy issues. These committees have reported on such things as the nature of American military preparedness and the direction of its foreign aid programs. Seven of the eight most important committees concerned with foreign policy matters were chaired by corporate executives; the eighth chairman was the president of the Massachusetts Institute of Technology.[15] The research and discussion groups referred to are organizations such as the Council on Foreign Relations, the Committee for Economic Development, the Foreign Policy Association, the Trilateral Commission, and RAND, many of whose members and boards of directors come from a big business background.

All these groups act as links between corporations and government officials, and they ostensibly provide expert but nonbiased advice from nongovernmental sectors. In fact, though, the interests, perspectives, and alternatives advantageous to business are conveyed to governmental decision makers through the activities of these groups. These transmission belts sponsor formal face-to-face meetings that allow their largely business membership to exchange ideas and information with American and non-American foreign policy officials. These information and access advantages, combined with good organization and competent staffs, mean that these groups are able to develop thoughtful and comprehensive recommendations about foreign affiars. Indeed, there are almost no other sources outside of the government that can consistently provide such well-informed and coherent analyses of foreign policy issues of direct relevance to foreign policy officials. In other words, these transmission belts enjoy a virtual monopoly of effective interest representation regarding foreign economic and political policy. Moreover, the similar background characteristics of

[15]Ibid., p. 46.

business and government elites ensure the receptivity of the latter to the concerns of the former.

This influence relationship is fostered as a result of the social, intellectual, and value similarities between foreign policy officials and the active membership of these transmission belts. This both follows from and leads to these groups serving as a major source of recruitment for high-level foreign policy officials. As an example of the two-way flow of personnel, prior to becoming secretary of state for President Kennedy, Dean Rusk was president of the Rockfeller Foundation. In the opposite direction, McGeorge Bundy left his position as national security advisor to the White House to become president of the Ford Foundation. There are many more such examples.

Domhoff suggests that the Council on Foreign Relations is probably the most important transmission belt for foreign policy matters. The large foundations and a number of major corporations provide the prime financial support for the council. In addition, top corporate executives are members of boards of directors of the major foundations and are also members of the Council on Foreign Relations. Thus, according to Domhoff, it should not be surprising that the council consciously attempts to increase the interaction between Washington officialdom and its largely corporate membership. These efforts have obviously paid off. For example, John J. McCloy, who has been among many things chairman of the board of Chase Manhattan Bank, high commissioner for Germany, and coordinator of American disarmament activities, once remarked, "Whenever we needed a man [to help direct foreign policy activity during World War II] we thumbed through the roll of Council members and put through a call to New York."[16]

To stimulate this interaction, the council arranges off-the-record speeches and question-and-answer sessions by important foreign policy officials of the United States and other countries. The information learned, the insights gained, and the views exchanged draw together more closely corporate interests and Washington officials. In addition, the council publishes a number of important books and reference works as well as the prestigious journal, *Foreign Affairs,* which frequently contains articles by foreign policy officials.

However, Domhoff feels that the most important activity of the council is the discussion and study groups that examine a specific issue in great detail. Twenty-five business executives, government officials, a few military officials, and a small number of nonradical scholars conduct extensive discussions, often off the record, which eventually result in a book that presents a thorough statement of the problem. Some of the topics considered by these study groups have been instrumental in shaping U.S. policy regarding the nature of the United Nations charter and the development of the

---

[16]Quoted by Joseph Kraft, "School for Statesmen," *Harper's Magazine,* July, 1958, p. 67.

Marshall Plan for European recovery and in the early 1970s a full-scale reassessment of American relations with China. In sum, the council, along with the other groups mentioned, serves to encourage business participation in the formulation of foreign policy and to transmit business influence to foreign policy officials in multiple ways. At the very least, such institutions provide an important means of access to and maintenance of contacts with foreign policymakers.

A more recently founded vehicle for implanting corporate views in the councils of governments is the Trilateral Commission. One radical critic referred to it as "the executive committee of transnational finance capital."[17] It is important to note that this organization is comprised of government officials and private persons from the United States, Japan and countries in the European Common Market. This internationalism is an attempt, some would say, to ensure cohesion within the capitalist class across national boundaries and to maintain the dominance of the international capitalist system.

The basic argument of the instrumentalist view is that American foreign policy reflects and represents the interests of big corporations in foreign affairs. Whether governmental political objectives conveyed through state capitalism lead to foreign economic involvement, or vice versa, is not a crucial distinction for our purposes. Either way, the result is a foreign policy that is linked closely and substantively to the interests of corporate America through a foreign policy formulation process that is subject to immense and almost exclusive influence from big business on the executive branch of the government. Congress, the radical analysts feel, is a largely impotent body in foreign policy matters since it often meekly upholds the policies and actions of the executive without acting as an alternate decision-making center. Consequently, corporate efforts to influence foreign policy are logically directed primarily to the executive branch.

A different view, that of the structuralists, rejects the notion that the actions of the state are determined by members of the capitalist class occupying positions of power or influencing those in such positions. Instead, the structure of society and that of the state are the driving forces behind the formulation of state policy. Without examining the complexity of the argument fully, the state structure is dominant because it sets limits for the policy options available and also determines which parts of the state apparatus and society are critical to the policymaking process. Furthermore it ensures the development and survival of those structures that will reinforce the predominance of capitalism in foreign (and domestic) policies.

There are other radical explanations of the foreign policymaking process, but there is substantial agreement that the United States, as the premier power of the world, is largely unconstrained by the interests and concerns

---

[17]Jeff Frieden, "The Trilateral Commission: Economics and Politics in the 1970's," *Monthly Review*, 29, no. 7 (1977), p. 11.

of other countries and thus enjoys a correspondingly wide decisional latitude. American political and military policies, in conjunction with foreign economic policies that change economic partners into economic dependents, have enabled the United States to ensure the compliance of most states to its wishes. The radical literature is replete with examples of how the United States has imposed its will on recalcitrant friends and enemies to enrich itself and its corporations and to extend its global dominance at the expense of other countries. Thus, the United States has consciously attempted to structure and use the global economic system in a way that promotes its economic and political hegemony and the subjugation of other states. As a result of this process, American policy is largely unfettered by the wishes and constraints that are imposed by other countries. This gives American business interests free rein to develop and implement the kinds of policies that will advance their interests the most.

A CRITIQUE OF THE INSTRUMENTALIST RADICAL VIEW

Admittedly, this brief sketch of several radical conceptions of the American foreign policymaking process fails to do full justice to both the richness of the arguments and the many significant differences that do exist among radical analysts. Nevertheless, it is appropriate to raise questions about the substance of the instrumentalist view, the methodology used to develop these positions, and the way in which each contributes to an understanding of the foreign economic policymaking process.

Historically, much of the instrumentalist argument has been based on an analysis of American foreign political, security, and military policy. The role of domestic U.S. interests in these policies has been examined extensively, but far fewer attempts have been made to focus on how foreign economic policy has been made. One of the results of concentrating on political and military policy as the outcome of the policymaking process is that frequently there has been much greater unanimity within the United States on these issues because of the perception of serious external threats. Given the Cold War environment as the historical (though not the only) focus of the instrumentalists,[18] the coincidence of national policy and economic interests is not surprising. With large segments of the American population perceiving the existence of the Soviet Union and other communist states as having broad and largely singular implications for all of American society, the concept of bipartisanship or the submerging of different and parochial interests was undertaken for the sake of national unity against a common threat. Business, labor, and government all joined to-

---

[18]Most radicals say that the Cold War was contrived by the United States. See Joyce Kolko and Gabriel Kolko, *The Limits of Power* (New York: Harper & Row, 1972).

gether to protect the American system from what was perceived to be both a political and economic threat. Thus, the view of business dominance is based largely upon an analysis of political and security issues on which there was wide agreement as to the nature of the situation and American objectives.

A Multiplicity of Business Interests

By focusing on such political, security, and military issues, instrumentalist critics have largely neglected a rich panoply of bureaucratic and political maneuvering that is found in the making of foreign economic policy. Here, the common perception of threat and the unified external posture (with many internal differences and disputes about tactics) dissolves into wrangling associated with the promotion of specific and contradictory objectives by many competing economic and business interests. Thus, the concept of a business interest dominating the foreign policymaking process seems inappropriate for those foreign economic groups that are often at odds with one another. In short, because the instrumentalist view is founded primarily on analyses of overarching political, military, and security issues, some serious problems are created in the transferring of their conclusions to discussions of the formulation of foreign economic policy.

As a result, the analysis fails to define, much less operationalize, the notion of *the business interest*. Instead, it is asserted categorically that a single unified business interest exists. An examination of the policy formulation process on trade or investment issues reveals something quite different. In the first place, different types of industries disagree greatly about the consequences of various foreign economic policy alternatives. For example, imposing tariffs or import quotas to protect the steel, textile, and shoe industries in the United States has been resisted by those industries who can successfully meet foreign competition and who themselves export to other countries. They fear that protectionist moves by the United States will be countered with similar actions by other countries and that their export activities will thereby be harmed. To illustrate these differences, consider this partial list of industries and products that were the subject of congressional testimony by interested unions, trade associations, and companies on the Trade Reform Act of 1973–74:

Agriculture	Musical instruments
Automobiles	Petroleum
Bicycles	Potash
Chemicals	Poultry
Clay	Shears
Dinnerware	Shoes
Eggs	Steel
Flowers	Textiles
Glue	Tools
Leather goods	Vegetables
Marbles	Wine

These specific groups differed greatly on their positions regarding the desirability of raising or lowering tariffs. Moreover, some of them have changed their views since that time, such as the auto industry. A precise and unanimous business interest cannot be observed among these industries, as a brief review of some of the conflicting testimony will indicate.

On certain issues, different firms within the same industry perceive different patterns of gains and losses to result from foreign economic policy. In the coffee industry, giant multinational corporations such as General Foods, Procter & Gamble, and Coca-Cola disagree over the nature of American policy toward the International Coffee Agreement. General Foods was quite concerned about the import of soluable coffee products from abroad, but P&G and Coca-Cola, joined by other smaller firms, did not wish to stem the flow. Quite naturally, each side used political influence in an effort to ensure that its position was advanced or protected by the policy that emerged.

An issue such as tariff reform may also highlight the very real areas of disagreement among different divisions of a multiproduct firm. In their careful study of the politics of tariff policy, Bauer, Pool, and Dexter point out that within the Dupont corporation the division manufacturing paint supported liberalization of trade whereas the rayon yarn division tended to be protectionist. Other parts of the corporation were little interested in the issue.[19] Similar differences can be observed within other corporations that manufacture a variety of products.

In the area of foreign economic policy, at least, American business interests rarely support a single policy position solidly except on the broadest levels, such as enthusiasm for the concept of private enterprise. Instead, the various alternatives available have different implications for different industries, firms, and divisions within specific corporations. As a result, the process by which foreign economic policy is made seems to be subject to the same type of political struggles thought to be characteristic of the domestic policymaking process.

Foreign economic policy has important and varying implications for businesses. Thus, businesses and other economic interests—including unions and a potpourri of various social groups each with their own conceptions of desirable goals—become actively involved in the domestic political process to influence the outcome of policy deliberations. As a result, the formulation of foreign economic policy provokes extensive and at times heated domestic political activity. For example, the hearings before the House Ways and Means Committee on the 1973 Trade Reform Act produced testimony by 96 industry associations and trade groups, 36 companies, 18 union organizations, 17 agricultural groups, 15 public interest groups and 15 individuals. In addition, the committee received written statements from 111 other such groups and individuals. An examination of the hearings em-

[19]Raymond A. Bauer, Ithiel de Sola Pool, and Lewis Anthony Dexter, *American Business and Public Policy* (New York: Atherton, 1963), p. 270.

phasizes the lack of consensus among these groups or within each type of group. The positions advanced reflected very specific conceptions of self-interest—not some overall consensus position by business.

Business executives tend to become preoccupied with and most active in specific issues that have definite implications for their business. They are not usually trying to establish and promote a grand design regarding the foreign political and economic posture of the United States. For instance, there is some suggestion that business involvement in organizations such as the Council on Foreign Relations amounts to little more than political dilettantism. Even a leading radical analyst, Domhoff, quotes a study by Bernard C. Cohen that concludes that members of the Foreign Policy Association "seldom seriously discuss political policies at all, let alone alternative policies. They tend to keep discussions apolitical, emphasizing the social, economic, cultural, and historical aspects of foreign affairs."[20] Barnet claims that corporate executives "do not seem to know how to manipulate this great wealth to influence the great decisions of war and peace. Nor do they seem to be particularly interested in doing so."[21]

Differences Within Government

The political, military and security perspective of the radical analysts has led them to understand the governmental process in a way that may not be applicable to the formulation of American foreign economic policy.[22] Just as they assert *a* business interest, so also do they perceive *a* government view of U.S. foreign policy. Such an approach ignores the significance of the different perspectives and interests of various government agencies. Moreover, it neglects the specialized clientele and constituents of each department. Thus, the departments of Labor, Commerce, and Agriculture have different interests and objectives regarding American foreign economic policy as a result of the different sets of pressures they are subjected to by labor, business, and farmers and as a result of different conceptions of the nature of their tasks. Furthermore, within these broad economic sectors and within each of these departments there are disagreements on the consequences of policy alternatives. Thus, it is an oversimplification even to view various departments as passive instruments of their constituencies (labor, business, farmers, and so on) in society, for these groups themselves are not united on all issues.

Another critical assumption at the base of the instrumentalists' view of the American foreign policymaking process involves the nature of the relationship between business and government. As we discussed earlier, they feel that business interests dominate the government. However, there

[20]Domhoff, "Who Made American Foreign Policy 1945–1963?" p. 61.

[21]Barnet, *The Roots of War*, p. 186.

[22]This topic is discussed at greater length later in this chapter when we examine the pluralist view of the foreign economic policymaking process.

are numerous examples of U.S. policy that contradict this view. The Trading with the Enemy Act prohibits U.S. firms and their subsidiaries from trading with specified enemy countries in a number of defense-related products. In the mid-1970s and early 1980s, this act inhibited some business interaction with the Soviet Union and Cuba, in spite of the requests of American firms to rescind its restrictive provisions. Antitrust concerns of the Department of Justice have also served to retard the growth and success of the foreign subsidiaries of American firms. Moreover, the years of Cold War between the Soviet Union and the United States as well as the many years of American nonrecognition of China meant many missed opportunities for doing business with these countries. The inability of American business to change government policy on these matters long after allies and their corporate competitors had opened lucrative business and political contacts is another important instance in which the interests of many corporations were not served by government policy. Despite official U.S. government hostility toward the Marxist regime in Angola, Gulf Oil successfully pursued its oil-drilling operations in that country with excellent relations with the government. Thus, one has to question the degree to which business in fact controls government policy.

Bauer, Pool, and Dexter suggest that in many ways Congress tends to use business lobbyists, rather than vice versa.[23] This study, which examines business and government interactions on the question of tariff reform, indicates that lobbyists are most effective when they aid an already favorably disposed legislator in the attempt to sway colleagues in the House or Senate. Moreover, members of Congress frequently utilize lobbyists to obtain information about an issue so that they can make up their minds on the issue. Although practices obviously vary widely, the basic conclusion of the authors is that Congress is not captive of business lobbyists, or of any lobbyists for that matter.

However, instrumentalist radical critics feel that the legislative branch is relatively impotent in the foreign policymaking process. Thus, much of their argument is based on the extent of business control over the administrative branch. Basically, some radical thinkers *infer* business control from the socioeconomic backgrounds of top-level officials recruited into executive agencies, without offering substantial evidence as to the precise nature of the linkage between background and decision making.

Such critics insist that former corporate employees carry their predispositions and parochial interest directly into their positions in government. Although there is substance to this argument, it is possible that the new experiences and role expectations accompanying their office expand the horizons of former corporate executives beyond their previous views. For example, in assessing the influence of foreign travel on business executives' conceptions of self-interest, Bauer, Pool, and Dexter found that it

[23]Bauer, Pool, and Dexter, *Americn Business and Public Policy* p. 488.

"made a man see the trade issue in national terms, rather than in the parochial terms of his own industry."[24] One cannot help but wonder whether journeys into government service do not have a similar effect.

The radicals insist that the legislative branch has little to do with the making of foreign policy on political and security issues. (This is the view of many nonradicals as well.) This is probably not the case in regard to international economic issues having important domestic implications. In these instances, different business interests and other economic interests actively urge members of Congress to represent their concerns in the legislative process. The administration's trade bill in 1973 and 1974 stimulated great pressure on Congress from numerous economic groups, and the passage of the bill was delayed by Congress until December, 1974. Congress does fulfill an active and important role in many issues involving foreign economic policy. Yet this role is disregarded by most radical analysts because their frame of reference tends to be focused on military and security issues. It is useful to note, though, that national security policy and executive branch leadership in such matters often overwhelm strong domestic economic interests. The Carter administration's imposition of a grain embargo on the Soviet Union in response to the invasion of Afghanistan is a case in point.

The instrumentalist conception of American foreign policymaking implies or asserts that only high-level political appointees determine the content of foreign policy. Barnet suggests that these national security managers revel in their jobs because of "the sense of playing for high stakes."[25] These foreign policy officials are exhilarated and "intrigued by power, more than money and more than fame."[26] Even if we accept Barnet's characterization, it is hard to imagine these national security managers experiencing much thrill and excitement over attempts to get Japan to reduce automobile exports to the United States or attempts to change the discriminatory trade policies of the European Common Market. Participation in many of these economic issues does not often yield fascinating memoirs testifying to one's diplomatic astuteness and importance.

Instead, many of these economic issues involve exceptionally technical details that are managed more competently by the technical experts in the civil service who inhabit the departments of Treasury, Commerce, and Agriculture. Thus, the important role of the technostructure, on economic issues at least, should not be, but often has been, ignored by some critics, who perceive American foreign policy to be the preserve of a small number of political appointees in the State and Defense Departments. It is important to note that there is much more diversity in social backgrounds, educational experience, and career patterns among career civil servants than there is

[24]Ibid., p. 168.
[25]Barnet, *The Roots of War*, p. 98.
[26]Ibid., p. 97.

among the top political elites, upon whom some radical critics focus. Moreover, the relationship between the bureaucracy and business interests, especially where regulation is concerned, is often adversarial, reflecting in part the lack of common objectives and career backgrounds.

The point is that business control of government, as proclaimed by followers of the instrumentalist approach, is probably overstated. Radical thinkers fail to specify either what they define as control of foreign policy or the precise nature of the foreign policy decision-making process. They presume that broad conclusions about overall policy outcomes and the backgrounds of certain types of government officials are sufficient evidence to infer the control of business interests over the American foreign policy process. But radical analysts do not tell us what control is and how it can be observed. Their concept of the foreign policy decision-making process is developed from the presumption that a highly unified business interest dictates government policy. No inputs into the foreign policy process other than business interest are examined seriously. The role of Congress and the intense struggles among and within executive agencies, if they receive any attention at all, are considered inconsequential for American foreign economic policy.[27]

Nonetheless, the analyses of the instrumentalist and structuralist critics do provide important insights into the nature of foreign economic policymaking. Whether through the prevalence of common backgrounds or interests among officials or through the structure of the state allowing participation in the process only to those societal institutions that foster the prevailing view, there are wide areas of consensus. In spite of conflicting and vigorous expressions of self-interest about the nature of U.S. foreign economic policy, the fundamental concepts of capitalism and the internationalism of capitalism are widely accepted and rarely debated seriously, much less challenged seriously, in the United States.

THE PLURALIST PERSPECTIVE

There are a number of different liberal views of American foreign economic policy and the process by which it is formulated. While some analysts feel that there are basic differences between how foreign economic policy is made and that of foreign political and national security policy, others do not observe such differences. Still others classify the foreign policymaking process (economic or not) by the types of issues involved.[28]

[27]This point is made by Gabriel Kolko, *The Roots of American Foreign Policy* (Boston: Beacon Press, 1969), pp. 4–5.

[28]McGowan and Walker, *"Radical and Conventional Models,"* pp. 365–77, provide a useful interpretation of the issue-area analysis approach as it relates to the formulation of foreign economic policy. See also William Zimmerman, "Issue Area and Foreign Policy Process," *American Political Science Review*, 67 (December 1973), p. 1204–12.

However, for purposes of highlighting differences with the radical views discussed, in this section we will examine a perspective that is based on the concepts of pluralism and bureaucratic politics.[29]

Rather than a dominant business interest, the pluralist approach perceives the existence and importance of a wide variety of internal interests and constraints that greatly complicate foreign economic policymaking. Second, this view contends that American foreign policy in the economic arena is constrained severely by the economic objectives and actions of other states, whose own domestic groups have a vested interest in their government's actions.[30] In short, the process by which U. S. foreign economic policy is formulated is subject domestically to widespread political bargaining and maneuvering and internationally to the actions and concerns of other states.

Domestic Constraints on Foreign Economic Policy

The extensive domestic political activity associated with American foreign economic policy occurs because some domestic interest groups stand to gain or lose as a result of the particular policy adopted. To achieve an outcome that is favorable to their particular set of interests, each of the affected groups mobilizes to protect and advance its concerns. For example, trade issues have both international and domestic implications; thus, labor, business, consumer, and other groups who feel that they may be affected by the U.S. policy will seek to influence it. A proposal to reduce tariffs in the 1973 Trade Reform Bill received the support of such diverse groups as the Aerospace Industries Association of America, the American Importers Association, the National Grain and Feed Association, the National Farmers Union, the League of Women Voters, and the U.S. Council of the International Chamber of Commerce. Those seeking to maintain the current tariff structure or to increase the duties included the Manufacturers of Small Tools and Metal Fasteners, the National Association of Marble Producers, the American Iron and Steel Institute, the United Rubber, Cork, Linoleum and Plastic Workers of America, the Nationwide Committee on Import-Export Policy, the AFL-CIO , and the Liberty Lobby.

Investment issues provoke the same type of widespread and deeply committed interest-group activity and conflict. As we discussed in Chapter 4, the AFL-CIO and some of its affiliates were active promoters of the Burke-Hartke Bill to restrict the ability of American corporations to invest

---

[29]Two books that represent this view are Bauer, Pool, and Dexter, *American Business and Public Policy;* and Morton H. Halperin, *Bureaucratic Politics and Foreign Policy* (Washington, D.C.: The Brookings Institution, 1974). A useful analysis of the U.S. foreign economic policymaking process can be found in Robert Pastor, *Congress and the Politics of U.S. Foreign Economic Policy* (Berkeley, Calif.: University of California Press, 1980).

[30]The international constraints on foreign economic policy making are examined in Robert O. Keohane and Joseph S. Nye, *Power and Interdependence: World in Transition* (Boston: Little, Brown, 1977).

abroad. This pressure was countered by the activities of numerous multinational corporations that were designed to protect their interests. Other American firms had little interest one way or the other in the proposed restrictions. Again, the determining factor of interest-group involvement is the perception that self-interest may be advanced or injured by the various policy options available. However, the critical point is that foreign economic issues directly affect various domestic interests in different ways, and these interests in turn seek to influence the substance of U.S. foreign economic policy by actively engaging in the policymaking process.

Regarding foreign economic matters, especially those involving trade issues, Congress is an important target of interest-group pressures and conflicts. The various interests affected by specific legislation and policy decisions present their concerns to individual legislators, who represent a region according to how that region stands to gain or lose as a result of the policy adopted. For example, on trade issues, labor and/or business interests are able to demonstrate precisely how an increase or decrease in tariffs will lead to more or less business and consequently to more or less employment in a specific geographical area. Since the policy has a direct impact on constituents, the congressperson at least takes notice. When determining the overall impact on the district in light of his or her own interests in future elections, the representative may well actively seek to champion the interests of those groups with electoral power who will be significantly affected by governmental policy.

The nature of most foreign economic issues is such that different regions of the country are affected differently by a policy. Thus, the textile interests in the South have obtained widespread support for their attempts to reduce foreign competition by enacting protectionist legislation. Similarly, Senator Edward Kennedy and other members of Congress from New England have advocated measures to protect the domestic shoe industry. And in steel-producing areas, such as Pittsburgh, local members of Congress are leaders in protecting companies and unions who are disadvantaged by the imports of foreign steel. However, regional coalitions such as these face opposition from American farmers, who wish to reduce trade barriers, not increase them. Representatives from the Midwest advocate a free trade position, especially with respect to EEC barriers, because it will aid their farming constituents. They are joined by other representatives whose constituents would benefit from a reduction of trade obstacles. The politically conservative farmers of the Grain Belt objected strongly to "punishing" the Soviet Union for invading Afghanistan by withholding grain shipments.

It is important to note, however, that with respect to trade reform these coalitions of interests and representatives from many parts of the country join together for the purpose of advancing common interests only at the most general level. These are coalitions of convenience and self-interest, not coalitions reflecting deep-seated consensus on the nature of American foreign economic policy. Large multinational firms may be concerned about how a policy under consideration affects their global operations. Executive branch career civil servants and technocrats may have their eye on how certain policy proposals affect the fortunes of their department or office within the U.S. government apparatus. Members of Congress, state and local officials, and most business and labor groups evaluate policy proposals in terms of the potential effect on production and employment in their particular geographic area or economic sector. The policy process in the United States must accommodate *all* these important economic and political forces. As a result, foreign economic policy involves much more, and usually produces much less than does a coherent strategy that maximizes American power and advances American·private interests around the world.

Many interest groups supplement their efforts to influence congressional deliberations with a strategy to gain access to decision makers in the executive branch. There are two basic objectives associated with such efforts: to influence the specific policy alternatives proposed and choices made as they emerge from the bureaucracy and to influence the technocrats within the bureaucracy as they implement the policies established in the legislative or administrative sectors of government. In either case, interest-group involvement in the executive branch is frequent and wide-spread. Moreover, the congressional allies of interest groups also attempt to influence the appropriate parts of the bureaucracy through well-established patterns of communication and what amounts to congressional lobbying of the executive agencies. Thus, the pluralistic struggles of interest-group activity are carried directly into the bureaucracy.

According to the bureaucratic paradigm, the various agencies and departments within the bureaucracy engage in severe conflict among themselves. There are important differences among the perceptions, attitudes, goals, and operating procedures prevalent in different administrative units. Moreover, these units have different constituencies, whose views they are likely to adopt to at least some degree. Thus, in general, the Department of Agriculture represents the interests of farmers, the Department of Labor promotes the labor view, the Treasury Department looks after the concerns of banks and financial organizations, and the Department of Commerce tends to represent business. However, as we discussed earlier, it is inappropriate to speak of a single labor view or a single business view on specific issues, such as tariff reform. Various units or bureaus *within* the agencies have their own, more specialized constituencies, whose interests they often seek to represent and from whom they often receive support during budgetary allocations and other intradepartmental conflicts. It is also misleading to assume that the agencies are total captives of their natural constituency in society. A former official in the international division of the Bureau of the Budget has noted, "Perhaps more than in any other area of policy international trade pits agency against agency, advisor against advisor."[31]

These conflicts produce intra- and interagency struggles in which the many parties to these disputes utilize a host of political techniques to represent their concerns. In their relations with one another, they resort to the use of raw power, appeals to higher authority (the president), persuasion, manipulation, negotiation, and bargaining. The result is often a policy that is a mixture of the contending positions. Rarely does one set of interests succeed in obtaining all its objectives, for this essentially legislative process involves bargaining and compromise over different goals and strategies, and the eventual acceptance and incorporation of contradictory positions in the policy adopted. Thus, political conflict and political maneuvering are characteristic of the bureaucratic policymaking process regarding foreign economic issues. The differences within society are mirrored in and affect the nature of the decision-making process in the bureaucracy. The substance of foreign economic policy reflects the results of these intense battles in the policymaking process.

This tendency for a fragmented and political decision-making process to occur in regard to foreign economic policy is heightened by the fact that during most of the postwar period few high political officials have taken much interest in the specific issues raised. The president and his major advisors have not been much concerned with the rather mundane and often exceedingly complex and technical matters of international economics. This is illustrated by President Nixon's response to being told that the chairman of the Federal Reserve, Arthur Burns, was concerned about the speculation against the Italian lira. His response, as captured on the White House tapes of June 23, 1972, was, "Well, I don't give a (expletive deleted) about the lira (unintelligible)." Similar disinterest was expressed about the problems of the British currency.

Moreover, these issues, because of their domestic content and their repercussions in the many countries concerned, often involve long, drawn-out negotiations and trade-offs among technical specialists who are subject to severe domestic pressures and constraints. It is difficult to emerge from such a grueling process with an international reputation that will have much historical impact. In the absence of the direct and continuing interest and participation of top political officials, these difficult and technical matters have tended to be the concern of bureaucratic technocrats. These specialists do not operate according to some grand design, but rather in a professional but limited way to advance their bureaucratic and constituent interest.

---

[31]Donald S. Green, "Government Organization for Policymaking and Execution in International Trade and Investment," in Commission on International Trade and Investment, *United States International Economic Policy in an Interdependent World*, Vol. II (Washington, D.C.: 1971), p. 420.

Thus, the political disputes are frequently carved out in a bureaucratic arena that is not at the top level of political officials. This lack of ongoing involvement by high-level political actors emphasizes the importance of interest groups promoting their objectives at the level of bureaucratic implementation, for sometimes the decisions of consequence are made during this implementation process.

This situation has changed somewhat as international political relations increasingly involve questions of access to oil and raw materials, global inflation and recession, and other economic questions.[32] But the change is taking place slowly. Moreover, as the Reagan administration focuses attention on security and defense issues and the threat from the Soviet Union, foreign economic policy may once again be pushed down in the order of priorities. U.S. foreign economic policy has proceeded in fits and starts and has continued by and large to be the preserve of technocrats while various high political officials have wrangled with one another over who would provide titular leadership of American foreign economic policy. Harald Malmgren, a former deputy special representative for trade negotiations, observed that for the most part the State Department has "consistently avoided taking the necessary steps to deal directly with domestic political and economic interests."[33] Instead of incorporating and organizing for these matters, the Department of State has been willing to allow other agencies to handle functionally or politically related matters. One result is that at one time in the 1970s over sixty agencies, departments, or other institutions had "direct interests and decision-making powers in international economic issues."[34] Consequently, there is extensive interagency bargaining and compromise on such matters but very little central planning and direction regarding U.S. foreign economic policy. The proliferation of multiagency coordinating committees in which some of this negotiation occurs is evidence of the fragmented nature of the process by which American policy and actions are developed. Indeed, Malmgren wishes that American foreign economic policy exhibited the degree of coherence and consistency imputed to it by radical analysts.

Malmgren also notes that White House involvement in foreign economic policy often results from the implications of foreign economic issues for questions of domestic politics, and from the actions of contending domestic interest groups in regard to these issues. Thus, the White House is called upon to make decisions on international economic matters, but from the perspective of their effect on domestic politics. Consequently, the president and his advisors respond to specific issues and concerns without the

[32]See Chapter 2 for a discussion of the political effects of some of these issues.

[33]Harald B. Malmgren, "Managing Foreign Economic Policy," *Foreign Policy*, No. 6 (Spring, 1972), p. 46.

[34]Ibid., p. 43.

benefit of an overall international economic policy, but instead in the context of furthering domestic political advantages. Examples from the Nixon administration serve to illustrate this point. Part of the Nixon reelection strategy in 1972 was to obtain the support of labor and the South. The former was accomplished in part by securing official AFL-CIO neutrality in the election in exchange for provisions in the administration's trade bill that would to some degree meet labor's concerns regarding foreign competition and U.S. multinational corporations. A cornerstone of the Southern strategy was the administration's willingness to heed the concerns of the Southern textile industry regarding the proposed trade bill and the government's textile negotiations with Japan. In both cases, U.S. foreign economic policy was perceived as a mechanism for obtaining domestic political support in the 1972 election. Further evidence of the general link between domestic politics and foreign economic policy can be found in the 1973–74 Trade Reform Act, which sought to make it necessary to secure congressional authorization to negotiate for higher as well as lower tariffs. A consistent and coherent U.S. policy on trade reform that was divorced from domestic interests and politics would have attempted to obtain permission either to raise tariffs or to lower them—not to do both depending upon the domestic and international circumstances. Another example of the influence of domestic political concerns on foreign economic policy was provided in the early months of the Reagan administration. As a candidate, Ronald Reagan stressed the inappropriateness of lifting the grain embargo imposed by President Carter after the Soviet Union sent troops to Afghanistan. As president, Reagan halted the embargo within six months of his inauguration despite his hardline attitude voiced so often during the campaign.

External Constraints on Foreign Economic Policy

The pluralist approach also differs from the radical view with respect to the importance of external constraints on the policymaking process. It recognizes that the objectives and desires of other states are difficult (though perhaps not impossible in every case) for the United States to disregard. In regard to economic issues, other countries have political and economic objectives that sometimes contradict the policies of the United States. During the early 1970s, France had views on tariff reform, monetary reform, and relations with petroleum-producing countries that were very different from those of the United States. In spite of the February 1974 Washington conference of petroleum-consuming countries, which pledged to try to coordinate Western energy policies in response to the actions of OPEC, Japan and many of the European Common Market states proceeded to make separate arrangements with the Arab petroleum producers. The summer 1981 conference in Canada among the leaders of the seven most highly industrialized nations in the non-Socialist bloc illustrated once again the differences over international economic policy and how domestic actions affect other countries. For instance, some of the European leaders experienced concern about the damaging effects of high interest rates in the United States on their own economies. In these cases, the ability of the United States to formulate and execute its policy effectively without considering the actions and reactions of other states was quite impossible. Clearly, it was beyond the capacity of the United States to control the actions of its allies.

As we pointed out earlier in our analyses of trade, monetary affairs, and investment issues, other nations are subject to pressure by powerful domestic groups seeking to advance and protect their interests, as is true in the United States. These countries are not able to disregard their domestic pressures in favor of faithfully following American directives. Through political activity, the French farmers make it very difficult for the French government, even if it wishes to do so, to agree with the American position on reduction of trade barriers in the agricultural sphere. Negotiations on this and other issues are extremely difficult because each state's ability to compromise is restricted by the important positions held by various economic groups in domestic politics. Consequently, the link between domestic economics and politics and economic relations with other countries serves to reduce the decisional latitude of any single country, including the United States.

As we have seen throughout this study, the United States and other advanced states have a wide range of economic linkages with one another. Trade among advanced states accounts for the largest volume of international trade. A sizable majority of the funds invested by multinational corporations flows to facilities in other advanced economies. As a consequence of these factors and of a similar situation regarding other international transactions (such as tourism and shipping), the critical global economic issues for such states primarily involve their relations with one another. For advanced states, these linkages with one another are both numerous and intensive in terms of their impact on a variety of domestic interests. As a result, any advanced state—and the United States in particular, as the leader among the center states—is limited in its ability to formulate and implement a foreign economic policy without engaging in complex bilateral or multilateral negotiations to accommodate the interests of others.

Moreover, the United States is constrained by the fact that it is the most important economic and political power. Consequently, there have been some occasions where the necessity of being a reliable leader of the international political economy has forced it to forego policies of narrow self-interest. The underwriting of European economic recovery, maintaining the role of the dollar as the key international currency facilitating international transactions, accepting European and Japanese protectionist policies to facilitate their economic revival, providing military security for both Europe and Japan, thereby relieving them of huge expenses—all are examples of American actions designed to aid allies in spite of some costs to the United States. This does not mean that the United States did not also reap benefits from these actions, but international obligations muted American opposition to some of its allies' policies.

In brief, the effect of many of the external constraints identified can be summed up by the concept of interdependence.[35] Because of the interdependent nature of the global economic system, the United States does not have the requisite degree of autonomy to implement successfully whatever policies it would like. Indeed, there is a similarity between a situation of dependence and interdependence. Both imply that there are severe constraints on the ability of a state to control effectively its own relations with the global economic system and other states. In the dominant subordinate situation that the radical analysts visualize in the global political economy, the dependent state alone is constrained. In an interdependent economic system, *all* parties have lost some degree of autonomy, although some may be more constrained than others.

It is appropriate to recognize the limiting effect of other countries and their domestic economic and political systems. The view that the United States can, and does, do whatever it desires seems to be a relic of the days of American leadership of a devastated Western world confronted with a unified Communist camp during the height of the Cold War. Moreover, this perception is based largely on observations of international political issues during these relatively few years and not on international economic matters over a longer span of time. It is possible that on any single issue the United States can call upon its reserves of political and economic influence to obtain its own objectives at the expense of other advanced industrial states. For example, in 1981 extreme pressure was brought to bear on Japan to reduce its automobile exports to the United States. In the long run, however, such a policy is likely to be self-defeating, since other states have gained economic strength relative to the United States; too much American pressure now will probably heighten their resistance to accommodate the United States on other issues.

A CRITIQUE
OF THE PLURALIST VIEW

The pluralist view of foreign economic policymaking requires criticism, just as the radical view did. The image of extensive conflict among interested economic groups, among various agencies in the fractionalized executive bureaucracy, and between Congress and the White House suggests a degree

---

[35]The concept of interdependence was discussed in Chapter 3.

of anarchy and overall purposelessness that is hard to accept. On specific issues various groups in society and the government do differ and clash over objectives and strategies, but, more generally, there also seems to be a consistent thrust to the foreign economic policies of the United States. Chaos and competition have not become so pervasive as to produce a system incapable of identifying or furthering economic and political goals that are widely held among important and interested segments in society. Moreover, although various government agencies may seek to advance their particular interests, and those of their constituents, it is inappropriate to assume that foreign economic policy is totally uncoordinated. High political leadership and coordination may be missing, but among bureaucrats and technocrats below the highest levels of government there are numerous interagency coordinating groups that do seek to achieve a degree of consistency and coherence in policy. The output of such groups may be a series of compromises and agreements to disagree on certain specific issues, but to describe this system as one of unfettered conflict and confusion is just not accurate.

Stephen Krasner addressed this issue by suggesting that there is an overarching national interest that is pursued at the highest levels of the American government. Krasner advances the notion "of a state as a set of rules and institutions having peculiar drives, compulsions, and aims of their own that are separate and distinct from the interests of any particular societal group."[36] Note that, whereas Krasner criticizes the pluralist view, his argument is also at odds with radical thought that purports that the state serves the interests of the dominant financial and corporate sectors. Moreover, in Krasner's view, issues of national security as represented and upheld by the top levels of the government dominate more narrowly held and precisely targeted economic and business issues.

His study of American raw materials policy establishes the preeminence of broad foreign policy objectives as defined by the White House and the State Department acting on behalf of the entire nation. The economic goal of low prices as urged by specific interest groups takes a subordinate position. Continuity and direction in the general area of American foreign economic policy is fostered further by the widespread acceptance of capitalism and the American business ethic. Radical thinkers have pointed out quite correctly that leading corporate and political officials tend to come from similar backgrounds and, thus, tend to have common interests, values, and perceptions—even if the radicals may have overstated the consequences of these tendencies for policy. Perhaps even more important is the fact that a great majority of congresspersons, government bureaucrats and members and leaders of economic interest groups have been raised in a culture that approves of the American brand of capitalism. Consequently,

[36]Stephen Krasner, *Defending the National Interest* (Princeton, N.J.: Princeton University Press, 1978), p. 10.

many responsible individuals in government and society act in ways that are consistent with a positive view of American business. This does not mean that there will be no conflicts over specific issues; it does mean that most actions and proposals will not fundamentally contradict the milieu provided by American history and society. The importance of these general predispositions toward American business and private enterprise is illustrated by a State Department paper drafted in 1972 to consider alternative postures toward American direct foreign investment.

This position paper outlined three possible approaches. The negative alternative examined ways in which the government could actively seek to inhibit the activities of American-based multinational corporations. The positive position suggested ways of promoting American investment in other countries. The third view—in the paper's terms, a "neutral" approach—was to maintain the existing policy of neither promoting nor hindering multinational enterprises. This "neutral" view failed to recognize the supportive character of the important set of incentives that is offered by the U.S. government for foreign investment. Tax credits, tax deferrals, a host of preinvestment services, and many other policies cannot be termed a neutral approach to American investment abroad. Neutrality, like beauty, is in the eyes of the beholder, and the neutral view of the State Department and American society is based on an acceptance and approval of American business and private enterprise.

The process by which foreign economic policy is formulated does entail conflict over specific issues, as the pluralist orientation suggests, but the conflict takes place within a capitalist system. Consequently, there is and has been an overall thrust toward liberal economic solutions in America's approach to international economic relations. This prevailing theme evolves from the nature of the contemporary American system as well as from its history. There is nothing surprising about this, as the radicals sometimes suggest; nor should it be ignored, as it has been at times by pluralist and bureaucratic analyses of American foreign economic policy.

Moreover, while recognizing the external constraints on American foreign economic policy, it is important not to overlook the political and economic strength that the United States does bring to any controversy. If events of the 1960s and 1970s have shown that Europe, Japan, and the oil-producing countries can themselves wield significant amounts of political and economic influence, events have also shown that none of them has the combination of size, unity, industrial and technological capability, and natural resource and food reserves that the United States possesses. These strengths, combined with the military might and the wide-ranging political and economic activity of the United States, ensures it of a critical and powerful position in conflicts with other countries. The United States cannot often dictate international economic policy in its relations with other advanced states. It is quite a bit less than dominant, but it is also something more than the equal of any of its major economic partners.

Methodologically, the pluralist thinkers exhibit some of the same failings as the radical critics. Their reliance upon pluralist and bureaucratic models of the policy formulation process determines largely the nature of what they analyze and therefore conclude. Pluralists study interest-group and bureaucratic conflicts and quite naturally ascribe great importance to them. Their presumption of conflict among disparate interest groups and agencies of government tends to prevent their consideration of larger forces that unite officials representing conflicting interests and that confine conflicts within rather narrow bounds. Pluralist and bureaucratic analysts discussing foreign economic policy tend to ignore the fact that some interests generally prevail over others, even if they document the existence of conflict surrounding all questions of American foreign economic policy.

Our purpose is not to designate one view or another as being the accurate or most useful perspective on how American foreign policy is made. Instead, the examination of different views should emphasize again the complex interactions between domestic matters—government, politics, social structure, interest groups, and ideology—and the global political economy. To some extent, foreign economic policy is composed of all these ingredients, though, as this chapter has indicated, the importance ascribed to each varies widely. Much can be learned from examining the concepts of contending approaches that clarify each other's shortcomings and have so much to offer in an understanding of U.S. policymaking.

CHAPTER NINE
INTERNATIONAL POLITICAL ECONOMY
*Current Problems
and Future Needs*

Writing a conclusion for this book is a difficult task, for its intent is to introduce the subject, to identify and describe relationships, to expose political and economic dilemmas, to demonstrate policy prescriptions based on alternative theoretical orientations, and, we hope, to stimulate further analysis and research. Instead of seeking to gather together and integrate the most important points examined in earlier chapters, we will discuss several fundamental characteristics of the field of international political economy that have crucial implications for scholarly analysis and policymaking. These characteristics apply to all the substantive areas examined in this study.

As an academic discipline and as an area for policy analysis, the politics of global economic relations have only recently been analyzed extensively. Some of the reasons for this neglect were examined in Chapter 1, but there are two conceptual aspects of the problem upon which we would like to elaborate. First, the study of the international political economy, and thus policymaking, is complicated by the existence of multiple sets of substantive interconnections that refuse to fit comfortably into well-established and traditional academic or bureaucratic departments. As a result, and this is the critical second point, there are few useful conceptual frameworks or theories that are comprehensive or sensitive enough to incorporate and build upon these interconnections. Since the subject is rarely approached as a substantive and conceptual whole, the related disciplines of economics and political science, as well as their bureaucratic counterparts, have generally been content to focus only on that part of the interconnection that is familiar and comfortable. Economists focus almost exclusively on the economic dimensions of these issues, either ignoring the political aspects or merely "playing" with the political angle without the benefit of any systematic theory. On the other hand, some political scientists ignore the economic dimension altogether. Others recognize its importance but treat it merely as an issue area, not as an integral part of international politics. Thus, the development of theory to accommodate these interconnections has been slow in coming and even then has not been widely accepted by the field. This has presented severe obstacles to policymakers and academic analysts alike. Policy prescriptions generated within government, or by many academicians and others, have been based primarily on different sets of values and assumptions rather than on a full appreciation of the variety of political and economic interrelations that only a comprehensive theory of political economy can provide.

RECOGNIZING CRUCIAL INTERRELATIONSHIPS

A complete understanding of the international political economy (and an adequate comprehensive theory of it) requires, at the minimum, a systematic examination of several sets of interrelationships. These are the interrelationships among various substantive issues, between political and economic matters, between the domestic and international arenas, and between governmental and nongovernmental actors at all levels of domestic and international society. It is important to appreciate the fact that these various sets of interrelationships are themselves linked to one another. The inordinately complex nature of the global political economy behooves us to think more in terms of identifying empirical interdependencies and their effects on various actors than in simple cause-and-effect terms. The latter can occur only after the former has been accomplished.

All analysts embrace the notion that there are many interconnections among the various substantive issues regarding the international political economy. But there is repeated evidence of a lack of comprehension of precisely how these issues are related to one another. The significance and character of the interconnections become evident only after events occur that wreak havoc on national and international economics and politics.

The oil embargo and price increases imposed by oil-producing states during 1973 and 1974 are a dramatic example of how interconnections between substantive economic issues transmit shocks throughout the global political economy. The actions produced an energy shortage and staggering import bills that curtailed general economic production in rich and poor states. They also produced simultaneously a fertilizer shortage that aggravated an already precarious global food situation; huge balance-of-payments deficits in virtually all rich states; increased needs for foreign exchange by poor states in amounts that exceeded their total foreign aid receipts in 1973; a revolutionary alteration of the distribution of monetary reserves within the global economy; and a dramatic boost to an already unprecedented level of inflation plaguing the global economy, along with a rapidly spreading economic downturn in many countries. This is not to mention the effects of the actions by oil-producing states on international and domestic political coalitions. Although everyone agrees that there are important interconnections between oil supplies and other aspects of international economic and political relations, no one, before the fact, clearly recognized the scope of these first-order and other consequences of the use of oil as a political weapon by Arab states and the control of oil prices by a cartel of oil-producing states.

The existence of interconnections among various forms of transnational economic relations not only transmits shocks throughout the world, it also poses great problems for a state attempting to protect itself from certain aspects of international economic relations. Unless the nature of these interconnections are understood fully—and they usually are not—the cure chosen by a state may be worse than the disease. For example, in the early 1900s Canada was greatly concerned about its high degree of dependence upon products imported from the United States and the stiff competition that Canadian firms faced from their American counterparts. As a consequence, it erected tariff barriers to keep out American goods, only to find that American firms secured and expanded their Canadian markets by drastically expanding investments in Canada. Now more than 50 percent of Canadian manufacturing is owned by American investors. Further it has been alleged that the shock of exploding oil prices has had a substantial influence on productivity in industrial countries. Uncertainty about oil supplies has resulted in delayed investment plans. In other cases, the high cost of oil has led to shifts in investment toward more labor-intensive and less capital-intensive processes. These and other instances of interconnections among various forms of international economic relations are appreciated but not fully comprehended by analysts and/or policymakers.

There are also interconnections among what have traditionally been identified and dealt with as economic or political issues. This is demonstrated clearly in the alternative means by which the United States might reduce its balance-of-payments deficit. What at first appears to be a series of economic decisions becomes transformed into a series of political decisions about America's power profile in the world and about which elements of American society will bear the brunt of the adjustment process. If internal adjustment measures are adopted, will multinational businesses, tourists, laborers in noncompetitive American production, or all of us as consumers assume the burden? Alternatively, will American defense capability around the world be reduced? Perhaps the costs of adjustment should be transferred to other countries and their economic health and that of their workers? Similarly, manifestly political issues, such as whether the United States should interrupt all relations with regimes such as those in the Soviet Union, Cuba, Nicaragua, South Africa, Argentina, Angola, or Poland have substantial economic implications for special interests within the United States and for their competitors abroad. In all societies, economic interests are expressed through political as well as economic activity. Political and economic analysts tend to consider only the dimensions of these challenges and processes with which they are most comfortable, even though few important issues are either purely economic or purely political in their implications.

Interconnections between domestic concerns and processes and international relations are particularly evident in analyses of international political economy. Analysts of world politics have always noted the existence of these interconnections, but they frequently leave the systematic examination of domestic political processes to their colleagues in American or comparative politics. Neither government officials nor students of international political economy can afford the luxury of such a fine division of labor. For example, it is simply impossible to comprehend the trade dilemma facing the United States and Europe with Japan regarding automobile exports without directly examining the domestic as well as international linkages that define the dimensions of the problem. Demands by European and American workers and corporations threatened by Japanese auto imports have resulted in the erection of trade barriers that hinder the free flow of automobiles. The United States urged voluntary restraints on Japanese manufacturers and the French have imposed far more direct limits. The complex interplay between domestic interests, national governments, and negotiations between the United States and Japan are diagrammed in Figure 9-1.

While recognizing the integral relationship of behavior in both the domestic and international arenas, it is increasingly important to examine nongovernmental as well as governmental actors in analyses of international political economy. It seems likely that the role of nongovernmental organizations will continue to increase as international economic interdependence becomes more pervasive. This is bound to stimulate greater activity by nongovernmental interests seeking to secure advantage from direct participation in transnational economic relations.

Specifically, the multinational corporation is one of the major vehicles by which the economies of states are linked. Consequently, both analysts and policymakers need to account 'for the behavior and interactions of these nongovernmental actors in their assessments and predictions regarding the international political economy.

In addition to multinational corporations, many other important nongovernmental actors—such as international banks, international trade union secretariats, domestic pressure groups, international money speculators,

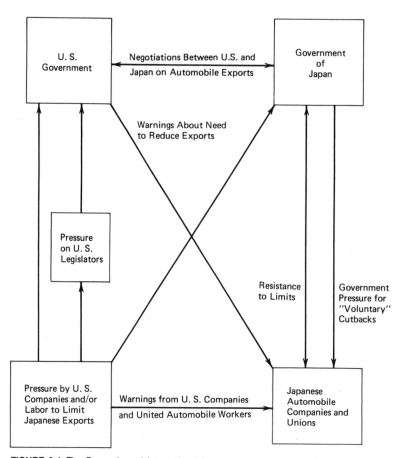

FIGURE 9-1 The Domestic and International Interconnection: Japanese Automobile Exports to the United States

and a host of other organized interests—are concerned about various aspects of the international political economy. Some of these nongovernmental organizations can be found active in any of the issues discussed in this book; some restrict their direct activities, though not all their consequences, to the domestic level; others focus on international activities; and still others are active both within states and between states. Similarly, some of these actors are most concerned with political issues, others are most concerned with economic issues, and some fail to see the distinction and act accordingly. The interconnections among states are less bothersome to truly transnational nongovernmental actors, for they develop attitudes among their personnel, processes, and institutions that are designed to be responsive to and effective in the global economic system.

The influence of these nongovernmental actors is exerted in several different ways. Some of these groups, domestic interest groups particularly, attempt to advance their objectives by pressuring their local and national governments to act in ways favorable to their specific interests. The normal techniques of interest-group representation that are characteristic of a particular political system are pursued in the attempt to influence government policy at all levels of domestic society. The activity of these nongovernmental groups has often strengthened the hands of states as they confront problems of international economic policy. They now have substantial domestic support to back up their positions. Sometimes and at the same time, the domestic interests are contradictory.

Other nongovernmental actors, such as multinational corporations and regional and international trade union organizations, seek to advance their particular interests by participating directly in the global economy. These institutions are truly transnational actors: even though they may have national components, the scope, nature, and target of their activities are international in character. Of course, some also engage in subnational and state-oriented activities, and in this respect they differ little from the actors in the previous category. However, their uniqueness and importance in the study of international political economy is that they themselves have become international in orientation because of the necessity of representing their interests and pursuing their activities on an international basis.

Figure 9-2 illustrates the various ways in which nongovernmental actors exert influence on the global political economy. As can be seen, not only do nongovernmental actors affect national and international or regional actors, but some of them also act on the international level without the need for governmental intermediaries.

The existence of domestic and transnational nongovernmental actors reduces the decisional latitude of national governments to the extent that they must be responsive to the demands of these groups. Since developments in the global economic system have widespread consequences for domestic interests within states, the governments are likely to be subject to extensive and conflicting pressures regarding appropriate policy postures. This type of interest-group activity is likely to delay the development of policy, hinder the establishment of clear and bold directions in policy, confuse the implementation of policy, and generally complicate the policy-making process.

The following list outlines specific relations identified in Figure 9-2:

1. The International Labor Organization sets labor standards strengthening the bargaining position of domestic labor unions with management and with the state (e.g., Poland).
2. National trade unions in Europe seek to influence EEC law requiring companies to share plans with unions twice a year.
3. The Council of the Americas tries to modify provisions of the investment code of the Andean Common Market.
4. The United Nations attempts to draw up a code of conduct regulating activities of multinational corporations.

5. Belgium attempts to change EEC ruling on the inappropriateness of its investment incentives.
6. The EEC seeks to legitimize and also limit the emergency measures of Italy to overcome balance-of-payments problems in 1974.
7. The International Metalworkers' Federation works against the antitrade union policies of the Brazilian government.
8. South Korea pursues policies designed to attract multinational corporations.
9. Unions from Germany and the Netherlands apply pressure to a European multinational chemical firm.
10. Henry Ford visits the United Kingdom and urges the British people to adopt measures to improve the chaotic labor relations climate in the United Kingdom.
11. The UAW pressures the U.S. government to restrict the inflow of Japanese automobiles.
12. The French government assures its farmers that, in return for their support of the EEC, policies will be adopted to inhibit competition from American agricultural imports.

The existence and increasing activity of international nongovernmental actors means that some developments in the international political economy are beyond the control of individual states and also international governmental organizations. Thus, a state's monetary, trade, or pollution policy may be thwarted by nongovernmental actors that know how to operate effectively in the international system in their own behalf to bypass government constraints. We discussed in Chapter 4 how nations are concerned about the ability of multinational corporations to circumvent or ignore national policy. The problem is compounded by the fact that governments have had difficulty developing effective multinational intergovernmental institutions to try to control or counterbalance the effective

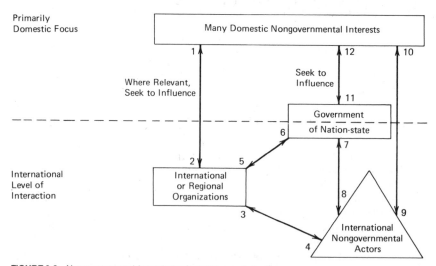

FIGURE 9-2 Nongovernmental Actors in the Global Economic System

maneuvers of such organizations. The point is that both analysts and policymakers must take into account the actions of such organizations, their
ability to impede governmental policies, and their role in structuring the
substance and process of the global economic system.

These various interconnections complicate the tasks of critical analysis
and policy prescription by requiring a more comprehensive and systematic
view of the relationships and problems involved in international political
economic relations. Any approach employed by decision makers or academicians that focuses on only one aspect of the field, to the exclusion of
other relevant linkages, will be incomplete, simplistic, and very likely misguided. Similarly, each set of interconnections is interrelated with the others,
thereby demanding analysis and policymaking that take into account sec-
ond- and third-order consequences and linkages of major importance. In
sum, this is an exceptionally complex set of policy concerns, which is currently being dealt with in the absence of a well-developed conceptual or
empirical understanding of the precise character of these crucial
interrelationships.

THE LINKAGE AMONG VALUES,
THEORY, AND POLICY PRESCRIPTION

The field of international political economy is itself intricate. However,
adding to the difficulty of making policy or conducting useful analysis is
the fact that the issues of importance generate extensive disagreement over
what is a desirable state of affairs, the causes of various problems, useful
remedies, and the consequences of various policies. More fundamentally,
policymakers and scholars in rich states and poor states, as well as those
within any specific state, often have sharply divergent sets of values regarding the international political economy and its consequences for states
and the global system. These conflicting sets of values often produce contradictory perceptions of the problems, their causes, and their solutions.
Even where there is agreement on values and objectives, there may be
substantial differences of opinion regarding the best strategy with which
to seek common goals.

In this book, the beliefs and analyses of the radical view have been
juxtaposed with those of the classical liberal perspective on a variety of
substantive problems in international economic and political relations. However, disputes over desirable objectives and appropriate strategies do not
exist solely between the radicals and the classical liberals. Indeed, as we
mentioned often in earlier chapters, there is no single radical view, nor is
there a universally embraced traditional liberal perspective. Instead, there
are many shades and nuances within each viewpoint. What policymakers
and analysts share in each perspective is a set of basic values and assumptions that essentially predetermine their explanations of international po-

litical economy. Students, analysts, and policymakers must strive to understand the value positions and primary assumptions of a particular analyst to evaluate their assessments of the nature of the problem, desired goals, or reasonable solutions. This is important not only for constructive criticism of others' perspectives, but also for achieving a genuine dialogue among analysts and policymakers of different analytical persuasions who now usually talk past each other.

THE CONCERNS OF RICH
AND POOR STATES

Throughout this study we have examined the major challenges to both advanced industrial states and less developed countries as they relate to the global political economy. Advanced industrial states are preoccupied with the conflicts and problems that affect them the most. Generally, the critical issues faced by advanced states involve difficulties that stem from interdependent public and private relationships with other industrialized countries. These problems tend to be particularly conflictive and intense since most advanced industrial states have highly developed pluralist political systems, with numerous domestic groups seeking to influence state policy in support of their interests. Because of internal pressures and the nature of the external problems, advanced state policymakers concentrate on ways in which to adjust and enhance economic transactions among themselves. For example, industrial states' proposals for structural reform in the trade or monetary system naturally tend to focus on how changes would facilitate economic relations among the advanced countries.

This orientation of advanced industrial states is understandable given the fact that a significant majority of their trade, monetary, and investment transactions are among one another. However, this concentration on advanced state concerns has contributed to insufficient attention paid to the different but severe set of problems faced by the developing countries, whose international economic interactions are primarily with advanced states, not with other less developed countries. Major international economic organizations have begun to address seriously the issues confronting less developed countries, for, historically, their focus on advanced states' issues has reflected the dominance of these states in these organizations.

Recent events such as the oil embargo and the rising prices of petroleum, shortages of other natural resources, food shortages, and in general the use of economic clout by poor states over rich states have forced the latter to become cognizant of the developing countries. However, the primary reaction of the advanced states has been one of trying to protect themselves against this newly found and exercised power enjoyed by some of the developing countries. While attempting to deal sensitively with the concerns of the poor states, many of the industrialized countries seek primarily to circumvent this economic pressure by finding and developing new supplies of scarce commodities, by instituting programs of conservation and recycling, and by unleashing research and development funds to find substitutes for the critical resources. They exhibit much less interest in attempting to develop mechanisms that integrate the poor states more closely and equitably into the global economic system so that their critical problems become of paramount concern to the entire system.

In summary, the development of a community of interest regarding the international political economy between rich states and poor states, and within each of these two types of countries, will be hindered by the fact that each perceives a different set of problems to be the most critical. Advanced states seek to facilitate the extensive international economic interactions that they enjoy with one another. Developing countries would like the system to be more responsive to the needs of development. Perceiving different problems, having different priorities and domestic pressures, enjoying vastly different influence capabilities, it is not surprising that there is little agreement between advanced states and developing countries on the appropriate nature of the international political economy or on suggestions for its reform.

CONCLUSION

The complexity of global economic relations has several important implications for policy prescription. First, it argues strongly for a global, multilateral approach to the many critical issues of the global political economy. Even problems that used to be perceived as domestic, such as inflation, are now global; thus, they must be resolved at the international level. As we have indicated with respect to trade, monetary, investment, technological, and developmental issues, unilateral measures by a single state generally have the effect of imposing costs and creating problems for other states. As a result, the affected countries often retaliate in a fashion that imposes new problems and costs on the initiating state. The basic point is that problems involving global interaction cannot be resolved by the actions of individual states; multilateral approaches are required.

However, we are well aware of the difficulty in organizing and achieving satisfactory multilateral approaches. There are well-developed institutions, such as the IMF and GATT, in the monetary and trade areas, but these have no meaningful counterparts in the areas of investment or technology transfer. Moreover, neither the IMF nor GATT as they currently exist are confronting effectively the full range of problems in their respective areas. In addition, of course, the problems we have discussed rarely fit neatly into the jurisdiction of one international institution without having widespread effects on the others.

Probably an even greater hindrance to the development of global approaches to global problems is the fact that, within each state, politically powerful domestic groups concerned about their immediate interests and problems exert great pressure on their governments to advance their particular values. To such groups in advanced states and developing states, counterarguments pointing out the aggregate or long-run benefits of a different policy will not be accepted. Thus, governmental officials are faced constantly with the dilemma of promoting national or global economic welfare in the long run at the expense of well-organized special interests. These officials are very likely to suffer domestic political retaliation if they ignore special interests. On the other hand, they advance the demands of special interests at the risk of disrupting relations with other states and with other nongovernmental actors. Those states and nongovernmental actors hurt by the disruptions are likely to retaliate in a manner that ultimately prevents the achievement of the domestic goals being pursued and imposes unpopular domestic costs on the originating state. This basic conflict cannot be ignored, nor is it easily resolvable.

In addition, interdependence has meant that actions taken by states for domestic reasons sometimes have severe repercussions for other states. Aspects of this interconnection have been discussed in earlier chapters, especially in those dealing with trade, the monetary system, and technology transfer. During much of the 1970s, the industrial partners of the United States urged it to adopt internal measures to reduce inflation and the size of the balance-of-payments deficit. By 1980 and 1981, the tight money policy of the Federal Reserve Bank and other actions designed to control inflation resulted in high interest rates. These rates attracted European, particularly German, capital in increasing amounts and the dollar strengthened in international markets. To counteract these capital exports, European states were themselves forced to impose high interest rates. Consequently, domestic U.S. monetary policy confronted its economic partners with inflation, declining currency values, and an economic stagnation. At a summit meeting in Canada in the summer of 1981, the German prime minister, joined by some of his European colleagues, strongly urged the Reagan administration to back away from the very economic policies that the Europeans had recommended only a few years earlier. This example is illustrative of the disruptive foreign effects of domestic policies.

Recognizing the extraordinarily complex nature of the problems resulting from these interconnections, our very general recommendations for policy constitute a multi-pronged strategy. First, we clearly recognize the need for global approaches to international problems. Consequently, states as well as international institutions need to develop the basic orientation that multilateral action is required for the establishment and maintenance of an international political economy that facilitates economic interactions and yet is responsive to the less fortunate states. The problems confronting advanced states and developing countries are resolvable only by international action and cooperation. This international strategy needs to be based upon courageous and creative leadership by national officials. It also demands a more conscious and comprehensive attempt to develop workable and broadly responsive international institutions. These organizations not only need to attack their particular problems more vigorously; they must also interact with one another more constructively to develop an approach that is effective across the broad spectrum of international economic issues. They also need to be sensitive to the domestic economic and political problems and pressures associated with international political economy issues. Nations and international organizations have much room for improvement in these directions.

The second part of our recommendations concerns the development of domestic policies that are designed to ease the disruptions and dislocations caused by the increased interdependence of states. Actions at the international level must be combined with attitudes and programs that consciously reduce the costs of a closer integration between particular states and the international economic order. In the United States, important segments of society have suffered severe dislocations as a result of global interdependence. Unemployment in the steel, auto, textile, and shoe industries has been extensive. Skyrocketing costs for fuel have made it difficult for fixed income households to pay heating bills. There are many other examples of similar adjustment problems in other countries. While the solutions are not easy, nations like the United States must find ways of easing the transition for affected groups. There is no way to avoid the disruptions and dislocations; the transition is inevitable. The challenge is how to make it occur most effectively and smoothly.

In sum, we are calling for a national and international approach to the evolving global economic system. Neither strategy can work effectively without the other. Moreover, given the nature of the international political economy, no other set of strategies will work either. However, having indulged in a bit of preaching about appropriate policy directions, we are well aware of the immense operational difficulties implied by these recommendations, in addition to the obvious political problems at both the national and international level. Indeed, we are recommending the conscious creation of a system that increases interdependency among states and thus reduces the individual state's autonomy. The political implications and obstacles to such an approach are enormous. Frankly, we doubt very much the existence of a necessary degree of commitment by rich and poor states, as well as by various domestic groups. Moreover, we are concerned that the requisite political and economic skills have yet to be developed and refined. Yet we see no other reasonable course likely to produce acceptable results.

INDEX